M-H

10

18ª

ggbumz

Joseph Conrad

Commemorative Essays

Selected Proceedings of the International Conference of
Conrad Scholars, University of California, San Diego
August 29 — September 5, 1974;
Chairperson, Suzanne Henig;
Program Chairman, Adam Gillon.

Edited by
ADAM GILLON
and
LUDWIK KRZYŻANOWSKI

assisted by
David Leon Higdon
Donald W. Rude
Krystyna M. Olszer

ASTRA BOOKS,   NEW YORK

ISBN: 0-913994-24-3

ASTRA BOOKS, NEW YORK
Order Department
Box 392, Times Square Station
New York, N.Y. 100036

EDITORIAL DEPARTMENT
Suite 906
369 Lexington Avenue
New York, N.Y. 10017

DISTRIBUTED BY
Twayne Publishers: A Division of G. K. Hall & Co.
70 Lincoln Street
Boston, Massachusetts 02111

CONTENTS

CONRAD

In London at Bessborough
Gardens
He suddenly said:
"You may clear the table."
(It was an empty cup.
A plate with leftovers of bacon,
A little marmalade and toast.)
Upon the empty table
He smoothed a sheet of paper
Hesitating long.
Pondering half in French
And half in Polish,
Drafted the first word:
T H E .
Having written these
Three letters,
(Pronounced tee, aich, ee),
He bypassed the thicket
Of his native Eng, Ong, Sh, Tch.
Bypassed the flat bank
Of the shallow river
And sailed onto the broad ocean
Of Anglo-Saxon speech,
Where he beheld
The three letters:
T H E .
Across the milky mists
The faint dawn seeps onto
The bobby's helmet
and Barclay Street.
The fireplace crackles.
Dickens, Mark Twain.
A pipe. Big Ben tolls.

5

A tranquil dream.
And there it was Vologda,
Zhitomir and Tchernikhov,
A mother crying softly,
And a Tsarist soldier behind the door.

But neither silence, nor mist—only the storm
Could allay the anguish here, this burden,
Strangling the heart.
There is an English saying:
To travel means to conquer.
To conquer means redeem.

And he sailed the measureless ocean,
Released from his fetters.
And he returned no more to his own home.
For his house in the county of Kent
Was not his home.

When the eternal pilgrims sailed
Into the black, star-studded night,
Upon the deck, swathed in cocoons of silk,
Dark, their feet like stains of pink,
Dreaming of distant Meccas,
I also heard, as did Lord Jim,
The voice that tempted: "Jump!"

1960

Translated from the Polish by
Adam Gillon

(From Antoni Słonimski's *Poezje 1916-1961,* Warsaw, 1961)

DR. JACOB BRONOWSKI

PREFACE

The selections in this volume are from papers read at the International Conference of Conrad Scholars, held at the Revelle Campus of the University of California at San Diego (August 29- September 5, 1974), and organized by Professor Suzanne Henig of San Diego State University. The aim of the Conference was to offer yet another tribute to Conrad on the fiftieth anniversary of his death. The number and range of the papers offered were indeed impressive; unfortunately, however, this made the publication of the entire proceedings impossible, due primarily to space limitations of The Polish Review. *Thus, some papers meriting publication had to be left out after many agonizing hours of reflection by the editors. I offer my sincere apologies to the authors who were asked to submit their papers for any inconvenience caused by our negative decision, and I thank them for their patience.*

I am sure that the community of Conrad scholars and readers will share my gratitude to the many people who made the Conference and this volume possible, especially the following whom I must single out for their dedication and assistance: Professors Suzanne Henig, Elaine Boney and Florence Talamantes, of San Diego; Dr. Eugene Kusielewicz, President of the Kościuszko Foundation; The Polish Institute of Arts and Sciences and Dr. Ludwik Krzyżanowski for devoting a double issue of The Polish Review *to these Commemorative Essays; the editorial staff of* The Polish Review, *particularly Krystyna M. Olszer; Professors David Leon Higdon and Donald W. Rude of Texas Tech University.*

No anthology of essays can aspire to any definitive appraisal of a great artist's work. I fondly hope that the collection which is here offered is an ample testimony that age cannot wither Conrad's infinite variety.

Adam Gillon
Program Chairman,
International Conference
of Conrad Scholars

7

DR. JACOB BRONOWSKI

Opening address by the Chairperson, Fiftieth Commemorative Anniversary International Conference of Conrad Scholars, University of California, San Diego, 28 August, 1974

Jacob Bronowski was to have delivered a major introductory talk to you this morning. Instead of introducing him as it would have been my profound pleasure, it is my unhappy duty to inform you that Jacob Bronowski died last Thursday while on holiday in New York. Instead of listening to his remarks about Conrad, I would like to say a few words about him, his life-long curiosity about everything around him, his erudition and devotion to learning, his genius, and his great, great kindness to everyone.

I came to know Jacob Bronowski almost accidentally last year at Salk Institute at a luncheon presided over by Françoise Gilot. He came in unexpectedly, joined us, and stayed. During the course of the conversation, I discovered he did not like Virginia Woolf, whom he knew, one of my favorite authors, but that he did like Conrad, also one of my favorites. Although he was a mathematician by training, he was in the tradition of the true Renaissance men of letters. He had produced one of the finest books on Blake and a book on poetic criticism. I asked him whether he would address this conference. He didn't hesitate for a moment. "I love Conrad," he said, "and I would very much be honored to address your conference."

I saw Bronowski several months after this luncheon when John Lehmann, the distinguished British poet, was visiting me. He and Bronowski had known each other years before at Cambridge, I called Bronowski to invite him and his wife to visit us, but he was too busy working on a bicentennial project with visiting scientists, museum directors and foundation heads to accept my invitation, so John Lehmann and I went instead to visit him for Sunday brunch. He drove in promptly at noon while many other cars followed him and we had a memorable time, he and John reminiscing about their student days, Bronowski discussing the "Ascent of Man" T.V. program that had recently received such high praise in London and which would be here in the autumn.

Atlantic had asked me to do an article on him to coincide with the T.V. series and I asked his permission. Within a month I was at his office for the interview which was to have lasted one hour but which lasted five instead. During the course of our talk he discovered to his horror that I did not understand Einstein's theory of relativity and so, for almost an hour, he interrupted our discussion to teach me how relativity worked. It is the greatest compliment to his skill as a teacher that I, who had failed high school calculus, could not only follow his diagrams with ease but understood the theory well enough afterward to explain it to another poet.

We spoke of many things from philosophy to biology to the evolution of man in the future and what he said will be published shortly. But here I only wish to adumbrate his feelings about man and science and life and death which seem appropriate at this moment.

He had a marvelous sense of humor and later in the afternoon, with a visiting expert of medieval biology from London and two officers from H.M.S. Kent, his secretary, beloved editor and I, Bronowski regaled us with a story about the time he was Scientific Deputy to the British Chiefs of Staff Mission to Japan. He had to make an official report for England on the devastation of the atomic bomb over Hiroshima. "I lived on a destroyer for three to four months in Hiroshima Harbor in the middle of '45. Quite the most unpleasant quarters I've ever lived in," he said. "A physicist from the Department of Industrial Research discovered an isotope of nickel that had a long decaying period so he could measure the exact moment the bomb fell on Hiroshima by measuring the nickel's radioactivity. To this end, he collected several hundred vacuum cleaners and sewing machines and asked the government to send a ship for them." The British government wired Bronowski asking what they should do with this shipful of vacuum cleaners and sewing machines, Bronowski sent word to his officers that whenever anyone came across a vacuum cleaner or sewing machine, "Bury it." He mused as we sipped our tea how sometime in centuries to come when other cultures dig up our ruins and find these machines all over Hiroshima what will they think? He laughed. Our interview was over. We went to hear Dr. Talbert lecture and before I left Dr. Bronowski suggested I call him "Bruno" as he shook my hand.

Bruno felt the supreme achievement of his life had "to do with the sort of revolt I brought about in 1953 in *Science and Humanistic Values* in making scientists aware that the most distinctive faculty of man is the ability to gain communal knowledge. That faculty is

not a mechanical one but becomes an unique character of imagination
. . . Man is a knowledge-getting creature."

He believed the sense of human dignity is inherent in human evolution itself. And finally we spoke of death. He said, "I don't think about it. I am bothered about living carefully enough to finish my work. Death is disappearing from one's own consciousness, but living in the consciousness of one's friends, relations, readers." Today Jacob Bronowski lives here in this room. This conference which was originally to be dedicated to the memory of Joseph Conrad is now also dedicated to the memory of Jacob Bronowski and it will appear in the publications which emanate from the talks we shall hear today and over the next few days.

I want at this time to call on Dr. Jonas Salk, distinguished scientist, who was instrumental in bringing Jacob Bronowski to Salk Institute and who was his friend and colleague for a decade.

IN TRIBUTE TO JACOB BRONOWSKI
AND JOSEPH CONRAD

It seems most appropriate that this conference has been dedicated both to Jacob Bronowski and to Joseph Conrad. We are here, in a sense to commemorate, and also to celebrate genius, a quality manifested both in Bronowski and in Conrad. Their books and their recorded thoughts stand as lasting monuments to Man and to his uniquely human strengths. As we consider the lives of Bronowski and Conrad and study their works, we may come to understand the underlying structures and patterns that give rise to the kind of genius exemplified in these men.

It was his book *Science and Human Values* that drew me to Dr. Bronowski. I saw the book for the first time during the Spring of 1960, a time when plans for the Institute were being conceived. I also recall a time in England when I met with Bruno, who was then working with the Coal Board. As we sat in his London office, I could see that he wanted to escape from the activities that were interfering with his creative work, and I saw an opportunity to help him. I described the Institute for Biological Studies soon to be born in La Jolla. His response was memorable: "You have just changed the course of my life. I would very much like to become part of what you have in mind."

Dr. Bronowski spent the last years of his life at the Institute, a place where he worked and, I should add, played; at that time in his life, his work and his play were one. The architecture of the Institute, designed to evoke the most creative human qualities, seemed to influence him. The fact that Dr. Bronowski flourished here was for me a source of personal reward, for the Institute was and is in thought the fulfillment of a vision about science and human values, a place designed to bridge the so-called "world of science" and the "world of the humanities." It was our mutual desire to help build such a bridge, to show the unity in these two aspects of a complementary dualism. In both his person and his works, Jacob Bronowski dedicated himself to this task over the past several decades.

As you may know, Dr. Bronowski had planned to address this conference, and, as was his custom, he intended to speak extemporaneously.

11

His performance before an audience was always remarkable to witness. Although he cannot speak today, his words remain with us. He has left a great legacy of written works, books and essays which illustrate one of his most outstanding talents: his supreme command of the English language. As Warren Weaver once said, "He writes like an angel."

As we think of the talent of linguistic expression, it is interesting to consider some of the obvious similarities between Dr. Bronowski and Joseph Conrad. Having been born in Poland, each acquired a second language: Bruno, German and Conrad, French. Later, both became students and masters of the English language. While each possessed inherent qualities of genius, there is probably more than a casual significance in the effect that their acquaintance with differing languages had upon their abilites to think and to communicate. These linguistic experiences allowed for the expression of special latent qualities the qualities of genius that we can perceive through their work. During his twenty years at sea, Conrad learned first to love and then to grasp another language, the outlook of another people and the shape and texture of their art. With this experience, he uncovered the gifts and passions that made him a master. "I, too," said Bronowski, "came to England as a stranger speaking another language. Learning a new language is a tremendous experience." Certainly, both men shared a reverence for the English language. As Bronowski remarked, "Learning at the age of twelve as precise and cogent, as exact and detailed a language as English really was a most moving experience. The exactness of the language, the way the words march one after the other . . . to this day gives me pleasure in the reading and in the hearing." Speaking about the nature of symbolic communication, Bronowski said:

Human beings have, in speech and in other symbols, the means to bring to mind that which is absent; and, in a sense, this recall creates the thinking mind. It gives men the capacity to manipulate a number of things in their minds at once, to form general concepts and to note the regular laws which they obey.

In each of his works, Bronowski has demonstrated his ability to use language as a tool for thought, as has Conrad in his mastery of the English novel and short story. Both of these men also possessed remarkable skill as they employed the precise yet multifarious quality of language as a tool for communication. Said Bronowski, "Speech has, from the outset, had the power not merely to enrich the experience of one man, but to make it part of the experience of others." And so it is that each of these men, Bronowski and Conrad, has left to us a rich inheritance of experience.

I Joseph Conrad – A Comparative View

ADAM GILLON

JOSEPH CONRAD AND SHAKESPEARE:
PART FIVE*
"King Lear" and "Heart of Darkness"

If one were to establish valid grounds of comparison with Shakespeare on the strength of Conrad's own pronouncements about his literary background, one would have a difficult case to prove. In 1898, for instance, he protests vehemently: ". . . really I read nothing and never look at the papers so I know nothing of politics or literature. . . . This is the whole truth."[1] Fortunately for the critic, however, such statements need not be taken at face value; if anything, Conrad's correspondence reveals his extensive reading and often a fairly erudite approach to literature, indicated by numerous analytical comments on other writers. And since Shakespeare was Conrad's earliest reading fare, it is not surprising to find many references to the Bard in the novelist's letters.

For example: "Hang it. Now if that astonishing Lord Roseberry gives peerage to Sir John Falstaff and makes Bardolph Secretary of State . . ."[2] This statement was made in 1895, in a letter to Edward Garnett. It is

---

* "Joseph Conrad and Shakespeare," Part I, *Conradiana*, vol. I, No. 1, 1968; Part II, *Ibid.*, vol. I, No. 2, 1968; Part III, *Ibid.*, vol. I, No. 3, 1969; Part IV, *Ibid.*, vol. VII, No. 3, 1975.)
    Unless otherwise stated, the page numbers referring to Conrad's text are those of the Edition of the Complete Works, Garden City, New York, Doubleday, Page & Co., 1924. All references to Shakespeare's text are from William Shakespeare, *The Complete Works*, edited by Alfred Harbage, Penguin Books, Baltimore, Maryland, 1969.
    [1] G. Jean-Aubry, *Joseph Conrad: Life and Letters* (2 vols., Garden City: Doubleday, Page & Co., 1927) I, pp. 263-4. Letter to A. Zagórska.
    [2] *Ibid.*, p. 175. See also Edward Garnett, *Letters from Conrad, 1895 to 1924.* (London: The Nonesuch Press, 1928), p. 132: "In the matter of R. (*The Rescue*) I have lost all sense of form and I can't see *images* . . . But what to write I *know*." (Conrad's italics)

interesting to observe how Conrad expresses his bleak mood during the
month of December 1897. On December 5, he writes to Garnett of
a night spent with Steven Crane, whom he describes in Hamletian
terms: "With his rapidity in *action* . . . with that amazing *faculty* of
vision . . . He is not to be *questioned* . . . This is my *flesh* you slip out
of his hand .. . It is perhaps my own self that is slippery. I don't know
. . . *No matter* . . . My soul is like a stone within me . . . Death is
nothing . . . The *wrong* seems too *monstrous* to be lived down. *Yet* it
must. And I don't know *why, how, wherefore* . . . Manifold *torment* . . .
Some day I will *tell* you the *tale*. I can't write it now. But there is a
psychological point in it. However, this also *does not matter* . . . I struggle without pleasure like a man *certain of defeat* . . ."[3]

Indeed, there is a psychological point in Conrad's stylistic borrowings
from *Hamlet*. Any doubt that these Hamletian echoes are pertinent is
dispelled when one peruses the letter Conrad wrote to R. B. Cunninghame Graham on the following day, in which he observed, among other
things: "No man can escape his fate . . . It is *written!* It is written!"[4]
Here Conrad delivers a diatribe against actors, while confessing that he
greatly desires to write a play himself. This is his ". . . *dark* and *secret*
ambition."[5] He continues: ". . . To look at them breeds in my *melancholy soul, thoughts of murder and suicide* — such in my *anger* and
my *loathing* of their transparent pretences."[6]

Eight days later (Dec. 14, 1895), in another letter to Graham, Conrad
is still harping on *Hamlet* when he speaks of Singleton: "If it is the
knowledge of *how to live*, my man essentially possessed it . . . *Nothing
can touch him*, but the curse of decay, — the eternal decree that will
extinguish the sun, the stars, one by one, and in another instant shall
spread a *frozen darkness* over the whole universe . . . Understand that
you are *nothing*, less than *a shadow*, more *insignificant* than a drop

---

[3] *Ibid.,* I, pp. 211-212, my italics.
Hamlet: I loved you ever. But *it is no matter*. (V, i, 278, my ital.)
        But thou wouldst not think how ill all's here about
        my *heart. But* it is *no matter*. (V, ii, 202, my ital.)
        No, not for a king,
        Upon whose property and most dear life
        A *damned defeat* was made?   (II, ii, 55, my ital.)
        O, I could tell tell you —
        But let it be.   (V, ii, 325, my ital.)
        And in this harsh world draw thy breath in pain,
        To *tell my story*.   (V, ii, 337, my ital.)
Macbeth: But *wherefore* could not I pronounce 'Amen'?   (II, ii, 30, my ital.)
[4] *Ibid.,* I, p. 213. My italics.
Cf. *Hamlet:* There's a divinity that shapes our ends. (V,i, 10)
        We defy augury. There is a special providence in the fall of a sparrow . . . .
        The readiness is all!   (V,, ii, 207)
[5] *Ibid.,* my italics.
[6] *Ibid.,* my italics.

of water in the ocean, more fleeting than *the illusion of a dream . . ."*[7] In a letter to Edward Garnett (of September 29, 1897), Hamlet's voice is heard again: "I am hoist with my own petard." (*Hamlet*, III, iv, 208[8]) On December 28, 1897, the Calderonian and Shakespearean concept of *Life Is a Dream* again appears in a letter to E. I. Sanderson, although the mood is somewhat brighter. Conrad addresses Sanderson thus: *"Methinks,* O most fortunate of men . . . The future is as mysterious as ever and every added happiness is another *terror* added *to life.* Sometimes I think that I am following an *ignis fatuus* (Conrad's italics) that shall inevitably lead me *to destruction . . .* Here you have *the essence of my existence* unveiled . . . think of me often . . . Our friendship can withstand *silence,* — because *silence* is not *forgetful."*[9]

In my four preceding essays (see Note * above). I have listed a number of such Shakespearean echoes in Conrad's correspondence and text, concluding with the images of the pitiless storm of *King Lear* in Conrad's *Victory.* The storm image is a fitting accompaniment to the theme of moral darkness. The darkening sky and other aspects of elemental fury usually attend upon Conrad's exploration of this theme in which he showed interest from the very first.

In *Almayer's Folly,* the novelist was concerned with man's moral predicament in his "endeavor, the test, the trial of life" *(Youth and Two Other Stories,* p. 12), revealed in the struggle against the fury of the elements (the sea or the jungle) or in the contest with the savagery of man. In "Youth," the ship *Judea* is suspended ". . . between the *darkness* of earth and heaven . . .burning fiercely . . . upon a disc of water glittering and *sinister* . . . a *lonely* flame . . . the *black smoke . . . mournful* and imposing like a *funeral* pile kindled in the *night . . .* A magnificent *death . . .* the vast *night* lying *silent* upon the sea . . ." (pp. 34-35, my ital.) Young Marlow's recollection of his glamorous and adventurous youth is obviously rendered in *dark* colors.

Man's true identity in Conrad or, to use a more contemporary form of reference, man's existential authenticity is unfolded in this kind of contest, as the Shakespearean tragic hero bares his soul in the battle against Destiny's odds and those of his own nature. Young Marlow

---

[7] *Ibid.,* I, pp. 214-215. Conrad uses similar language at the end of *Lord Jim:* " '*Nothing can touch me,*' he said in a last flicker of superb egoism." (p. 413, my ital.) Not surprisingly, the novelist continues in a rather theatrical, fairly Elizabethan fashion. " 'Ah! but I shall hold *thee* thus,' she cried . . .' *Thou art mine!*' " (*Ibid.,* my ital.)

[8] Jean-Aubry, *op. cit.,* I, p. 93.

[9] Once more Conrad has adopted Hamlet's idiom: "And yet to me what is this quintessence of dust," finally speaking to Sanderson in the mode of dying Hamlet to Horatio: "If thou didst ever hold me in thy heart, absent thee from felicity awhile... the rest is silence." (V, ii, 335).

describes his exaltation in terms which could be applied to a Romeo or a Hamlet: "The *deceitful feeling* that lures us on to joys, to perils, to *love,* to *vain effort* — to *death;* the *triumphant conviction of strength,* the heat of life in the *handful of dust,* the *glow in the heart* that with every year grows *dim,* grows old, grows small, and expires, too soon, too soon, before life itself. (*Ibid.,* p. 37, my ital.)

The conception of the Shakespearean hero implies a certain delusion of sense as well as the ultimate recognition either by the hero himself or by the audience of the flimsiness of human existence. Shakespeare's references to dust are too numerous to be cited here, but even a random quotation can establish the affinity between Shakespeare's view of life and that of Conrad.

At least two prominent modern writers have made use of Conrad's (or Shakespeare's) phrase: "handful of dust": T. S. Eliot in *The Waste Land* ("I will show you fear in a handful of dust." In his "The Hollow Men" there is a motto from *Heart of Darkness:* "Mistah Kurtz, he dead."), and Evelyn Waugh in the title of his novel, *A Handful of Dust* (which offers four lines from *The Waste Land* as an epigram, including the one mentioned above).

While Conrad's dark comments about man's brief sojourn on this earth are close to Shakespeare's tragic mood, the "romance of illusions" described in "Youth" (p. 42) is reminiscent of *Twelfth Night* and *As You Like It,* which portray a "happy" shipwreck and the sweet uses of adversity; or of the Sicilia in *The Winter's Tale* and the enchanted island in *The Tempest* — all of which convey tragic undertones. "Youth" is an exception in Conrad's canon, being one of the few "happy" stories, in the sense that Shakespeare's comedies or romances are "happy," though they depict exile, treachery, and the winter wind of man's ingratitude.

As Juliet McLaughlan reminds us, Conrad considered the *Youth* volume as one artistic unit, stating that *Jim* "has not been planned to stand alone. *H of D* was meant in my mind as a foil, and *Youth* was supposed to give the note."[10] Though Conrad contradicts himself (as he often does) in proclaiming there is no bond between the three stories except that of the time in which they were written, and that there is "no claim to unity of artistic purpose (Author's Note, p. ix),[11] the stories, according to McLauchlan, represent three Ages of Man. The

---

[10] Juliet McLauchlan, "Conrad's 'Three Ages of Man': the *Youth* Volume," paper read at the International Conference of Conrad Scholars, San Diego, California, August 29, 1974. This essay appears in the present volume of the *Proceedings* of the Conference.
[11] *Youth and Two Other Stories,* Vol. XVI.

Marlow of *Heart of Darkness* is certainly and older and a wiser man, and it is not the ship that goes down in a lonely flame and at night; it is Kurtz, the non-heroic hero who is consumed by the horrors of the Congo jungle and those of his own heart.

This essay is an attempt to examine the Shakespearean motifs in *Heart of Darkness,* mainly from *King lear.* The analogy between the two at first seems rather tenuous; one cannot point to *obvious* resemblances such as can be seen between Lord Hamlet and Lord Jim; between Duke Prospero and Baron Heyst. Moreover, when one begins to seek for firm clues linking the story to an appropriate Shakespearean tragedy, one can hardly resist drawing an analogy with *Macbeth* rather than with *King Lear.* This is not merely because one's sleuthing instincts are aroused by a phrase from *Macbeth,* repeated twice: "That animal has *a charmed life,'* he said; 'but you can say this only of brutes in this country. No man — *you apprehend me?* — no man here *bears a charmed life.'* " (p. 84, my ital. Cf. *Macbeth:* "I bear a charmed life . . ." V, vii, 12). There is the common theme of an essentially good man whose moral nature is weak and can be destroyed by an evil temptation. Macbeth is a noble and brave soldier, a loyal subject to his King Duncan. Kurtz is an inspired idealist who hopes to reform the savages of the Dark Continent, to bring the enlightment of modern civilization to them. Both yield to the persuasive voice of the "Prince of Darkness" (*Lear,* III, vii, 134),[12] turning into savage devils themselves, ultimately destroyed by their own "vaulting ambition."

Macbeth, too, might have suggested to Conrad the powerful evocation of darkness, which Macbeth and Lady Macbeth seek to cover up their evil thoughts and deeds; the "seeling night," the horror, the nightmares, the ghosts, the witches; above all, the pervasive atmosphere of fear and gloom, of madness and despair.

Yet though this analogy could be developed in textual detail, showing a number of close correspondences. I choose to discuss the less ostensible but perhaps the more profound affinity between *Heart of Darkness* and *King Lear,* two works in which a paradoxical view of man is offered, with evil and goodness as two necessary aspects of human nature. One of Shakespeare's principal observations on man in the play is: "Humanity must perforce prey upon itself, / Like monsters of the deep." (IV, ii, 49) Marlow has a vision of Kurtz" . . . opening his mouth *voraciously* as if to *devour* all the earth with *all of its mankind.*" (p. 155, my ital.)

Conrad made a similar comment on humanity at the time he was

---

[12] See also *All's Well That Ends Well:*
    The Black Prince, sir, alias *the prince of darkness,* alias the devil.
                               (IV, v, 39, my ital.)

writing *Heart of Darkness,* in a letter to R. B. Cunninghame Graham (February 8, 1899), in which he also spoke of the narrative method employed in the story:

L'homme est an animal méchant . . . Le crime est une condition nécessaire de l'existence organisée . . .
    La société est essentiellement criminelle, — ou elle n'existerait pas. C'est l'egoisme qui suive tout, — absolument tout, — tout ce que nous abhorrons, tout ce que nous aimons."[13]

Conrad explained his deliberate use of images in the story:

I am simply in the seventh heaven, to find you like the *H of D* so far. You bless me indeed. Mind you don't curse me bye and bye for the very same thing. There are too more instalments in which the idea is so wrapped up in secondary notions that You — even You! — may miss it. And you also must remember that *I don't start with an abstract notion. I start with definite images* and as their rendering is true some little effect is produced.[14]

A careful study of these "definite images" will indeed render the "secondary notions" which surround Conrad's central ideal. I believe that the imaginative tapestry of this short novel parallels the linguistic and the philosophical revelations of Shakespeare's great tragedy. In both the hero must learn the difference between language and truth. Lear and Gloucester on the one hand, and Marlow and Kurtz on the other, discover the gap between the expressions of emotion and idealism, and love that needs no words or decency that demands no high-sounding slogans. Language itself becomes an index of truth. Lear's initial utterance is Latinite, elaborate; Goneril's and Regan's speeches are full of insincere hyperbole. At the end of the play the language changes; there is a predominance of simple, Saxon vocabulary; there is repetition of a key word, as in the unforgettable trochaic line": "Never, never, never, never, never." (V, iii, 308-9)

As the ironic stress of Conrad's tale grows more intolerable, the tension is also conveyed by similar rhetoric. The Intended, like Lear, refuses to accept the fact of her beloved Kurtz's death: "I cannot—I cannot believe—not yet. I cannot believe that I shall *never* see him

---

13 "Man is a wicked animal... Crime is a necessary condition of organized existence. Society is essentially criminal—or it wouldn't exist. It is egoism that saves everything, — absolutely everything, — everything that we hate, everything that we love" One should, however, bear in mind the fact that the first lines of Conrad's pessimistic statement might have been suggested by Anatole France's *Les Opinions de M. Coignard* (Calmann Lévy, Paris, 1893), p. 23, which is strikingly similar:
    "L'homme est naturellement un très méchant animal, et... les sociétés ne sont abominables que parce qu'il met son génie à la former." Quoted by C. T. Watts in his *Joseph Conrad's Letters to Cunninghame Graham* (Cambridge University Press, Cambridge, 1969), p. 121.
14 *Ibid.,* p. 268, my italics.

again, that nobody will see him again, *never, never, never* . . . *Never* see him!" (p. 160, my ital.) After this word is repeated five times within two short paragraphs, Marlow refers to her in the "generic" term of Shakespeare's art: ". . . I shall see her, too, a *tragic* and familiar Shade, resembling in this gesture another one, *tragic* also . . ." (*Ibid.*, my ital.) Marlow's "dull anger" at this point is not unlike Lear's "This is a *dull* sight "though, admittedly, Lear's use of the word implies his dimmed and tearful *eyesight;* or not unlike Kent's despair: "Is his the promised end?" (e.g., doomsday); or Edgar's "Or image of that horror?" Conrad's scene is marked by iteration: "I would have treasured every sigh, every word, every sign, every glance . . . I want— I want— something— something — to live with; The horror! The horror! . . . I loved him— I loved him-— I loved him." (p. 161)

Kurtz has been entrusted by the International Society for the Suppression of Savage Customs with the making of a report for its future guidance. Lear wishes to entrust his kingdom to his three daughters for the sake of future peace in the realm. Each fails in his task abysmally and ironically. Marlow reads the report and is impressed: "It was eloquent, vibrating with eloquence, but too high strung." (p. 17) Lear listens to Goneril's and Regan's eloquent tributes and he too is duly impressed. Yet, in each case, the eloquence serves the ironic purpose of revealing the moral flaw, or fault, to use Lear's word, hidden beneath the elegant surface of the statement. The opening paragraph of "this beautiful piece of writing" struck Marlow as "ominous . . . in the light of later information." Marlow was moved by the unbounded power of eloquence, "of words — of burning noble words," (as Lear was moved by the flattery of his two daughters' utterance) until he saw the postscriptum scrawled at the foot of the last page: "Exterminate all the brutes" (p. 118) Though Marlow lauds the power of Kurtz's voice which induces in him a kinship with the man (Lear too is content with the sound of his two daughters' public voices), he must acknowledge, in due time, the nature of that eloquence which can be "bewildering . . . the illuminations, the most exalted and the *most contemptible* . . . the *deceitful* flow from the *heart* of an *impenetrable darkness."* (p. 114, my ital.) Lear will also acknowledge the difference between the voices of his two evil daughters and that of Cordelia: "Her voice was ever soft,/Gentle, and low . . ." (V, iii, 271). And Cordelia senses the deceit of her sisters at once, as she is "most loath to call [your] *faults* as they are named." (I, i, 269) In the end, Kurtz's faults must come to full light, as do those of Goneril, Regan and Edmund, whose confession, as he is about to die, is similar to Kurtz's whispered admission of his own horror (fault).

The novel's title aptly describes the major theme of Shakespeare and Conrad who are both concerned with the darkness of the human heart. The twin image of heart-darkness assumes a broad connotation. *Heart* is love, idealism, fidelity, the essence and kernel of things; *darkness* represents physical and moral decay, death, corruption, and the general monstrosity of human nature. Marlow and Kurtz, like Lear and Gloucester, must travel through a moral desert, a wilderness of which they themselves are a part; they all must have their choice of nightmares, to use Marlow's phrase, before they can begin to ascend to the region of enlightment. The purpose of these journeys, in the larger sense, is the same in both works: to learn the true meaning of love, of truth, and of justice; to show the existence of goodness without glossing over evil inherent in man's character.

The play and the novel begin with an emphasis on the word *dark* which implies mystery, secrecy, night, death, ignorance, amorality and evil. Gloucester *conceals* (keeps in the dark) Edmund's illegitimate origin, blushing to acknowledge his son, conceived "in the lusty *stealth* of nature" (I, ii, 1, my ital.). Kent cannot *conceive* him (the meaning of Gloucester's words is dark) until he is told of the *fault* which was attendant upon Edmund's making. Kent, *ignorant* of Edmund's background, professes to *love* him, suing to *know* him better. Neither, of course, knows the real Edmund. Gloucester and Lear do not know their children or themselves, any more than Kurtz knew himself before he was lost in the darkness of the Congo.

Lear's very first words foreshadow this progress from darkness to light: "Meantime we shall express our *darker* purpose," the King begins, ". . . Know that we have divided / In three our kingdom . . . while we / Unburdened *crawl* toward *death* . . . " (I, i, 36) Shakespeare associates the *darker* (or secret) intention of Lear with the idea of a child (or insect), and that of death. Immediately thereafter *heart* comes into play, either through the repeated use of *love* (and its equivalents) or the word itself: ". . . *loving* son of Albany . . . our younger daughter's *love* . . . *amorous* sojourn . . . Which of you shall we say doth *love* us most . . . Sir, I love you *more* . . . as child e'er *loved* . . . A *love* that makes breath poor . . . of so much I *love* you . . ."

Cordelia's *"Love* and be *silent"* is another example of the association of love with an equivalent of death; both Shakespeare and Conrad employ this association repeatedly. Regan's speech refers to her" true *heart,* deed of *love,* and dear Highness' *love.* "Cordelia's response proclaims her *"love's*/More ponderous than [my] tongue." Whereupon Lear addresses Cordelia (whose Celtic name literally means "daughter of the sea" but it could also suggest the connotation of *cordial,* stimulating the *heart*) as his "joy to whose young *love* / The vines of France and and milk of Burgundy / Strive to be interest." And so it goes on before the scene is completed, the words *love* or *heart* will be used again and again. Lear demands; "But goes they *heart* with this?" Cordelia shall be" . . . as a stranger to [my] *heart*. "Kent, defending Cordelia, offers" the region of [my] *heart* as a target to his King's wrathful bow.

The scene serves a dramatic as well as a didactic function. It raises the questions of Gloucester's and Lear's morality, their understanding of love. It is clear that each is deficient: Gloucester in his early practice of lust and his failure to render justice to his son or see the goodness of Edgar; Lear in his offer to Cordelia ". . . to draw / A third *more opulent than* your sisters." (I, i, 85, my ital.) in exchange for a public display of flattery that would outshine that of Goneril and Regan. The play will show that love is not something quantitative, a thing to be measured with eloquence or bought with flattery. Darkness envelops the two old men; they will have to descend into even darker regions before they acquire true sight and insight; Gloucester will be able to see though not with his eyes; Lear will lose his royal garments, his authority and finally his mind, yet, paradoxically, he will thus gain a new stature of humanity. Both will learn the meaning of justice, which Kurtz also claimed.

The iteration of this image (heart-love) is also associated with several equivalents of dissolution, death, monstrosity, shame, fault, imperfection, rashness and the notion of worth or price. For example, Edmund responds to Goneril's declaration of love for him, accompanied by her kiss and the giving of her "favor", with "Yours in the ranks of *death*." (IV, ii, 25, my ital.) Albany's words addressed to the absent father of Edmund a few moments later are: "Gloucester, I live / To thank thee for the *love* thou show'dst the King . . ." (*Ibid.,* 95, my ital.) When the Gentleman reports Cordelia's anguish to Kent, he links *heart* with *shame* and *night:* ". . . once or twice she heaved the name of father / Pantingly forth, as if it pressed her *heart;* Cried 'Sisters, sisters, *shame* of ladies, sisters) / Kent, father, sisters? What, in'th'storm in'th'*night?* (IV, iii, 25, my ital.) And again, Kent reiterates the cluster of heart-shame, adding *dog,* for good measure:: "A sovereign *shame* so elbows him . . . / gave her dear rights / To his *dog-hearted* daughters—these things sting / His mind so venomously that burning *shame* / Detains him from Cordelia." (*Ibid.,* 42, my ital.)

Other characters also employ the cluster association of heart (love) and darkness. The Fool for whom Lear keeps asking in the beginning of the fourth scene (Act. I), being the yet unacknowledged mentor of the king, sets the tone by his:

So out went the candle, and we were left *darkling*. (I, iv, 208, my ital.)
Whoop, Jug, I *love* thee! (*Ibid.*, 215, my ital.)

Lear follows with:

Darkness and devils!
. . . drew from my *heart* all *love*. (*Ibid.*, 260, my ital.)

Gloucester's "flawed heart" bursts smilingly "twixt two extremes of passion, joy and grief." Lear's heart, too, must be torn thus and will break in the final scene of the play. But earlier too, during the storm the old King utters the pathetic rhetorical question: "Wilt break *my heart?*" (III, iv, 4, my ital.) He goes on: "In such a *night* / To shut me out! Pour on; I will endure. / In such a *night* as this! O Regan, Goneril, / Your old kind father, whose frank *heart* gave all, / O that way *madness lies* . . ." (IV, v, 17, my ital.) *Heart* goes together with *night* (darkness, death) and *madness* (darkness of the mind).

When Lear's mind is dimmed, he waxes bitter on the subject of love, which he now perceives as a thing of corruption: lust or prostitution. This concept of debased love is also linked with images of darkness, hell, and death.

. . . *Die* for *adultery!* No, / The wren *goes to it*, and the small, gilded fly / Does *lecher* in my sight. / Let *copulation* thrive for Gloucester's bastard son / Was kinder to his father than my daughters / *Got 'tween the lawful sheets.* / To't, luxury, pell-mell, for I lack soldiers. / Behold yond simp'ring dame, / That minces virtue, and does shake the head / To hear of *pleasure's name.* The fitchew nor the soiled horse goes to't / With a more *riotous appetite* . . . But to the girdle do the gods inherit, / *Beneath* is all *the fiend's.* / There's *hell,* there's *darkness,* there's the sulphurous *pit;* burning, scalding, stench, *consumption* . . . it smells of *mortality.* (IV, vi, 110-132, my ital.)

Observing this strange encounter of wits between the raving Lear and his *blinded* father, Edgar responds to Gloucester's and Lear's reiteration of the former's state of darkness (blindness):

Lear: . . . No, do they worst, *blind* Cupid. I'll not *love* . . .
Gloucester Were all thy letters suns, I *could not see.*
Edgar: I would not take this from report — it is,/ And *my heart breaks* at it. (IV, vi, 136, my ital.)

Again, Lear connects the idea of love with death, using the phrase "will die" in its sexual connotation: "Why, this would make a man a man of salt. / To use his eyes for garden waterpots. / Ay, and laying autumn's *dust*. I *will die* bravely. / Like a smug *bridegroom* . . ." (IV, vi, 192, my ital.) Edgar follows with a similar connection of *death* (darkness) and *heart:* "He's dead; I am only sorry / He had no other *death*sman . . . / We rip their *hearts* . .". (IV, vi, 253, my ital.)

Cordelia, too, links the dark color of her mourning with *love:* "My *mourning* and important tears hath pitied / But *love,* dear *love,* and our aged father's right." (IV, iv, 183, my ital.) The Gentleman is another speaker who thus associates these two words: ". . . she heaved the name of father / Pantingly forth, as if it pressed her *heart;* / . . . What, i'th'*storm i'th'night?* (IV, iii, 25, my ital.)

Conrad's novel, like *King Lear,* begins on a note of darkness, and the double image of *dark-heart* appears on the very first page: "The air was *dark* . . . seemed condensed into a *mournful gloom, brooding motionless* . . . *trust* worthiness personified . . . *brooding gloom* . . . the *bond* of the sea . . Besides holding our *hearts* together . . ." (p. 45, my ital.) As the story progresses the images of darkness (including those that mean not merely absence of light, but absence of motion, sound, life, reason etc.) proliferate, often in a combination with *death, nothingness* or images of moral decay, distortion, unnaturalness and monstrosity. The next three pages contain the following: "We felt . . . fit for *nothing* but *placid* staring. Only the *gloom* to the west, *brooding* over the upper reaches, became more *sombre* every minute . . . the sun sank *low* . . . stricken to *death* by the touch of that *gloom brooding* over a crowd of men . . . the *dark* 'interlopers' . . . *mystery* of an *unknown* earth . . . the *dusk* fell on the stream . . . the place of the *monstrous* town was still marked *ominously* on the sky, a *brooding gloom* in sunshine, a *lurid* glare under the stars. 'And this also,' said Marlow suddenly, 'has been one of the *dark* places of the earth . . . *foreign* shores, *foreign* faces . . . *veiled* . . . by a slightly disdainful *ignorance* . . . the sea . . . is as *inscrutable* as Destiny . . . he finds the *secret* not worth *knowing* . . . haze . . . *misty hole* . . . *spectral* illumination of *moonshine* (pp. 46-48, my ital.)

When Marlow describes Kurtz's statuesque, savage woman walking to the steamer, he again employs the same association of images, joining *darkness* with *heart:* ". . . there was something *ominous* . . . in her . . . progress . . . *sorrowful* land . . . the immense *wilderness,* the colossal body of the *fecund* and *mysterious* life . . . image of its own *tenebrous* and passionate soul . . . *brooding* over an *inscrutable* purpose . . . she stopped as if her *heart* had failed her . . . swift *shadows* . . . *shadowy embrace* . . . formidable *silence* . . . the *dusk* of the thickets." (p. 136, my ital.)

Thus, the beginning of each work is marked by the welding of the two images, *darkness* and *love.* So is the ending of the play and of the novel, again demonsrating their stylistic affinity. The tragedy closes with images of darkness and death tied up with those of heart and love: "She's *gone* for ever, / I know when one's *dead* . . . If Fortune brag of two she *loved* and hated . . . / All is *cheerless, dark,* and *deadly.* /

Your eldest daughters have *fordone* themselves. / And *desperately* are *dead.* " "Break, *heart,* I prithee break!"

As Marlow prepares to utter his compassionate lie to the Intended, he is haunted by the phantom-like vision of Kurtz which "seemed to enter the house . . . a *shadow* insatiable . . . of *frightful* realities . . . a *shadow darker* than the *shadow* of the *night . . . gloom* of the forests . . . *murky* bends . . . beat of the drum, regular and *muffled* like the beating of *a heart*— the *heart* of a conquering *darkness.* It was a triumph for the *wilderness . . .*" (pp. 155-156, my ital.) The Intended's rhetoric fits into the growing redundance of "dark" images: "The *dusk* was falling . . ." The piano looks like "a *sombre* and polished *sarcophagus.*" (p. 156, my ital.) She came . . . all in *black* . . . floating . . . in the *dusk.* She was in *mourning.* It was more than a year since his *death* . . . The room seemed to have grown *darker . . . dark eyes . . .* look of *awful desolation* . . . his *death* and her *sorrow.* (p. 157, my ital.) "moment of his *death* . . . Cruel and absurd *mysteries . . . Love* him . . . unextinghishable *light of belief* and *love* . . . The *darkness* deepened." (p. 158, my ital.) ". . . *mystery, desolation* and *sorrow* . . . eternal *darkness . . . triumphant* darkness . . ." (p. 159, my ital.) ". . . of his noble *heart . . . nothing* remains . . . *nothing* but a memory . . . leave *nothing* but sorrow . . ." (p. 160, my ital.) ". . . stream of *darkness* . . . The Intended murmured in a *heart-broken tone* . . ." (pp. 160-161, my ital.)

The now familiar cluster of images comes to an iterative crescendo at the conclusion of the story. Marlow can hear Kurtz's whisper "The horror! the horror!" The Intended keeps repeating "I love him." Now comes Marlow's ironic lie: "I heard a light sign and then my *heart* stopped *dead* short by an exulting and terribly cry, by the cry of inconceivable triumph and of *unspeakable pain* . . . But *nothing* happened. The heavens do not *fall* for such a trifle . . . It would have been *too dark—too dark altogether* . . . The offing was barred by a *black* bank of *clouds* . . . the earth flowed *sombre* under an *overcast sky—* seemed to lead into the *heart* of an *immense darkness.*" (pp. 161-162, my ital.)

Shakespeare uses the image of darkness in other plays, too, but rarely as poignantly as in this tragedy. Consider these, for instance:

"Child Rowland to a *dark tower* came . . ." (III, iv, 173, my ital.)
"All is *dark* and *comfortless.* Where's my son, Edmund?" (III, vii, 85, my ital.)
"There's *hell,* there's *darkness,* there's the sulphurous *pit.*" (IV, vi, 188, my ital.)
". . . thus out of season, threading / *dark-eye'd night* . . . " (II, i, 109, my italics)

"The *mysteries* of Hecate and the *night* . . ." (I, i, 109, my ital.)
"The *dark* and *vicious* place where thee he got cost him his eyes." (II, i, 18, my ital.)

Even more than *Othello* and *Macbeth, King Lear* is the Dark Tower of Shakespeare's imagination, since its main concern is with men's spiritual darkness, which is portrayed in broad strokes, encompassing the whole universe. It is a cosmic view of darkness, engulfing man and his globe in catastrophic upheavals, spelling death and destruction, suffering, injustice, blindness, isolation, supernatural evil, and animal-like rapacity of humans.

Conrad shares this view in *Heart of Darkness,* where the world of unreason, of rapacious folly and madness dominates his narrative canvas. He also shares Shakespeare's artistic method of orchestrating his sounds and selecting his colors in a symbolic manner, to create a total vision of a darkened universe. Both writers use animals suggestively; *King Lear's* animal imagery reinforces his depiction of savagery in human beings. Conrad's snakes, vultures, flies, hyenas, alligators, magpies, horseflies ,mice, similarly emphasize the air of general decay and corruption of the primeval forest. In both works there are numerous references to bestiality. Men appear to be monsters. There are images suggesting the mutilation and tearing of human flesh. In *King Lear* we have the gouging of Gloucester's eyes, the physical torments of Lear, the Fool and Edgar; the hanging of Cordelia; the stabbings, poisoning and the pulling of hair from an old man's beard. In *Heart of Darkness* there are the shrunken heads of humans mounted on stakes; the speared helmsman thrown overboard; the emaciated bodies of beaten and starving natives; the blind firing of rifles into the bush; the mysterious and horrid rites remembered by the dying Kurtz.

Savagery afflicts the human body as well as the human spirit. Clothing, like civilized customs and social bonds, is rent, revealing the naked flesh, and the moral nakedness or the Heart of Darkness: the dissolution of human solidarity, to use a Conradian term. But, paradoxically, the journey to the Heart of Darkness by Lear, Gloucester, Kurtz and Marlow constitutes an ironic quest of truth, wisdom, justice; above all, a pursuit of love, of brotherhood and fidelity. Thus, Conrad's moral sense, like Shakespeare's, is expressed less in terms of a systematic ethical statement than through dramatic action, and the evocation of certain moods by means of suggestive imagery.

The analogy wih *King Lear* is further strengthened by other echoes from the play. The final lines of the story, for example, read like a critical commentary on the theme of *Lear.* The King's "How, howl, howl!" is "the Intended's cry of unspeakable pain." Neither Lear nor the Intended can accept the irrevocable decree of death that has taken away the person each loves. There is an ironic sense of triumph in the cry of exultation uttered by the Intended, as there could be a sense of hope in Lear's "This feather stirs; she lives! If it be so, / It is a chance which does redeem all sorrows / That ever I have felt." For all we know, his last words may also be testimony of his false belief that Cordelia is alive, after all: "Do you see this? Look on her! Look her lips, / Look there, look there . . ." Yet his followers, like the loyal Marlow, know the truth and must speak it before each story is brought to an end.

Though it is a tragic truth, it contains the element of hope; perhaps *because* it is tragic, since it contains the element of affirmaton, the possibility of change, unlike the comic view of man, which merely mocks man's static qualities of folly, his foibles and stupidity. Lear and Kurtz change greatly in the course of their lives.

What is unchanged, perhaps, is the loyalty and fidelity of those who survive the tragic protagonist. "The weight of this sad time" must be obeyed and observed by Kent, Edgar, Marlow and the Intended. Kent's unfaltering devotion to his master; Edgar's compassion and love for his father are paralleled by the spectacle of "Mr. Kurtz's *adorers . . .* keeping their weary vigil" (p. 140) and of "the wild and gorgeous apparition of a woman" (p. 135) whose face bears" a *tragic* and fierce aspect of wild sorrow and of dumb pain." (p. 136, my ital.) There is also the bepatched Russian, the Harlequin of the story, who slavishly follows his mad mentor and master.

The Harlequin can be considered as Conrad's counterpart of Fool and of Tom o' Bedlam who often speak in obscure riddles; Marlow's first contact with the "glamorous" Russian is through Towson's book, containing his strange notes: "They were in *cipher;* Yes, it looked like *cipher* . . . It was an extravagant mystery." (p. 99, my ital.) When he meets the author of these mysterious notes in person, Marlow's wonder is even greater: "There he was before me, *in motley,* as though he had absconded from . . . *a troupe of mimes,* enthusiastic, fabulous." (p. 126, my ital.)

Once again we find the concurrence of love (heart) and darkness. " 'Ah, he talked to you of *love,*' I said much amused . . . 'he made me see things, — things . . .' . . . *never, never* before, did this land, this river, this jungle, the very arch of this *blazing* sky, appear to me so *hopeless* and so *dark,* so impenetrable to human thought, so *pitiless* to human *weakness.*" (p. 127, my ital.)

Fool is also a key word in *King Lear,* where it appears 47 times (*foolish* — 10 times); in *Heart of Darkness* it is used 12 times; *folly* —

4 times and *foolish* 4 times. The Fool acts as Lear's teacher, taunting him but his sharp, caustic wit keeps Lear from going mad for a while. Perhaps Conrad's phrase "in motley" might have been suggested by one of the following passages:

Fool: The sweet and bitter fool
      Will presently appear;
      The one *in motley here,*
      The other found out there.
Lear: Dost thou call me fool, boy?
Fool: All thy other titles thou hast given away; that thou wast born with.
Kent: This is not altogether fool, my lord. (I, iv, 137)
Fool: I am a fool . . . thou art nothing. (I, iv, 183)

Lear must ultimately be transformed into a fool, "fantastically dressed with wild flowers" and in a state of madness (as Kurtz appears to Marlow). Furthermore, he will accept his new role:

Beat at this gate that let thy folly in . . . (I, iv, 262)
When we are born, we cry that we are come
To this great stage of fools. (IV, vi, 79)
I am even / . . . The natural fool of Fortune . . . (IV, vi, 188)
I am a very foolish fond old man. (IV, vii, 60)
I am old and foolish. (IV, vii, 84)

So does Gloucester: "Oh, my follies! / Then Edgar was abused." (III, vii, 91). Edgar too, adopts the garments and the demeanor of Fool-madman; he plays fool to his father and Lear, serving both as a guide and teacher. While the young Russian chooses motley, his function is reversed, for he is the one who learns from Kurtz who "enlarges" the young man's mind. But he, in turn, instructs Marlow, by appearing to him as "an insoluble problem;" by presenting an existence which "was improbable, inexplicable and altogether bewildering." (p. 196) Marlow confesses to having been *"seduced* into something like *ad-miration-*like envy." (*Ibid.,* my ital.) It is the Russian who finally reveals to Marlow the true nature of Kurtz's appeal.

There is another use of "fool" which suggests *King Lear* as a possible source. Marlow speaks of the "subtle *bond*" (p. 19, my ital.) with the savage black helmsman who is killed by a spear, and whose body he must throw overboard. Not, however, before recalling the dead man's last look which remains graven in his memory ". . . like a claim of distant *kinship* affirmed in a supreme moment." *"Poor fool!"* Marlow exclaims, describing how the helmsman's shoulders "were *pressed* to [my] *breast.* [I] hugged him from behind *desperately."* Soon thereafter he refers to his action which appears to the pilgrims aboard as his "*heartless* promptitude." (p. 120, my ital.)

Cordelia affirms her love for Lear thus: "I cannot heave / *My heart* into my mouth. I *love* your Majesty /

According to my *bond,* no more no less." (I, i, 92, my ital.) When Lear presses hanged Cordelia to *his* breast, he cries out: "And my *poor fool* is hanged." In each case, the word implies a term of endearment. One more possible correspondence occurs here. Marlow tips the dead body overboard and he "saw the body roll over twice before [I] lost sight of it *for ever.*" (p. 120, my ital.) Lear with Cordelia in his arms says: ". . . She's gone *forever . . .* "

The fools and madmen in each case stress the absurdity of human existence. Lear's initial materialism—his concern with his dignity, his status, his one hundred (or fewer) followers, is the epitome of human vanity and folly. He must be stripped of the external trappings of power, crazed with anguish and humiliation before he can begin his ascent towards true humanity. Similarly, Kurtz's voice rants with all the accents of royal authority, as he becomes the devil-god of the savages. He dreams of "*images* of wealth and fame revolving obsequiously round his unextinguishable gift of *noble* expression. *My* intended, *my* station, *my* career, *my* ideas." (p. 147, my ital.) He will be "buried presently in the mould of *primeval* earth" (*Ibid.,* my ital.) He is possessed by "the *diabolic love;*" his soul is "satiated with *primitive* emotions, avid of *lying fame,* of *sham distinction,* of all the *apperances of success and power.*" (pp. 147-148, my ital.)

Is this not a fitting analysis of Lear's desire to retain his image as the supreme ruler of the land, without being prepared to bear the full weight of his office? "Only we shall retain / The *name* and all *th'addition* to a king." (I, i, 135, my ital.) We recognize Lear's incipient madness, his second childishness, as do his two daughters, Goneril and Regan. Kurtz, too, "was contemptibly *childish.* He desired to have *kings* meet him . . ." (p. 184, my ital.) What Conrad says of Kurtz applies to Lear. His tempest of mind, his physical pain and his ravings all lead to the central thematic statement of identity: "I am a very foolish old man." The admission of his foolishness is the culmination of Shakespeare's ironic reversal, illustrating the contrast between what the hero has become and his appearance at the outset of the play.

A new dignity has been conferred upon the old and foolish man, for now we can feel a profound kinship with him, as Marlow experienced a sense of kinship with Kurtz. Lear, like so many Conradian heroes, has learned the lesson, has passed the supreme test, and has attained the ironic triumph. When he breaks Kent's heart, he touches ours. And when Kurtz cries at the "invisible wilderness" *"Oh,* but I will wring your *heart* yet!" he also declares his new identity, muttering, *"Live* rightly, *die, die . . ."* (p. 148, my ital.) Marlow listens, then unconsciously lapses into Kurtz's idiom, as he in turn cries: "Oh, I wasn't *touched.* I was *fascinated."* (p. 149, my ital.) As he lies "in the *dark* waiting for *death,"* Kurtz's face reflects "the extreme expression of *sombre pride,* ruthless *power,* craven *terror* of an intense and *hopeless despair.* Did he live his life in every detail of desire, temptation, and surrender during that *moment of complete knowledge?"* (p. 149, my ital.) This knowledge is manifested in his final cry of "horror." Kurtz is the unjust Lear of the early part of the play, proud, insolent, unfeeling. Yet he does change, for Conrad would have him attain, as every great tragic hero of Shakespeare must attain, "that moment of complete knowledge." The *darker* purpose of Lear is revealed after it has unleashed a storm of universal proportions. The darker purpose of Kurtz's mission also results in a tempestuous progression towards death. Yet in the end, both Shakespeare and Conrad have evoked a vision of evil; they have shown us the horrendous gulf between appearance and reality, and, through moving scenes of ironic recognition, hope and reversal, have offered eloquent testimony to man's potential for goodness.

In a letter to Edward Garnett (August 11, 1902) Conrad advised his friend: "And let 'all thy words bear the accent of heroic truth' properly seasoned by malice. But before everything switch off the critical current of your mind and *work in darkness* — the *creative darkness* which no ghost of responsibility will haunt."[15] I think Conrad followed his own advice, and out of his creative darkness came the best of his work, and some of his imagery derived from Shakespeare. This is no artistic sin, for William Shakespeare himself, whose power of adaptation often exceeded his power of invention, derived a great deal of his imagery and most of his plots from other writers. Admittedly, it is not easy to draw a clear-cut dividing line between invention and adaptation in great poetry. Yet much of Shakespeare's derived imagery is so thoroughly altered, so integrated into his dramatic or poetic intent, that it is often undetectable. But even when it is possible to identify passages from the Bible, from the Holinshed Chronicles, or from Greek or Latin sources, Shakespeare's achievement is not thereby diminished. So it is with Conrad.

---

[15] Edward Garnett, *op. cit.,* p. 298, my italics.
The cluster image of heart-death occurs also in Conrad's correspondence, e.g., "The generosity of your criticism (of *The Rover)* my dear Edward, is great enough to put *heart* into a *dead* man." (*Ibid.,* p. 330, my ital.)

His style is an ornate quilt, blending Shakespeare's rich hues with the sparkling blazes of Polish and Continental Romantics; it glows with the intense passions of a Dostoyevsky; it radiates the keen irony of a Flaubert. To some spectators, of course, this multicolored garment of Conrad's fiction must remain invisible, like the "clothes" of the gullible emperor. With their limited literary sight they must take the word of the critics whose tailoring skills they can admire in the abstract at best, or pretend to admire, as the case may be. Similarly, the adjectival gaudiness of the narrative fabric, the gossamer lightness of ironic threads can elude the impatient eye of the reader who demands action on every page, and a simplistic cut of character.

Those, however, who aspire to understand the art of Conrad's literary loom will try to discern the woof from the warp, without losing the effect of the total design. They will bear in mind Conrad's own artistic credo, stated in the Preface to *The Nigger of the "Narcissus."* "Confronted by the same enigmatical spectacle the artist *descends within* himself, and in that lonely *region* of stress and strife, if he be deserving and fortunate, he finds the terms of his appeal." (p. xii, my ital.) Perhaps Conrad did not borrow the word from Kent's admonition to Lear (quoted above in this essay), yet in the very same paragraph he does speak of the "invincible conviction of solidarity that knits together the loneliness of innumerable *hearts* . . ." And that other key term of *Lear* is also there: ". . . it becomes evident that there is not a place of splendor or a *dark* corner of the earth that does not deserve, if only a passing glance of wonder and pity."

Although the allusive texture of Conrad's narrative may indeed suggest the suit of motley worn by the glamorous Harlequin of *Heart of Darkness,* its character is definitely not "a thing of shreds and patches," — as Conrad remarked, again echoing a Hamletian dictum.[16] Nor is it "a thing of darkness," which Prospero had to acknowledge with some embarrassment, Conrad's imagery of darkness notwithstanding. His literary art is unique, unclassifiable; it is perhaps like Hamlet's soul — "a thing immortal."[17]

---

[16] Preface to *The Shorter Tales of Joseph Conrad* (Garden City, New York; Doubleday, Page & Co., 1924), p. x. Conrad writes about the problem of selection for this volume ". . . in the full consciousness of [my] feelings, [my] concern . . . to give it some unity . . . its own character. Character is not *a thing of shreds and patches.*" (My ital.) Cf. *Hamlet:* "A king of shreds and patches . . ." (III, iv, 102). I suppose, it is possible to assume that the phrase came to Conrad via Gilbert and Sullivan; but even if this is so, the latter took it from Shakespeare.

[17] *Hamlet*, I, iv, 67.

RUTH CHRISTIANI BROWN

"PLUNG'D IN THAT ABORTIVE GULF"
MILTON IN "NOSTROMO"

The relationship of setting and theme in *Nostromo* has absorbed the attention of many Conrad students, for clearly that imaginary South American republic combines the lure of a vividly portrayed locale with an insistent yet puzzling symbolism. A wealth of material has appeared probing both the actual and symbolic aspects of the setting, yet these explorations leave many questions unanswered concerning Conrad's "largest canvas." While Conrad insisted, "Costaguana is meant for a S. American state in general,"[1] his assertion has seemingly spurred on the efforts to link the place names of Costaguana to specific geographical areas and to trace the descriptions of both place and incident in *Nostromo* to the adventure and travel books which Conrad used. Opinions differ as to the effectiveness of the abundant and rich description, for in some sections Guerard has found the specificity too great to be artistically effective,[2] while for Tillyard the setting is of "compelling reality." He declares, "For the sustained compulsion to see and believe in an imagined town and its surroundings no English novel can challenge *Nostromo*."[3] Equally compelling is the symbolism of the setting, for each careful study of the text reveals an intricate interweaving of scene and theme. In the rich soil of Costaguana, details of setting like dragon's teeth give rise to an army of meanings. Grappling with the complex interpenetration of theme and setting, one may experience sensations like those of Conrad while in the throes of composition. He suffered, as he told Wells, "an uncomfortable sense of losing my footing in deep waters."[4]

Much of the difficulty may lie in a misunderstanding of Conrad's purpose and method, for as Tillyard suggests, "Critics of *Nostromo* are

---

[1] C. T. Watts, *Joseph Conrad's Letters to R. B. Cunninghame Graham*, (London, 1969), p. 157. Letter of 31 October 1904.

[2] Albert J. Guerard, *Conrad the Novelist*, (Cambridge, Mass., Harvard University Press, 1965), P. 179. While for the most part Guerard confirms the reality of the setting, he finds "regrettably, more description of furniture and decor than is usual in his writing" and "certain descriptions in an older manner are frankly 'written'; the blocks are wearily piled into place...."

[3] E. M. W. Tillyard, *The Epic Strain in the English Novel*, (London, Chatto and Windus, 1967), p. 138.

[4] G. Jean-Aubry, *Joseph Conrad, Life and Letters*, (London, 1927), p. 321.

agreed that Conrad controlled and shaped his matter with conspicuous success. Still, having underestimated the extent and variety of that matter, they have thereby underestimated the difficulty of the task to which he was committed."[5] That Conrad did indeed attempt a prodigious creative effort in *Nostromo* can no longer be doubted; clearly he sought far greater scope and significance than in any other work, achieving, says Tillyard, "the kind of variety and amplitude propitious to the epic effect."[6] I propose that in addition to the mythic, political, and philosophic themes which Conrad wove into the dense and intricate fabric of his modern epic, he also worked in repeated echoes of the great epic *Paradise Lost.* These echoes are not isolated and accidental but frequent and purposeful, and a careful tracing of their use greatly enhances the appreciation of Conrad's greatest creative achievement.

The most obvious link to *Paradise Lost* is to be found in the setting of *Nostromo* where the shining heights of Higuerota, the dark gulf, and the Isabel Islands offer a sensation of *deja vu,* an experience of familiarity rather than one of utter strangeness. A comparison of Curry's drawing of Milton's Cosmos (Plate I) with an artist's rendering of the world described by Conrad (Plate II) reveals why this is so. The two worlds exhibit a marked congruence. The unsullied heights of the Sulaco province lie in the position of Heaven, the one dominated by the mountain Higuerota and the other by "God the Father"; the great dark semicircular Placid Gulf lies below in the position of Chaos; the Isabels "basking in the sunshine just outside the cloud veil" which "strives for but seldom wins the middle of the gulf"[7] accurately reflect Milton's placement of the World, pendant from Heaven's gate with its nadir just the distance of its radius from the upper limits of Hell; the "line drawn between Punta Mala and the Azuera" where "the ships from Europe bound to Sulaco lose at once the strong breezes of the ocean" and "become the prey of capricious airs" thus corresponds to the upper boundary of Milton's Hell. The directions are also congruent, with Heaven lying toward the east and Hell toward the west. Furthermore, it is not just in the major features that the congruence applies, for the harbor of Sulaco lies in the position of the gate of heaven and many other portions of Conrad's world exhibit distinct features of Milton's world. As I deal with each particular of setting below, I will give further significant detail to support each identification. Thus the opening chapter of *Nostromo* appears to be an elaborate and emotionally

---

[5] Tillyard, p. 156-7.
[6] Tillyard, p. 128.
[7] Joseph Conrad, *Nostromo,* (London, Dent Collected Edition, 1966), pp. 7, 6. All subsequent references are to this edition. Quotations of more than fifteen words have been footnoted.

charged word painting with each of its major elements reflecting the setting of Milton's epic of the fall of man.

It would then appear that Conrad in his epic of the fall of modern man in an Eden being invaded by the forces of material interest has arranged that the salient features of his setting will relate to those of the earlier fall. In his epic of "men shortsighted in good and evil," Conrad has sought to arouse in the reader almost unconscious memories of the earlier loss of bliss through pride and treachery. I believe that these echoes are purposely unobtrusive, intended to intensify the emotional response of the reader even when they are not consciously observed. In their subtle presence they are like the underlying fairy-tale motif, pervasive yet unobtrusive, as Tillyard noted: "Conrad's triumph is that he has integrated his fairy-lore so beautifully with the whole complex of the book that readers have deeply felt rather than consciously perceived it."[8] Conrad has succeeded also in his use of the *Paradise Lost* motif, I believe, for it has contributed greatly to the emotional power of the work even while remaining undetected. The echoes of *Paradise Lost* are interwoven with consummate artistry yet unmistakably present.

Others have perceived the thematic link and have recognized *Nostromo* as an epic of a fall even though they have not linked it to *Paradise Lost.* Eloise Knapp Hay observes, "Inevitably this tale of temptation and corruption has some reverberations from the original Fall of Man. By taking our sights from the biblical prototype, we can see the political fable most distinctly."[9] Claire Rosenfield sees the Goulds as "the Adam and Eve who first yield to the temptations of power" and who destroy the ferny ravine, bringing the "new race into a demonic Eden."[10] Particulars such as the name "Nostromo" meaning "our man" echoing "Adam" or "a man," make the interpretation of the novel as the tale of the loss of a latter day Eden almost inevitable.

The power of the setting to arouse intense emotional response in the reader has been attested by innumerable critics, and I believe that much of the power arises from the remarkable fusion of the exotic and particular locale with the mythical elements found specifically in Milton's epic. Conrad's "twilight country with its high shadowy Sierra and its

---

[8] Tillyard, p. 135. Tillyard holds that the glowering Montero plays the part of the evil fairy at the birthday party of the new railroad. He mentions Emilia elsewhere as the good fairy, but he does not refer to her efforts to reduce the evil the railroad brings by saving the Viola's house. She is powerless to prevent the pleasure ground of the people from being taken, however. He points out several other fairy tale motifs.

[9] Eloise Knapp Hay, *The Political Novels of Joseph Conrad,* (Chicago, University of Chicago, 1963), p. 182.

[10] Claire Rosenfield, *Paradise of Snakes,* (Chicago, University of Chicago, 1967), p. 51.

misty Campo" gripped his imagination so powerfully that Bennett once wrote to Conrad, "I read Higuerota again not long since. I always think of the book as 'Higuerota,' the said mountain being the principal personage in the story."[11] For most readers the gulf swathed in palpable obscurity remains in vivid memory as the emotional center of the novel. To cite but one example, Cox describes entering the gulf as "a movement out of ordinary life into some underworld."[12] And again more recently he writes, "When the two men leave the jetty, it is as if they have jumped off the earth into a *condition of chaos before creation*."[13] (italics mine) Thus in his attempt to describe the powerful effect of this scene, Cox has employed some of the terminology and imagery which Milton's epic has made an integral part of our heritage. I believe such response arises because Conrad is using these dimly remembered passages to intensify our response to the tragedy that is overtaking Costaguana.

Although Conrad insisted that Costaguana was an imaginary country ("There was not a single brick, stone, or grain of sand of its soil I had not placed in position with my own hands"). Costaguana can be linked to an actual area with only two really important discrepancies, and those discrepancies, I believe, were introduced to link Sulaco more closely to Milton's Cosmos. After his excellent summary of the details of Costaguana's geography, Tillyard concludes, "Costaguana, then, is an imaginary republic on one or the other side of the Isthmus of Panama but so imagined as to be unidentifiable."[14] Yet the details he enumerates fit well the present day Colombia *before* the loss of its westernmost province which became the republic of Panama. Colombia-Panama (earlier New Granada) lies in a hot latitude, has precipitous mountains above the snowline, borders on two oceans, contains a broad central valley affording relatively easy communication for the eastern part of the country, contains the sources of great rivers (the Amazon and the Orinoco), lies between San Francisco and Valparaiso, and is separated from its western province by towering mountains. That western province (now Panama) contains the great Gulf of Panama which boasts not only the Azuero peninsula noted by Tillyard but also a Punta Mala. A minor discrepancy is the absence of a good natural harbor along Colombia's western coast, and for this Conrad apparently

---

[11] G. Jean-Aubry, *Twenty Letters to Joseph Conrad*, (London, The First Edition Club 1926), n.p. In this letter of 22 November 1912, one of the very few which Conrad saved, Bennett says that he considers *Nostromo* the "finest novel of this generation (bar none)," and also declares, "Only other creative artists can understand a creative artist."

[12] C.B. Cox, *Nostromo (Joseph Conrad)*, (Oxford, Blackwell, 1964), p. 7.

[13] C. B. Cox, *Joseph Conrad: The Modern Imagination*, (London, Dent, 1974), pp. 78-9.

[14] Tillyard, pp. 199-200.

reached down into Ecuador using the principal features of Guayaquil for his Cayta. Panama, like Sulaco, was the one province of intense interest to European capitalists, although Panama's coveted treasure was a short route to the Pacific rather than a silver mine. And as to Conrad's knowledge of affairs in Panama during the writing of *Nostromo* there can be no doubt since he wrote to Cunninghame Graham, "What do you think of the Yankee Conquistadores in Panama? Pretty, isn't it?"[15] Further parallel details such as the presence of an American warship in the gulf and the great haste with which the United States recognized the new republic offer further corroboration. Whether or not the maneuvering of the Frenchman Bunau-Varilla, the architect of the Panamanian revolt, contributed anything to the portrait of the boulevardier and expatriate Decoud does not concern us here, but it seems quite possible.

For the present inquiry, the two great differences between Colombia-Panama and Costaguana now become more important than the many similarities. The main physical difference between Panama and the Occidental Province lies in Panama's having a port on the east as well as on the west. Sulaco opens only toward the west. The isolation of the western province was essential to the drama of the invasion of an unviolated area by the forces of material interests, and it would seem that Conrad eliminated the easy access by sea between the two parts of Costaguana. Through this change in geography, Sulaco lies protected from the struggles which convulse the rest of Costaguana by the precipitous wall of the Sierra; Costaguanan and foreign invaders must enter either by scaling the mountains or sailing through the Placid Gulf. The second important difference is one of direction: the Gulf of Panama opens toward the south, while the Placid Gulf faces west. Both of these changes serve Conrad well in sharpening the dramatic conflict, but even more significantly, they coincide with essential features of the Miltonic Cosmos. Here also the unscaled heights lie toward the east, the murky and dark gulf opens toward the west, and within the gulf lies the untouched new world. The importance of this similarity to the theme and the strong verbal echoes in Conrad's description support the contention that such geographical changes were made purposely to link the later epic to the earlier one.

The extent of Conrad's knowledge of Milton has not been fully appreciated even though his use of an epigraph from "Comus" for his novel *Victory* indicated long ago that he knew and chose to use something from Milton's work. The Polish novelist Stefan Żeromski linked

---

[15] Watts, p. 149. Letter of 26 December 1903.

Conrad's work with *Paradise Lost* in his preface to the Polish translation
of the selected writings of Conrad where he declared that the power and
sonority of Conrad's description in *The Mirror of the Sea* was so great
that "English criticism did not hesitate to set those pages of his book
alongside the pages from Milton's *Paradise Lost*."[16] Żeromski here is
suggesting equal literary rank for the two writers rather than a structural
or thematic link. To my knowledge, no one has suggested specific
parallels between Conrad's work and that of Milton.

Quite obviously Curry's drawing which appeared in 1956 could not
have been seen by Conrad, and whether or not he knew the Globe
Edition of the poems edited by David Masson I cannot yet be sure,
although it is possible since Masson's was a popular edition, going
through fourteen printings between its appearance in 1877 and 1903
when Conrad was writing *Nostromo*. If he had access to this edition,
he would have seen several diagrams of the Cosmos, the most complete
being that reproduced in Plate III. These plates were accompanied by
a careful exposition of the nature and dimensions of Milton's setting
for *Paradise Lost*, yet such explanations and representations would not
have been essential for Conrad's visualization of this great scheme,
for Conrad as well as Masson could discover it in the text itself.
Nonetheless, it is interesting to observe that such diagrams existed
and were readily available and that the diagram coincides in its
principal characteristics with the great passages describing the Occidental
Province.

Let us now examine each of the principal features of Conrad's setting
to discover wherein their relationships to one another resemble such
relationships in Milton's schema, to find verbal echoes of *Paradise Lost*
in Conrad's text, and to relate these elements to parallels in theme.
I will deal with the schematic parallels, the verbal correspondences,
and the relationship of these to the development of the theme for
each of the major features of the setting in turn.: first, "heaven,"
second, "chaos," third, "the world," fourth, "hell," and fifth, other smaller
settings in *Nostromo* which exhibit similarities to scenes in *Paradise Lost*.

The upper realm, "heaven" or "The Empyrean" is the abode of light
in Milton's Cosmos where God appears as a cloaked radiance:

> Fountain of light, thyself invisible
> Amidst the glorious brightness where thou sitt'st
> Throned inaccessible . . .   PL III, 375-7

---

16 Stefan Żeromski, Preface to Vol. I of *Selected Writings*, Joseph Conrad Ko-
rzeniowski, *Fantazja Almayera, Almayers Folly*, Opowieść o Wschodniej Rzece,
(Warszawa, Tow. Wydawnicze "Ignis" S. A. 1923), p. xxiv. Translated by Prof. M.
Mroczkowski for my use.

In *Nostromo* the wall of the cordillera is dominated by Great Higuerota, described in terms of aloofness, majesty, and radiance, and only its lower slopes can be challenged by the most daring men. The great peak stands in a position corresponding to the mountain "God the Father" in the drawing which Curry derived from Milton's text. Conrad insistently relates light to Higuerota through its "dazzling snow edge," its "snowy dome" and even personifies it in "the white head of Higuerota." The images are linked to sunrise and sunset, with the gleaming slopes of the peak holding the light and and dominating the panorama. Early in the novel Conrad stresses its infinite superiority, its disdain of the squabbles of the revolutionary rabble: "its cool purity seemed to hold itself aloof from the hot earth." The battle raging below seems "a violent game played upon the plain by dwarfs mounted and on foot, yelling with tiny throats, under the mountain that seemed a colossal embodiment of silence" (p. 27). Even as the omnipotent God takes no part in the three day battle of the revolted angels in heaven, so great Higuerota stands aloof from the petty three day upheaval which rocks Sulaco and he surrounding campo.

Both great eminences are shrouded in clouds, and the areas below them become darker by contrast:

> . . . but when thou shad'st
> The full blaze of thy beams, and through a cloud
> Drawn round about thee like a radiant shrine,
> Dark with excessive bright thy skirts appear,
> Yet dazzle heav'n . . . PL III 377-81

Higuerota towers over the other peaks and outdoes them in brightness: "The sunset rays striking the snowslope of Higuerota from afar gave it an air of rosy youth, while the serrated mass of distant peaks remained black, as if calcined in the fiery radiance" (p. 40). A light so powerful as to transform its surroundings as with the purifying fire of a furnace can hardly be characteristic of an ordinary mountain however lofty. The dark area around Higuerota not only emphasizes Higuerota's power and uniqueness, but also echoes closely "Dark with excessive bright thy skirts appear."

Higuerota functions also as a powerfully suggestive symbol which I am not alone in linking to a royal throne. Tillyard draws attention to Conrad's phraseology in the essay "Autocracy and War," written just after *Nostromo* and closely linked to it in ideas, where Conrad wrote:

It is the bitter fate of any idea to lose its royal form and power, to lose its "virtue" the moment it descends from *its* solitary throne to work its will among the people. (p. 142)

Tillyard comments, "Transferred to the context of *Nostromo,* the phrase 'solitary throne' makes us think of the eternal snows of Higuerota; as it should do, for Higuerota is not only a most convincingly real snow-peak . . . but a permanent symbol of ideal truth, sometimes forgotten but ever there in the background." Tillyard's experience of this symbol and that of many other readers thus supports the interpretation of Higuerota as an embodiment of purity and power. Such qualities along with the physical description of its radiance argue strongly that it is indeed a counterpart of Milton's "fountain of light" which is the source of good.

Further evidence of Higuerota as the embodiment of the ideal appears when one examines the relationship of the descriptive passages to the various characters in the novel. The close linking of Higuerota to the old white-haired Garibaldino has been frequently noted, but Tillyard shows that the mountain is mentioned in conjunction with many other characters, and always at a time when they are revealing some idealism or honor in themselves.[17] The moments when they aspire to generous or brave deeds are linked to descriptions of Higuerota's shining head. Tillyard further reminds us that our one close view of the mountain serves to sharpen the contrast between Sir John and the chief engineer, who are "as elementally different as fire and water." Sir John sees in the great peak only "the hostility of nature which can be overcome by the resources of finance," but the chief engineer stands in awe before it:

[He] had contemplated the changing hues on the enormous side of the mountain, thinking that in this sight, as in a piece of inspired music, there could be found together the utmost delicacy of shaded expression and a stupendous magnificence of effect. (p. 40)

The chief engineer is not deaf to the music of the spheres as is Sir John, and he reminds Sir John of the supremacy of Higuerota, saying with a humility rare among the arrogant men in *Nostromo.* "We can't move mountains." The chief engineer, one of the most selfless and admirable characters, speaks here for those men whose skill and devotion bring about the advancement of the railroad in this perilous outpost. Conrad reserves his scorn for the financial manipulators like Sir John and Holroyd; for the men who serve as the front line troops in the army of progress he shows respect, reminding us that some of them will die before their purpose is achieved. He treats with some irony the almost religious zeal which the very young bring to the cause.

Despite the invulnerability of Higuerota and the awe which it in-

---

[17] Tillyard, pp. 142-4.

spires, its effect upon Sulaco has been benevolent, its shadow lying late upon the flower stalls of the market place more protective than threatening, yet that sun bursts upon Sulaco at the fulness of its noonday power just as the technological revolution strikes Sulaco with the full force of its highly developed economic power. The mountains have shielded Sulaco from the fret of commerce as well as from the riots and political broils of the rest of Costaguana; now her defenses are breached by the steamship and the locomotive and she is "on the point of being invaded by all the world." The beneficent nature of Higuerota is further emphasized by the name which means "gigantic fig tree." The mountains seem to symbolize the inviolable fortress of nature, not inveterately hostile to man, but demanding respect, even reverence. In his shortsighted attack on the natural order, majestic and invulnerable, man destroys only himself. Higuerota needs no defense, just as God needs no defense when the rebellious angels wage impious war in heaven with their ingenious machines. But just as those rebels brought about their own ruin and that of the newly created world, so the invaders of Costaguana seem to be bringing about the destruction of a simpler and more humane way of life, and Conrad has used the metaphor of the destruction of Eden.

In the description of Higuerota at close range through the eyes of the character who climbs the highest and sees it most perceptively, the chief engineer, Conrad uses an image similar to Milton's gateway which stands "in utmost longitude, where heav'n / with earth and ocean meets." It is on the far side of Higuerota at the highest point the railway will reach:

Pillared masses of black basalt framed like an open portal a portion of the white field lying aslant against the west. (p. 40)

While Milton describes the gate thus:

> . . . It was a rock
> Of Alabaster, piled up to the clouds,
> Conspicuous far, winding with one ascent
> Accessible from earth, one entrance high;
> The rest was craggy cliff, that overhung
> Still as it rose, impossible to climb.
> Betwixt those rocky pillars . . . PL IV, 542-8

Higuerota thus stands like the great gate to Paradise in Milton's epic, the one legitimate way of entering the unspoiled home of man. This great gateway is linked with the chief engineer, confirming his positive qualities, for he more than any other character in *Nostromo* truly appreciates Higuerota and throughout the novel he acts bravely and generously.

In marked contrast to the shining heights of Higuerota is the Placid Gulf, a "vast semicircle of waters" whose nature and limits bear the mark of Milton's Chaos; the Placid Gulf is a region of "impenetrable darkness" where "sky, land, and sea disappear together out of the world." When the blanket of clouds lies over it, no light can penetrate its stygian shades.

The few stars left below the seaward frown of the vault shine feebly as into the mouth of a black cavern. In its vastness your ship floats unseen under your feet, her sails flutter invisible above your head. The eye of God Himself . . . could not find out what work a man's hand is doing in there; and you would be free to call the devil to your aid with impunity if even his malice were not defeated by such blind darkness. (p. 7)

Decoud and Nostromo struggle to cross this gulf at night in a lighter heavy with silver in the most vividly realized experience in the novel, and during their laborious passage the gulf reaches the apex of its symbolic power. The description of Chaos as Satan begins his journey to the newly created world offers strong parallels:

> . . . a dark
> Illimitable Ocean without bound,
> Without dimension, where length, breadth, and highth,
> And time and place are lost . . . PL II, 891-4

In Conrad's gulf with "the restlessness of the waters crushed by the weight of dense night," under a "veil of obscurity warm and hopeless," motion becomes imperceptible and all sense of direction is lost. Only by putting his hand into the black water can Decoud determine whether or not the boat is moving. In the "great recrudescence of obscurity" Nostromo must steer by the feel of the wind on his cheek, with no idea of his direction nor of his position in the gulf.

In both works the darkness is described as having substance, as when Beelzebub, pretending to seek a volunteer to undertake the journey across the frightful waste toward the new abode of man asks,

> . . . who shall tempt with wandring feet
> The dark unbottom'd infinite Abyss
> And through the palpable obscure find out
> His uncouth way . . .   PL II, 404-7

Conrad shows Decoud exulting in the solidity of the darkness:

The darkness of the gulf was no longer for him the end of all things. It was part of a living world since, pervading it, failure and death could be felt at your elbow. And at the same time it was a shelter. He exulted in its impenetrable obscurity. "Like a wall, like a wall," he muttered to himself. (p. 283)

Later to Nostromo also the darkness becomes substantial when he makes his way from the Great Isabel toward the harbor, looking back, he sees "nothing but smooth darkness like a solid wall."

In the Placid Gulf as in the great abyss of Chaos there are no steady or predictable winds. Ships within the gulf find themselves "the prey of capricious airs," amid unpredictable showers and great masses of moving mist. In Chaos, "hot, cold, moist, and dry, four Champions fierce / Strive here for Maistrie" (II, 898-9), and Satan entering Chaos is first swept upward but soon becomes the sport of the unreliable currents:

> As in a cloudy chair ascending rides
> Audacious, but that seat soon falling meets
> A vast vacuity.   PL II, 930-2

In the same way Nostromo and Decoud set out with a fairly good wind to drive them, one which Mitchell had thought to the better than usual for a journey across the gulf, but they are soon utterly becalmed in the vast emptiness of the dark gulf.

In the gulf, as in Chaos, all are prey to accident with no ability to foresee or to control events, for "eldest Night and Chaos . . . hold / Eternal anarchy. . ." (PL II, 894-6)

>   Chaos Umpire sits,
> And by decision more imbroiles the fray
> By which he Reigns: next him high Arbiter
> Chance governs all.   PL II, 907-10

In the gulf the rule of chance or accident makes man's trusted weapons worthless. Both Decoud and Nostromo are stripped of the means by which they have achieved their position in life: Decoud cannot use his sharp intellect.

Intellectually self confident, he suffered from being deprived of the only weapon he could use with effect. No intelligence could penetrate the darkness of the Placid Gulf. (p. 275)

Nostromo cannot use the strength and skill of which he is inordinately proud.

"I have been sent out into this black calm on a business where neither a good eye, nor a steady hand, nor judgment are any use." (p. 276)

The presence of Hirsch on the lighter comes about by pure chance, as does the collision with the troopship which carries him away clinging to its anchor. "The fate of Senor Hirsch remained suspended in the darkness of the gulf at the mercy of events that could not be foreseen" (p. 275). And Nostromo calls the whole adventure "a blind game with death." And chance still seems to rule the gulf when the bobbing little boat from which Decoud had plunged to his death meets the troopship of the returning Barrios at the same point, "just one hour's steaming from Sulaco," where the original collision occurred. For the captain of Sotillo's ship had declared then, "that in an hour he would be alongside the Sulaco wharf." No one could plan or arrange such meetings, chance governs in the gulf and in Chaos.

In one important way the gulf and Chaos contrast sharply, for Chaos is filled with the confused noise of winds, while the profound silence of the gulf is broken only by the whisper of showers, the throbbing of the steamer's engine, and the unearthly shrieks of Hirsch.

Yet both of the journeys across dark and confused areas entail great "difficulty and labour hard" which eases toward the end. The final stages of Satan's voyage are couched in the metaphor of a damaged ship: "a weather-beaten Vessel" with "Shrouds and Tackle torn" which "with less toil, and now with ease / Wafts on the calmer wave by dubious light" (II, 1041-2). So the final stages of Conrad's pair are aided by a "gentle but steady breeze," as the lighter, crippled by the collision, its rigging torn by the anchor of the troopship, slides ashore on the narrow beach under the cliff of the Great Isabel.

In both cases the darkness thins as the travelers arrive:

> . . . the sacred influence
> Of light appears, and from the walls of heav'n
> Shoots far into the bosom of dim Night
> A glimmering dawn . . . PL II, 1034-7

In *Nostromo* "The darkness had thinned considerably towards the morning though there were no signs of daylight as yet."

The emotional impact of the gulf upon both Nostromo and Decoud seems to echo Milton closely, for the loss of self which each experiences is carefully developed. When Satan enters Chaos, Milton describes his first shock thus:

> . . . the void profound
> Of unessential Night receives him next
> Wide gaping, and with utter loss of being
> Threatens him, plung'd in that abortive gulf.
> PL II, 438-41

Decoud's eerie sensations at the beginning of the journey are described in terms of detachment from self, and Nostromo also feels threatened with loss of being.

The enormous stillness, without light or sound, seemed to affect Decoud's senses like a powerful drug. He didn't even know at times whether he were asleep or awake. Like a man lost in slumber, he heard nothing, he saw nothing. Even his hand held before his face did not exist for his eyes. The change from the agitation, the passions and dangers, from the sights and sounds of the shore, was so complete that it would have resembled death had it not been for the survival of his thoughts. (p. 262)

Conrad then portrays Decoud as experiencing the sensations of a non-corporal being, a disembodied spirit, his mind the only portion of his being that remains:

In this foretaste of eternal peace they [his thoughts] floated vivid and light, like unearthly clear dreams of earthly things that may haunt the souls freed by death from the misty atmosphere of regrets and hopes. Decoud shook himself, shuddered a bit, though the air that drifted past him was warm. He had the strangest sensation of his soul having just returned into his body from the circumambient darkness in which land, sea, sky, the mountains and the rocks were as if they had not been. (p. 262)

The loss of self is experienced both as slumber and as a separation of the soul from the body, a subtle and complex experience, in harmony with his intricate patterns of thought. The mind, the essential core of his being, has been separated from his body and even the physical universe has seemed non existent. For Nostromo the loss of self occurs here simply as the familiar loss of consciousness of self which sleep induces. His experience is primarily physical, in harmony with his nature:

Nostromo's voice was speaking, though he, at the tiller, *were also as if he were not.* "Have you been asleep, Don Martin? Caramba! If it were possible, I would think that I, too, have dozed off." (p. 262) (my italics)

Conrad greatly augments the concept of "utter loss of being" later in the tale, for it is in the gulf that Decoud commits suicide after he has lost all sense of his own identity; so completely does he lose faith in his selfhood that it is as if he has ceased to exist even before his death. He doubts that "Antonia could have ever loved a being as impalpable as himself." Decoud's disintegration occurs under the pall of silence on the Great Isabel; he sees no other creature and hears not even the cry of a bird. Yet it is on the gulf that he breaks the cord of silence after twelve days of solitude: "The cord of silence could never snap on the island. It must let him fall and sink into the sea . . ." (p. 499). After an all night vigil in the dinghy, he shoots himself and plunges into the "glittering" gulf annihilating himself. Within the gulf Nostromo loses not his physical life but his integrity, his selfhood, when he is transformed from a vain and childlike being who deals openly with all men into a secretive and tormented captive. Nostromo's sense of outrage and betrayal arises from the discovery that his exploit with the silver and he himself are hardly worthy of notice. Nostromo's change also occurs in the dinghy, for returning to Sulaco in Barrios' transport he sees the empty boat floating and leaps into the shining gulf where he becomes another person. He feels that Decoud has placed the boat thus to assure the swift destruction of the old Nostromo:

> And now, with the means of gaining the Great Isabel thrown thus in his way at the earliest possible moment, his excitement had departed, as when the soul takes flight leaving the body inert upon an earth it knows no more. Nostromo did not seem to know the gulf. For a long time even his eyelids did not flutter once upon the glazed emptiness of his stare. Then slowly, without a limb having stirred, without a twitch of muscle or quiver of an eyelash, an expression, a living expression came upon the still features, deep thought crept into the empty stare—as if an outcast soul, a quiet brooding soul, finding that untenanted body in its way, had come in stealthily to take possession (p. 493)

Nostromo and Decoud have both stared long and unwinking at the glittering water, and both have experienced a loss of being: Decoud in losing his life and Nostromo in exchanging the inner core of his self for that of another. Here one is reminded of Decoud's soul which floated over the darkened gulf as the journey in the lighter began, for Nostromo becomes much like the cynical Decoud after this transformation. Shortly after his "loss of being" on the gulf, Nostromo's downfall is completed when he decides to keep the treasure.

When the link between the settings of *Nostromo* and *Paradise Lost* becomes clear, other portions of the description appear in a new light. Several times Conrad refers to scenes in which air and water appear to be confounded, a peculiar emphasis which links Conrad's world even more closely to Milton's Cosmos. When the journey across the gulf begins, Decoud feels as though he hangs suspended in space:

> it seemed to him that the wharf was floating away into the night . . . the effect was that of being launched into space . . . the big, half-decked boat slipped along with no more noise than if she had been suspended in the air. (p. 260-1)

Another similar example occurs after the torturous journey when

Nostromo has regained the mainland and has slept the day through
in the ruined fortress:

The three Isabels, overshadowed and clear cut in a great smoothness con-
founding the sea and sky, appeared suspended, purple-black, in the air.
(p. 411)

With this vision of the Isabels floating in the air, Conrad describes
Nostromo as awakening "with the lost air of a man just born into the
world." Thus just before the journey and at its close, the boat and
the Isabels are described as "suspended," a most evocative link to
Milton's "hanging in a golden chain / This pendant world."

The position of the three uninhabited islands, the Isabels, coincides
well with that of the Starry Universe in the Miltonic Cosmos. Lying
a little more than half way across the gulf, they are frequently described
in relation to the Sulaco harbor, a direct line from the low end of the
Great Isabel straight into the harbor of Sulaco figuring several times
in the text. While such a line surely need not be equated to the golden
chain from which the World hung, the image of the islands thus
connected to the harbor mouth is clearly established. And the details
concerning the harbor support the relationship: The mouth of the
harbor, "as abrupt as if chopped with an axe out of the regular sweep
of the coast," affords the only entry to the land lying beyond, for the
shores of the gulf are "steep-to all round." Through the harbor entrance
the "square blunt end of the wooden jetty" of the Oceanic Steam
Navigation Company is large enough to be visible from the beach of
the Great Isabel two miles away. The O. S. N. jetty thus stands in the
position of the gate of heaven in the Miltonic cosmos, (Plate I) and the
names of the ships which ply in and out of this gateway reinforce
Conrad's ironic intention for this detail. The ships bear the names of
the luminaries of the Greek pantheon: "The *Juno* was known only
for her comfortable cabins amidships, the *Saturn* for the geniality of
her captain . . . whereas the *Ganymede* was fitted out mainly for cattle
transport . . . " (p. 9-10). They ply up and down a coast "that had
never been ruled by the gods of Olympus," and are thus interlopers as
the objects worshipped by the invaders. These vessels are the modern
gods to which such simple men as Mitchell offer their whole devotion,
with Mitchell claiming for the O.S.N. the godlike quality of infallibility
—"We never make mistakes." The theme of the worship of materialism
finds greater and more serious development when the foreigners in
the Casa Gould wax ecstatic over the rich resources of the country,
causing Decoud to comment ironically, "Those gentlemen talk about
their gods," but the gate of heaven with its chugging steamers provides

a most amusing ironic metaphor for the worship of technological progress.

The gate to the harbor contrasts sharply with the pillars of basalt on the high slope of Higuerota, a gateway of an entirely different kind. And throughout *Nostromo* various features of the setting appear to be linked in pairs. Both the ravine in which the San Tomé Mine was built and the small ravine on the Great Isabel have a stream of pure water; the one has been destroyed and the other is threatened by the hidden silver. The edenic features of these ravines are echoed even within the Casa Gould during other parts of the novel as will be shown below.

The islands themselves serve well as a metaphor for the World or Starry Universe newly carved out of Chaos: the Great Isabel with its stream of clear water, its two great trees, and its high cliff toward the west offers parallels with Eden, contrasting with the other two islands, the bare cinder ironically called "Hermosa," or "beautiful," and the round desert of the Little Isabel. The name itself offers correspondence, for "Isabel," a variant of "Elizabeth," comes from the Hebrew meaning "God has sworn." Milton has the fallen angels describe the proclamation of God concerning his creation of the new world in terms of swearing an oath:

> There is a place
> (If ancient and prophetic fame in Heav'n
> Err not) another World, the happy seat
> Of some new Race call'd Man, about this time
> To be created like to us, though less
> In power and excellence, but favour'd more
> Of him who rules above; so was his will
> Pronounce'd among the Gods, and by an Oath
> That shook the Heav'ns whole circumference confirm'd.
> PL II, 345-53

While Conrad may well have chosen the name for its euphony or may have taken it from the large Galapagos island "Isabella" off Ecuador, the relationship of a name meaning "God has sworn" to "by an Oath . . . confirm'd" should not be disregarded.

Other details suggest the Great Isabel as Eden, with Nostromo as its first inhabitant, for he once spent a Sunday all alone on the island exploring its every valley and finding the water "sweet and good." The impression of timelessness on the island is also edenic. Significantly, after the terrible labors of the night on the gulf and with yet more exhausting work to complete before dawn, while the yet unfallen Nostromo is on the island, his anxiety leaves him and he loses all sense of time. Leaning against the great tree under whose roots he has just hidden the silver, "he spoke slowly, almost lazily, as if there had been a whole leisurely life before him instead of the scanty two hours before daylight" (p. 296). The island also resembles Eden in that its eastern end allows easy entrance with a gradual slope while the western end has an abrupt wall-like cliff, the first entrance of Decoud from this difficult side echoing somewhat imperfectly the leaping of the wall by Satan:

> One gate there onely was, and that look'd East
> On th'other side; which when th' arch-fellon saw
> Due entrance he disdaind, and in contempt,
> At one slight hound high overleap'd all bound
> Of Hill or highest Wall . . .   PL IV, 178-82

The contrast between Nostromo's open and secret visits to the island, the one up the easy slope from the east and the other crawling up the steep cliff, also repeat the theme.

The two large trees on the Great Isabel are reminiscent of Eden, with the hoard of silver in the roots of one symbolizing its change from an earlier and happier state. Under this tree Decoud suffers the psychic disintegration which leads to his suicide:

The tree under which Martin Decoud spent his last days, beholding life like a succession of senseless images, threw a large blotch of black shade on the grass." (p. 553)

And it is there "where the shade was blackest" that Nostromo receives the wound which kills him. The account of Decoud's downfall through isolation includes reminders of the beauty of the Great Isabel with its spring of pure water which Decoud cannot enjoy. Decoud echoes Satan's misery in Eden. Like Satan who despairs, "For onely in destroying I finde ease / To my relentless thoughts" (IX, 129-30), Decoud discovers that robbed of his opportunities to attack all he sees with his sardonic wit, he cannot exist.

Solitude from mere outward condition of existence becomes very swiftly a state of soul in which the affectations of irony and skepticism have no place. It takes possession of the mind, and drives forth the thought into the exile of utter unbelief. (p. 497)

Like Satan, Decoud also "Saw undelighted all delight" (IV, 286). For plunged in melancholy he looks back toward the high cliff of the Great Isabel, "warm with sunshine, as if with the heat of life, bathed in a rich light from head to foot as if in a radiance of hope and joy"

(p. 500). Beholding this he rows steadily away toward the west until the darkness of the gulf shrouds him. The following morning he shoots himself and plunges into the gulf.

Another detail reminding one of Eden is the persistent serpent imagery. On the day after his arrival on the island, Decoud lies for an entire day inert and sleepless: "from sunrise to sunset he had been lying prone on the ground, either on his back or on his face." The added emphasis of the word "prone," which hardly seems necessary to the sense, makes the image of unmoving length more vivid. After Nostromo's transformation, he too grovels along the earth:

His soul died within him at the vision of himself creeping in presently along the ravine, with the smell of earth, of damp foliage in his nostrils— creeping in, determined in a purpose that numbed his breast, and creeping out again loaded with silver, with his ears alert to every sound. (p. 542)

Such snake imagery is repeated for the ferny ravine in which the San Tomé Mine has dumped its tailings, for before the coming of the mine it was called "a paradise of snakes." The evil which has come along with the development of the mine is referred to as "disturbing a good many snakes." But it is the Isabels, particularly the Great Isabel, that remind the reader most forcibly of the lost Eden, for the untouched islands become ever more important in the action, and their spoliation parallels the fall of Nostromo.

The final major feature of the setting to be dealt with is the opening at the head of the gulf, bounded on the north by the rocky Azuera and on the south by Punta Mala. That opening lies in the approximate position of the opening of Hell in Milton's Cosmos. The references to the forbidding approaches to the area support the relationship, for the Azuera, growing not "a single blade of grass, as if blighted by a curse," is haunted by the lost souls of the gringos who sought its legendary treasure. Both Punta Mala, "an insignificant little cape" and the Azuera peninsula are invisible from the middle of the gulf: only the steep hill back of Punta Mala "can be made out faintly like a shadow on the sky," while over the Azuera "a blue mist floats lightly on the glare of the horizon." Unlike the rest of the gulf, this area is associated with lightning, for here a dark storm cloud "bursts suddenly into flame and crashes like a sinister pirate ship of the air." All of these qualities link the area to an other worldly region, invisible and menacing. The entrance to the gulf is described in terms of smoke and fire and stains of blood:

The great mass of cloud filling the head of the gulf had long red smears amongst its convoluted folds of grey and black, as of a floating mantle stained with blood . . . The little wavelets seemed to be tossing tiny red sparks upon the sandy beaches. The glassy bands of water along the horizon gave out a fiery red glow, as if fire and water had been mingled together in the vast bed of the ocean. (p. 411)

The description of fire and blood reminds one more forcibly of Milton's design when it is linked to the image of the edge of the earth:

At last the conflagration of sea and sky, lying embraced and still in a flaming contact upon the edge of the world, went out. The red sparks in the water vanished together with the stains of blood in the black mantle draping the sombre head of the Placid Gulf . . . (p. 411)

Here the "black mantle" suggests death, and the region lying west of the gulf is portrayed as the source of violence and evil.

Apparently Conrad placed his gulf with its opening toward the west in order to use the western sky in creating these images of an infernal region lying just outside the gulf and spreading its baleful influence throughout the Occidental Province. The congruence of Conrad's directions to those of Milton in the entire schema should be borne in mind. The West also represents the colonizers and exploiters whose machines and weapons bring slaughter and devastation. Surely it is no mere sunset Conrad describes thus:

. . . the dusk and gloom of the clouded gulf, with a low red streak in the west like a hot bar of glowing iron laid across the entrance of a world sombre as a cavern . . . (p. 536)

The "sombre world" is not the gulf but the region beyond, and like Hell it is filled with the most omnipresent of industrial metals, iron. The opening to the gulf is also closed by a barrier of silver formed in the moonlight, and in this description it is the gulf itself that is the cavern:

. . . the moonlight in the offing closed as if with a colossal bar of silver the entrance of the Placid Gulf—the sombre cavern of clouds and stillness in the surf-fretted seaboard. (p. 552)

The closing of the gulf with a bar of silver has not been sufficient to hold the forces of "progress" back, for the baleful influence has engulfed Sulaco and the Occidental Province.

The clouds at the head of the gulf are consistently used in relation to evil coming upon the Isabels. Even when Sulaco burns as Barrios wrests it from the Monteros, the influence reaches the islands by way of these clouds:

The loom of a great conflagration in Sulaco flashed up red above the coast, played on the clouds at the head of the gulf, seemed to touch with a ruddy and sinister reflection the forms of the Three Isabels.   (p. 495-6)

There is no question that this portion of the setting intensifies the experience of the reader, and much of that effect arises from the mythic link to Milton's Hell, that realm of molten rocks rich in metal, the abode of fallen angels, and the source of sin and death.

In addition to these principal features of the setting, many other minor parallels become significant in the light of the whole. Although I have dealt with some of these in an earlier article, those which concern the setting will be considered here. These parallels also serve to support the tacit assumption in earlier parts of this paper that the role of Decoud is similar to that of Satan, an assumption which requires more support than it has thus far received in this study.

Strong evidence that Decoud functions as a devil figure appears during the meeting of the great men of Sulaco in the salon of the Casa Gould where the assembly resembles Milton's congress of devils in Pandaemonium. The devils "who seemd / In bigness to surpass Earth's Giant Sons / Now less than smallest Dwarfs, in narrow room . . ." (I, 777-9), whereas in the great high-ceilinged salon we find "Decoud almost disappearing behind the high backs of leather sofas." The uproar of voices in both scenes is couched in images of the roaring ocean:

> . . . such murmur filld
> Th' Assembly, as when hollow rocks retain
> The sound of blustring winds, which all night long
> Had rous'd the Sea . . .   (PL II, 284-7)

While in the Casa "the political tide . . . rising higher with a hum of voices" becomes a "boastful tumult."

The figures also echo the principal devils in Pandaemonium with Charles Gould described in terms very similar to Beelzebub, dignified, powerful, and towering over the assemblage as he receives homage. Gould, a figure of "imperturbable calm" in whose face nothing can be discovered except "a kind and deferential attention," stands "very tall and thin" and "a tall beacon amid the deserted shoals of furniture," reflecting the description of Beelzebub:

> . . . in his rising seem'd
> A pillar of State; deep on his Front engraven
> Deliberation sat and publick care;
> And princely counsel in his face yet shon,
> Majestic though in ruin, sage he stood
> With Atlantean shoulders fit to bear

The weight of mightiest Monarchies . . .
PL II, 301-7

Charles Gould's early idealism is in ruin at this moment, for he is prepared to destroy his mine, often described as rich enough to support the whole country. And Gould has the strength of Atlas to bear the burden alone: "his shoulders alone sustained the whole weight of the Imperium in Imperio, the great Gould concession whose mere shadow had been enough to crush the life out of his father" (p. 148).

The first clear suggestion of Decoud as a tempter occurs in this salon when he crouches behind Antonia's chair and talks "into her ear from behind softly" in a way strongly reminiscent of Satan "Squat like a Toad, close at the eare of Eve," attempting to arouse in her "Vain hopes, vain aimes, inordinate desires" (IV, 800-8). Decoud's rapid utterance becomes "more and more insistent and caressing," and Conrad points out that Antonia does not look at Decoud at all during this whispered conversation. In this she is like the sleeping Eve into whose ear the toad pours his venom. Antonia sees Decoud in the seduction scene which follows, when they are alone on the balcony where he lures her away from her father's party and secures her support for his scheme of revolution. Yet so great is the strength of Antonia's austere patriotism that she almost confounds the cynic; "she seduced his attention; sometimes he could not restrain a murmur of assent; now and then he advanced an objection quite seriously" (p. 183-4). As Tillyard has observed, this is the one time that Decoud appears near a description of Higuerota, and he suggests that in this scene Decoud is touched by idealism.[18] Whether or not Decoud is deeply sincere about his idea of an Occidental Republic, he wins Antonia's allegiance; she deserts her father's cause and devotes herself to Decoud's scheme to separate from Costaguana.

Decoud functions again as a tempter when he persuades Emilia to deceive her husband for the first and only time. By a devious ruse he meets her alone in a "dimly lit corridor" with "the restful mysteriousness of a forest glade." The salon lights give the patio plants the "brilliance of flowers in a stream of sunshine" and Emilia "the vividness of a figure seen in the clear patches of sun that chequer the gloom of open glades in the woods" (p. 210). Conrad here has Decoud speak English for the only time: he speaks well "but with too many z sounds." This hint of hissing accords well with the serpent image for his actions parallel those of Satan. He speaks English as he touches Emilia at her weak point, her compassion for the helpless: "Think also of your hospitals,

---

[18] Tillyard, p. 144.

of your schools, of your ailing mothers and feeble old men" (p. 217). Decoud then moves to oblique flattery as to her wisdom being superior to Charles' to lure her into a betrayal of trust: "Women are idealists; but then they are so perspicacious" (p. 219). Her breach of trust is to conceal from her husband the news of Ribiera's defeat so that the huge silver shipment will come down from the mine to the harbor. While Decoud does want the silver available as a lever, he need not have forced Emilia to deceive Charles; Decoud himself brought the alarming news which he persuaded her to conceal. Had he said nothing at all, the silver would have come down to the harbor as a matter of course. In seeking her collusion he actually endangers his scheme; the only real accomplishment of this encounter is Emilia's fall when she agrees to deceive Charles.

Decoud reaches Nostromo through flattery also, praising him for his expert work in quelling the riot, and under his influence Nostromo asks, "And how much do I get for that, Senor?" For the first time Nostromo thinks more about gain than about the glory of the moment. No longer does he live a day at a time, careless of all rewards save his matchless reputation; even before they enter the gulf, Nostromo speculates about his reward and when it will come, thinking for the first time about the future. Decoud has seen Nostromo's inordinate vanity:

Here was a man, Decoud reflected, that seemed as though he would have preferred to die rather than deface the perfect form of his egoism. Such a man was safe. (p. 301)

Certainly, whatever Decoud's intention, his actions serve to hasten Nostromo's downfall: not only does he leave the boat ready for Nostromo's swift return to the treasure, but he also leaves the spade exposed and makes Nostromo eager to see the treasure: "with the feel of the handle in his palm the desire to have a look at the horse-hide boxes of treasure came upon him suddenly" (p. 495-8). Whether or not Decoud sought Nostromo's fall, his use of the four bars of silver to weight his body becomes the means of assuring that fall. The blocks may be said to build the bridge whereby sin and death enter the Great Isabel. Nostromo has mistrusted Decoud, resented his presence on the lighter, and suspects that Decoud has taken the four ingots out of malice. "And four ingots! Did he take them in revenge, to cast a spell . . . ?" (p. 502). Whatever his motives, Decoud precipitates Nostromo's fall.

When the corrupted Nostromo first decides to keep the treasure and "grow rich slowly," he remembers Teresa's final admonition, that he save the children. He accepts wealth as the means of such salvation:

Well, he had served the children. He had defeated the spell of poverty and starvaton. He had done it all alone—or perhaps *helped by the devil.* (p. 502) (Italics mine)

Decoud has repeatedly told Nostromo that he could not have saved the lighter without his help, and here Nostromo seems to be naming the one who aided him a tempter, the one who made his acquisition of wealth possible was an agent of evil. Nostromo believes he has bought the treasure at an awful price, "a soul lost" (Teresa's) and "a vanished life" (Decoud's). But it is equally true to say that Nostromo's own soul and body have been sold for wealth. For the fallen man, the clouded dawn breaks "gray as ashes."

At the conclusion of the novel, however, Nostromo rejects the treasure as a means of saving the children; rather he gives Giselle into the care of Emilia. He thus renounces his reliance on wealth, unlike the gringos of the Azuera, and he also renounces his vainglory: he refuses to build up a legend of his greatness by giving the treasure to the "frail, bloodthirsty" little photographer. This scene parallels the one in which Nostromo flung his last coin to a beggar woman before he embarked on the gulf with the treasure. Before going out into the dark unknown of death, Nostromo could once again have made a grandeloquent gesture to make his name live. He refuses to fling his treasure to the people, knowing that it cannot purchase their welfare, and dies in silence as utterly alone as Decoud.

Another scene which links Decoud closely to Satan occurs in the great Sala of the Casa Gould where the "Junta of Notables," fearing the imminent arrival of the Monterist forces, has gathered to plan the surrender of Sulaco. This scene resembles the one in which the hellish peers gather again in Pandaemonium to welcome Satan home after his despoiling of Eden. Satan is greeted first with loud acclaim, then after boasting of his achievement in seducing man and creating easy passage for evil into the newly created world, he expects praise:

> . . . a while he stood, expecting
> Thir universal shout and high applause
> To fill his eare, when contrary, he hears
> On all sides, from innumerable tongues
> A dismal universal hiss, the sound
> Of public scorn.   PL X, 504-9

In his letter to his sister, called an "angel" by Conrad, Decoud describes his reception by his compatriots:

"They raised a cry of 'Decoud! Don Martin!' at my entrance. I asked them,

'What are you deliberating upon, gentlemen?' . . . They all answered together, 'On the preservation of life and property.' . . . It was as if a steam of water had been poured upon my glowing idea of a new State. There was a hissing sound in my ears, and the room grew dim, as if suddenly filled with vapour." (p. 235)

Both Decoud and Satan have first been hailed, then have had their works scorned, and finally are beset by an overwhelming noise of hissing. Conrad seems to be relating Decoud very closely to Satan, the one who negates, the one who corrupts through lies, and who becomes a great serpent.

Many other verbal echoes arise in the text, such as the San Tomé being called a "wound" in the mountain, just as Mammon, "the least erected spirit" is said to open a wound:

> Men also, and by his suggestion taught,
> Ransack'd the Center, and with impious hands
> Rifl'd the bowels of their mother Earth
> For Treasures better hid. Soon had his crew
> Op'nd into the Hill a spacious wound
> And dig'd out ribs of Gold.   PL I, 685-90

Nostromo is spoken of as "tossing on a sea of pitch" and tasting "the dust and ashes of the fruit of life into which he had bitten deeply in his hunger for praise." (p. 416). Were these echoes few in number and only casually linked to the theme, one could see them as usages that have arisen simply because Milton has become an integral part of the language. But the congruences are both numerous and coherent, giving to Conrad's epic a density and scope unparalleled in a modern novel. The immediacy and vividness of the setting of *Nostromo* save it from becoming a lifeless allegory, yet the close parallels to *Paradise Lost* add immeasurably to its depth and symbolic power. Truly Conrad aimed for no middle flight in *Nostromo,* and his integration of so much of *Paradise Lost* is a significant part of his triumph.

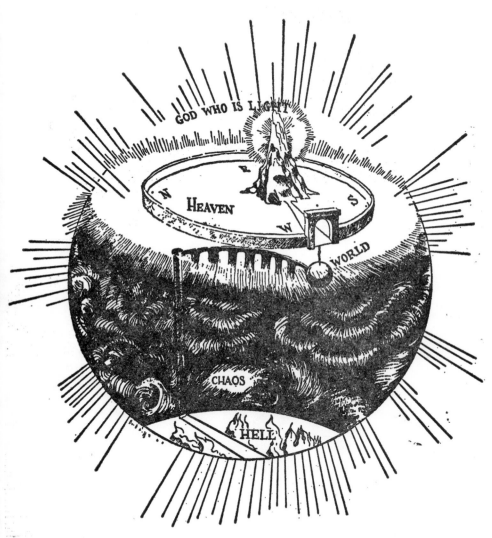

PLATE I

Walter Clyde Curry, *Milton's Ontology Cosmogony and Physics* (University of Kentucky, 1957), p. 156.

PLATE II

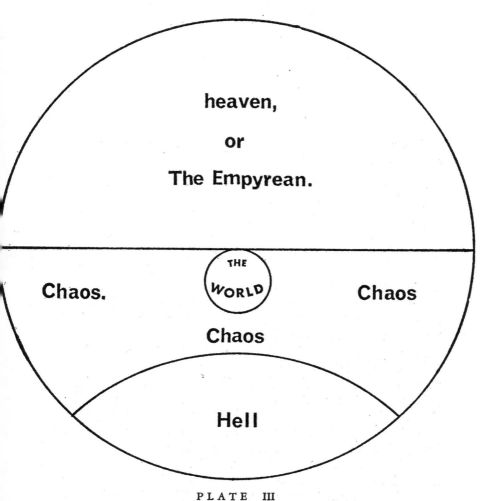

PLATE III

David Masson, "Introduction to Paradise Lost," in *The Poetical Works of John Milton,* (London, Macmillan, 1961), p. 22.

SUZANNE HENIG
and
FLORENCE W. TALAMANTES

CONRAD AND BALZAC

A Trio of Balzacian Interrelationships: "The Sisters," "The Tremolino," and "The Arrow of Gold"

I

Balzac was the first novelist to discover and use the literary device of having the same characters, at different stages of their lives, enter into his various novels, thus forming a subtle liaison of connection. Balzac's device, it must be remembered, was rooted in his art which documented *historically* Parisian life, manners, and customs. The story has become a legend how one morning in 1833 Balzac arrived at his sister's apartment in Paris and announced in an excited voice how he was about to become a genius. Mme. Surville recounted how her brother then proposed a fictional plan of a huge cycle of novels to be called *La comédie humaine* and with this plan his literary device emerged and was developed. The first work in which he utilized this device in order to assure the continuity of *La Comédie humaine* was *Histoire des Treize* which is composed of three parts.

Proust, Joyce, Woolf and Conrad continued to develop and use Balzac's device in this century. Proust and Joyce expanded the device through the addition of autobiographical elements. Woolf's usage was strictly Balzacian: a minor character of one novel became the major character in another novel (*e.g.,* Mrs. Dalloway, a minor personage in *The Voyage Out* becomes *Mrs. Dalloway,* the protagonist of a novel bearing her name, and Mrs. Hilbery of *Night and Day,* a major character, becomes a minor one in *Mrs. Dalloway.*) Conrad, however, used the device differently. Dona Rita, his *femme fatale* of *The Arrow of Gold,* first appears in his fiction as a child in the unfinished work *The Sisters,* which was started in 1896. She was still in his mind when he was working on *The Mirror of the Sea* (1903-1904) in his story called "The *Tremolino*" and she achieves penultimate development in

The Arrow of Gold which he worked on between 1917 and 1918. Unlike Balzac, he develops his repetitive character chronologically and organically. Her deprived childhood is documented in *The Sisters*, showing why she reacts to love and adventure as she does. Her involvement in the Carlist conspiracy is depicted in "The *Tremolino*." We are told in *The Arrow of Gold*, which goes much deeper into the Carlist conspiracy than "The *Tremolino*," about Rita's inability to love and her frigidity. That Rita as heroine intrigued Conrad is obvious, but that her delineation as a character is linked both to Balzac and to the Spanish Code of Honor is less so.

Conrad's knowledge of Balzac and his writings has been mentioned previously.[1] He knew Balzac's work intimately.[2] He told Walpole how "One can learn something from Balzac."[3]

Baines feels Conrad may have learned his technique of the time-shift from Balzac and cites the switches in *Almayer's Folly* which "almost exactly parallel those in *Le Curé de Tours*" (p. 145). *No one, however, has observed the more important device of recurrent characters which he learned from Balzac (e.g., Marlowe, Rita, etc.,) and no one has additionally shown his reliance on Balzac's "Histoire de Treize" as a major source for "The Sisters," "The Tremolino," and "The Arrow of Gold".* Conrad may have early identified with Balzac the man and writer because of Balzac's love affair and marriage with a Polish woman, Countess Hanska. Balzac and the Countess were married in Poland in the town where Conrad was later born at Berdichef in March 1850. The very first work of Balzac's, as noted earlier, which utilized his new device was *Histoire des Treize*. This was in Conrad's mind when he wrote "The *Tremolino*" for he writes:

> If the Mediterranean, the venerable (and sometimes atrociously ill-tempered) nurse of all navigators, was to rock my youth, the providing of the cradle necessary for that operation was entrusted by Fate to the most casual assemblage of irresponsible young men (all, however, older than myself) who, as if drunk with Provençal sunshine, frittered life away in joyous levity on the model of Balzac's *Histoire des Treize* qualified by a dash of romance *de cape et d'épée. (The Mirror of the Sea)*. London: J. M. Dent and Sons Ltd. Collected ed., 1968), p. 156.

The inevitable link between this work and Balzac is provided by Conrad himself. It is not even necessary for the critic to hunt for more than this internal evidence. Yet no writer on Conrad has ever mentioned this.

---

[1] See Baines, pp. 144-45, 203, 398.
[2] See letter to Galsworthy 9 April 1906, L L, II, 33.
[3] 7 June 1918, L L, II, 206.

In the first episode, *"Ferragus,"* Balzac describes the functioning of a secret brotherhood of thirteen members who pledge themselves to defy all legal and social codes. Scrupulously, they observe the conventions of the social mores which they scorn and adhere to a code of honor of their own devising. The fraternity risks adventure continuously. The hero, or anti-hero, is a notorious man with a past, *Ferragus* XXIII, who is also the parent of a beautiful daughter whose mother is Spanish. This fact furnishes Balzac's plot, and the juxtaposition of the devotion of the father to the daughter with his ultimate martyrdom constitutes the poetic vision of the novelist beyond the mere historicity of his depiction of Restoration days.

"The *Tremolino,"* like *Ferragus,* uses an historical background, the Second Carlist War (1872-1876). There is a fraternity among the four participants who are attempting to run guns, illegally, to aid the Carlists. There is a beautiful woman in the picture, and a martyred father-figure either in the brother of Dominic who is actual father to the hapless Cesar (he must go into hiding because of the death of the hereditary enemy of his family through the Latin Code of Honor), or in the person of Dominic himself who acts as surrogate father to Cesar.

Conrad recalls sadly the common enterprise first mentioned in "The *Tremolino"* years later in *The Arrow of Gold.*

At last came the day when everything slipped out of my grasp. The little vessel, broken and gone like the only toy of a lonely child, the sea itself, which had swallowed it, throwing me on shore after a shipwreck that instead of a fair fight left in me the memory of a suicide. It took away all that there was in me of independent life, but just failed to take me out of the world, which looked then indeed like Another World fit for no one else but unrepentant sinners. Even Dominic failed me, his moral entity destroyed by what to him was a most tragic ending of our common enterprise. (*Arrow,* p. 256).

That the partnership among the men in "The *Tremolino"* ended on a note of profound unhappiness can be seen from another allusion from *The Arrow of Gold.* "It seemed to me that all the things I had known ought to have come down with a crash at the moment of the final catastrophe on the Spanish coast" (*Arrow,* p. 257).

Balzac's insistence that one kills the thing one loves best can be seen in Conrad's transposing of the beloved object from a woman, as in Balzac, to the balancelle as in *The Arrow of Gold:*

— Pourquoi voulais-tu me tuer, mon amour? lui dit-elle.
De Marsay ne répondit pas.
— En quoi t'ai-je déplu? lui dit-elle. Parle, expliquons nous.

Henri garda l'attitude flegmatique de l'homme fort qui se sent vaincu;
contenance froide, silencieuse, tout anglaise, qui annonçait la conscience de
sa dignité par une résignation momentanée. D'ailleurs il avait déjà pensé,
malgré l'emportement de sa colère, qu'il était peu prudent de se commettre
avec la justice en tuant cette fille à l'improviste et sans en avoir préparé
le meurtre de manière à s'assurer l'impunité.

— Mon bien-aimé, reprit Paquita, parle-moi; ne me laisse pas sans un
adieu d'amour! Je ne voudrais pas garder dans mon coeur l'effroi que tu
viens d'y mettre. Parleras-tu? dit-elle en frappant du pied avec colère.

De Marsay lui jeta pour réponse un regard qui signifiait si bien *tu
mourras!* que Paquita se précipita sur lui.

— Eh! bien, veux-tu me tuer? Si ma mort peut te faire plaisir, tue-moi!
(Honoré de Balzac, *Histoire des Treize* [Paris: Éditions Garnier Fréres]
1956, pp. 446-47).

"Yes, we had to wreck the little vessel. It was awful. I feel like a murderer. But she had to be killed."
"Why?"
"Because I loved her too much. Don't you know that love and death go
very close together?" (*Arrow,* pp. 290-91).

The second episode of Balzac, *La Duchesse de Langeais,* which deals
with the hypocritical, calculating and unfeeling coquetries exerted by a
noble lady in *Faubourg Saint-Germain* can be said to correspond to the
portrait of the mature Rita in *The Arrow of Gold.* While her Basque
background provides her claim to nobility, she too—because of her
unhappy love experiences—is unable to reciprocate love.

— Je n'ai rien pu lui dire; en sa présence, je n'ai plus d'esprit. Elle ne
sait pas à quel point elle est vile et méprisable. Personne n'a osé mettre
cette créature en face d'elle-même. Elle a sans doute joué bien des hommes,
je les vengerai tous.

Pour la première fois peut-être, dans un coeur d'homme, l'amour, et la
vengeance se mêlèrent si également qu'il était impossible à Montriveau
lui-même de savoir qui de l'amour, qui de la vengeance l'emporterait. Il
se trouve le soir même au bal où devait être la duchesse de Langeais, et
désespéra presque d'atteindre cette femme à laquelle il fut tenté d'attribuer
quelque chose de démoniaque: elle se montra pour lui gracieuse et
pleine d'agréables sourires, elle ne voulait pas sans doute laisser croire
au monde qu'elle s'était compromise avec monsieur de Montriveau.
Une mutuelle bouderie trahit l'amour. Mais que la duchesse ne changeât
rien à ses manières, alors que le marquis était sombre et chagrin, n'était-ce
pas faire voir qu'Armand n'avait rien obtenu d'elle? Le monde sait bien
deviner le malheur des hommes dédaignés, et ne le confond point avec
les brouilles que certaines femmes ordonnent à leurs amants d'affecter dans
l'espoir de cacher un mutuel amour. Et chacun se moqua de Montriveau
qui, n'ayant pas consulté son cornac, resta rêveur, souffrant; tandis que
monsieur de Ronquerolles lui cût prescrit peut-être de compromettre la

duchesse en répondant à ses fausses amitiés par des démonstrations pas-
sionnées. Armand de Montriveau quitta le bal, ayant horreur de la nature
humaine, et croyant encore à peine a de si complétes perversités.

— S'il n'y a pas de bourreaux pour de semblables crimes, dit-il en
regardand les croisées lumineuses des salons où dansaient, causaient et riaient
les plus séduisantes femmes de Paris, je te prendrai par le chignon du cou,
madame la duchesse, et t'y ferai sentir un fer plus mordant que ne l'est le
couteau de la Grève. Acier contre acier, nous verrons quel coeur sera plus
tranchant. (*Histoire,* p. 289).

Suddenly my heart seemed torn in two within my breast and half of
my breath knocked out of me. It was a tumultuous awakening. The day
had come. Dona Rita had opened her eyes, found herself in my arms, and
instantly had flung herself out of them with one sudden effort. I saw her
already standing in the filtered sunshine of the closed shutters, with all the
childlike horror and shame of that night vibrating afresh in the awakened
body of the woman.

"Daylight," she whispered in an appalled voice. "Don't look at me,
George. I can't face daylight. No—not with you. Before we set eyes on
each other all that past was like nothing. I had crushed it all in my new
pride. Nothing could touch the Rita whose hand was kissed by you. But
now! Never in daylight."

I sat there stupid with surprise and grief. This was no longer the
adventure of venturesome children in a nursery-book. A grown man's
bitterness, informed, suspicious, resembling hatred, welled out of my heart.

"All this means that you are going to desert me again?" I said with
contempt. "All right. I won't throw stones after you . . . Are you going,
then?"

She lowered her head slowly with a backward gesture of her arm as if
to keep me off, for I had sprung to my feet all at once as if mad.

"Then go quickly," I said. "You are afraid of living flesh and blood.
What are you running after? Honesty, as you say, or some distinguished
carcass to feed your vanity on? I know how cold you can be—and yet live.
What have I done to you? You go to sleep in my arms, wake up and go
away. Is it to impress me? Charlatanism of character, my dear." (*Arrow,*
pp. 333-34).

Balzac's third episode, *La Fille aux yeux d'or,* has as heroine, Paquita
Valdès, who is the typical Spanish woman of mystery. She is a romanticized version of the female who is the symbolic eternal feminine. She
is befriended by a wealthy family and becomes an intimate of the wife,
named coincidentally Margarita, and falls in love with Margarita's illegitimate half-brother, then unknown to Margarita. Paquita is subsequently
murdered by Margarita in a perversion of the Spanish Code of Honor
and there are subtle suggestions of Lesbian domination as a subconscious
motivation. Balzac's method of presenting his hapless heroine, Paquita,
is similar to the method Conrad later adopts in presenting Rita of *The
Arrow of Gold.* He describes and weaves a legend about her before
she is actually presented to the reader.

— Paquita Valdès est sans doute la maîtresse du marquis de San-Real, l'ami du roi Ferdinand. Un vieux cadavre espagnol de quatre-vingts ans est seul capable de prendre des précautions semblables, dit Henri quand son valet de chambre lui eut raconté le résultat de ses recherches. (*Histoire*, p. 407).

"I am not an easy enthusiast where women are concerned, but she was without doubt the most admirable find of his amongst all the priceless items he had accumulated in that house—the most admirable. . ."
". . . but she radiated life," continued Mills. "She had plenty of it, and it had a quality. My cousin and Henry Allègre had a lot to say to each other and so I was free to talk to her. At the second visit we were like old friends, which was absurd considering that all the chances were that we would never meet again in this world or in the next. I am not meddling with theology but it seems to me that in the Elysian fields she'll have her place in a very special company." (*Arrow*, p. 23).

After such preparation for Dona Rita, Monsieur George exclaims, "The woman of whom I had heard so much, in a sort of way in which I had never heard a woman spoken of before, was coming down the stairs, and my first sensation was that of profound astonishment at this evidence that she did really exist. And even then the visual impression was more of colour in a picture than of the forms of actual life" (*Arrow*, p. 66). Implicit in Balzac's Margarita's murder of Paquita whom she adored is a sanctimonious sense of honor that Paquita is somehow guilty of incest.

Ford Madox Ford states in the introduction to *The Sisters*, "Incest as a subject seemed somehow predestined for treatment by Conrad" and that their first collaboration [*The Inheritors*] "has a faint and fantastic suggestion of—unrequited—love between brother and sister" (Introd. to *The Sisters*, p. 18). This unfinished novel was an early attempt at treating both the childhood of Rita and the subject of incest which Ford describes. The Slav painter "was to have married the older sister and then to have an incestuous child by the other." Ford said the novel was to have ended with the murder of the child and its mother by the fanatic priest (*Sisters*, p. 20). Balzac, it should be recalled, uses Margarita as a judgment figure to murder Paquita when the element of incest is suggested.

Another interesting parallel between Balzac and Conrad is that Balzac's lover of Paquita is named Henri de Marsay (cognate "Marseilles"). There was a well known contemporary of Conrad's, a painter named Raymond Allègre who lived in Marseilles. Conrad's Rita is a former mistress of Henri Allègre. It need hardly be mentioned that Marsay, member of a noted French family as was the Allègre family, is one of the personae employed by Balzac as the linking device in his

Comédie humaine so that he appears in more than just this work. A subconscious reliance on Balzac's creation as well as a mental connection with Allègre of Marseilles might have suggested Henri Allègre, who could just as easily have been called Henri de Marseilles or Henri de Marsay, so obvious is his line of historical descendency. Stephen, the Slav painter of Conrad's *The Sisters,* seems somehow to be related psychologically to Henri the painter of *The Arrow of Gold.* Indeed, Stephen, which means crown in Greek, is similar as a Christian name to Henri which means ruler of an enclosure or private property, for rulers wear crowns. Conrad always chose the names his characters bore very carefully.

Ford wrote, "Conrad meditated transporting the characters . . . both to Spain and to Russia so as to get the last drop of contrast out of opposed race natures." He didn't, but kept them in France. Balzac, it should be recalled, uses precisely this method to contrast the Spanish temperament of Paquita and her relations with the half-English Henri de Marsay.

. . . Dans une de ces joyeuses journées donc, un jeune homme, beau comme était le jour de ce jour-là, mis avec goût, aisé dans ses manières (disons le secret) un enfant de l'amour, le fils naturel de lord Dudley et de la célèbre marquise de Vordac, se promenait dans la grande allée des Tuileries. Cet Adonis, nommé Henri de Marsay, naquit en France, où lord Dudley vint marier la jeune personne, déjà mère d'Henri, à un vieux gentilhomme appelé monsieur de Marsay. Ce papillon déteint et presque éteint reconnut l'enfant pour sien, moyennant l'usufruit d'une rente de cent mille francs définitivement attribuée à son fils putatif; folie qui ne coûta pas fort cher à lord Dudley: les rentes françaises valaient alors dix-sept francs cinquante centimes. Le vieux gentilhomme mourut sans avoir connu sa femme. Madame de Marsay épousa depuis le marquis de Vordac; mais, avant de devenir marquise, elle s'inquiéta peu de son enfant et de lord Dudley. D'abord, la guerre déclarée entre la France et l'Angleterre avait séparé les deux amants, et la fidélité *quand même* n'était pas et ne sera guère de mode à Paris. (*Histoire, La Fille aux yeux d'or,* p. 389).

Conrad's duel, in fact, in *The Arrow* of Gold may even have been suggested by Balzac's hint of a possible duel which was to involve Henri's friend, Paul de Manerville. There are so many other parallel elements in the three episodes of Balzac and the three works of Conrad that a juxtaposition of quotations at this point should show adequately their artistic relationship. Balzac compares Paquita to a ravishing picture called *"La Femme Caressant sa Chimère."*

Elle est l'original de la délirante peinture, appelée *la femme caressant sa chimère;* la plus chaude, la plus infernale inspiration du génie antique; une sainte poésie prostituée par ceux qui l'ont copiée pour les fresques et les mosaïques; pour un tas de bourgeois qui ne voient dans ce camée qu'une breloque, et la mettent à leurs clefs de montre, tandis que c'est toute la femme, un abîme de plaisirs où l'on roule sans en trouver la fin, tandis que c'est une femme idéale qui se voit quelquefois en réalité dans l'Espagne, dans l'Italie, presque jamais en France. Hé! bien, j'ai revu cette fille aux yeux d'or, cette femme caressant sa chimère, je l'ai revue ici, vendredi. Je pressentais que le lendemain elle reviendrait à la même heure. Je ne me trompais point. Je me suis plu à la suivre sans qu'elle me vît, à étudier cette démarche indolente de la femme inoccupée, mais dans les mouvements de laquelle se devine la volupté qui dort. Eh! bien, elle s'est retournée, elle m'a vu, m'a de nouveau adoré, a de nouveau tressailli, frissonné. Alors j'ai remarqué la veritable *duègne* espagnole qui la garde, une hyène à laquelle un jaloux a mis une robe, quelque diablesse bien payée pour garder cette suave créature... Oh! alors, la duègne m'a rendu plus qu'amoureaux, je suis devenu curieux. Samedi, personne. Me voilà, aujourd'hui, attendant cette fille dont je suis la chimère, et ne demandant pas mieux que de me poser comme le monstre de la fresque. (*Histoire, La Fille aux yeux d'or*, pp. 401-02).

Conrad compares Rita similarly to a portrait of Theodosia in *The Arrow of Gold* (p. 28).

The Byzantine Empress was already there, hung on the end wall—full length, gold frame weighing half a ton. My mother first overwhelms the Master with thanks, and then absorbs herself in the adoration of the 'Girl in the Hat.' Then she sighs out: 'It should be called Diaphanéité, if there is such a word. Ah! This is the last expression of modernity!' She puts up suddenly her face-à-main and looks toward the end wall. 'And that— Byzantium itself! Who was she, this sullen and beautiful Empress?'

" 'The one I had in my mind was Theodosia!' Allègre consented to answer. 'Originally a slave girl—from somewhere.'

"My mother can be marvellously indiscreet when the whim takes her. She finds nothing better to do than to ask the 'Master' why he took his inspiration for those two faces from the same model. No doubt she was proud of her discerning eye. It was really clever of her. Allègre, however, looked on it as a colossal impertinence; but he answered in his silkiest tones:

" 'Perhaps it is because I saw in that woman something of the women of all time.'

"My mother might have guessed that she was on thin ice there. She is extremely intelligent. Moreover, she ought to have known. But women can be miraculously dense sometimes. So she exclaims, 'Then she is a wonder!' And with some notion of being complimentary goes on to say that only the eyes of the discoverer of so many wonders of art could have discovered something so marvellous in life. I suppose Allègre lost his temper altogether then; or perhaps he only wanted to pay my mother out, for all these 'Masters' she had been throwing at his head for the last two hours. He insinuates with the utmost politeness:

" 'As you are honouring my poor collection with a visit you may like to judge for yourself as to the inspiration of these two pictures. She is upstairs changing her dress after our morning ride. But she wouldn't be very long. She might be a little surprised at first to be called down like this, but with a few words of preparation and purely as a matter of art. . .' "

(*Arrow*, pp. 28-29). [punctuation sic].

Balzac made a profound impression upon Conrad and this is reflected in these three Conradian works in the presentation both of his characters and his method in the works themselves. And somehow this debt to Balzac is related to Conrad's use of the Spanish Code of Honor.

II

The Code of Honor

Dominic Cervoni of Corsica appears in "The *Tremolino*" and in *The Arrow of Gold*. In the former, he is a character both of comic irony and an embodiment of the Latin Code of Honor. He is almost the tragic hero of Conrad's story because he enters into the gunrunning activities with an endowment of hereditary deferences to the Code. A scion of an old and distinguished Corsican family, the Caporalis, which date back to the twelfth century, he is mindful of this heritage. But, as in *Romeo and Juliet*, the Caporalis had their Mantagues, the Brunaschis, and the feud between the two families proved to be the undoing ultimately of the little boat, the *Tremolino*.

In this way I learned that our Dominic had a brother. As to "going into the bush," this only means that a man has done his duty successfully in the pursuit of a hereditary vendetta. The feud which had existed for ages between the families of Cervoni and Brunaschi was so old that it seemed to have smouldered out at last. One evening Pietro Brunaschi, after a laborious day amongst his olive-trees, sat on a chair against the wall of his house with a bowl of broth on his knees and a piece of bread in his hand. Dominic's brother, going home with a gun on his shoulder, found a sudden offence in this picture of content and rest so obviously calculated to awaken the feelings of hatred and revenge. He and Pietro had never had any personal quarrel; but, as Dominic explained, "all our dead cried out to him." He shouted from behind a wall of stones, "O Pietro! Behold what is coming!" And as the other looked up innocently he took aim at the forehead and squared the old vendetta account so neatly that, according to Dominic, the dead man continued to sit with the bowl of broth on his knees and the piece of bread in his hand. This is why—because in Corsica your dead will not leave you alone— Dominic's brother had to go into the *maquis*, into the bush on the wild mountain-side, to dodge the gendarmes for the insignificant remainder of his life, and Dominic had charge of his nephew with a mission to make a man of him. (*The Mirror of the Sea*, "The *Tremolino*," pp. 164-65).

The senselessness of the hereditary ritual never enters into the thinking of the families; it is tradition and, therefore, to be accepted.

But if this hereditary feud is an important factor in Corsican life, it is even stronger as an influence in the Spanish and Basque territories and Dominic is to become the leader of the *Tremolino's* gunrunning activities for the Basque and Carlist cause. This devotion and loyalty to the Latin Code of Honor makes him, as Rita observes after their first meeting, just perfect.

But what exactly is the Code of Honor to the Latin? Revenge tragedy, as it has come to be known in English literature is known as "honor tragedy, (*comedia de capa y espada*—comedy of manners, and love-and-honor intrigue) to the Spaniards. Calderón de la Barca, one of the greatest of the Golden Age dramatists, interpreted the concept of honor as it was manifested in the society of his day in such plays as *El Médico de su honra* and *Casa con dos puertas mala es de guardar*. The point of honor itself (*pundonor*) and the resulting social complications is a complex notion.

Honor was sexualized and based primarily upon a sentiment of conjugal fidelity which, by extension, included all female relatives: daughters (married or not) or any other woman in the household. Since women were considered mere chattel, any demonstration in their direction would be considered an affront to the man, ostensibly the "owner" of his female chattel, and his "honor." If his honor were sullied, it had to be avenged. This sense of personal dignity and concern for his reputation became a matter of pride and self respect—and, more often, of life and death. Death was demanded by the Code (or marriage in the case of women whose honor had been unpugned as in the well-known case of the Cid's marriage to Dona Jimena after he had killed her father). Under the Code, all male members of a household were responsible for protecting the family name and for avenging the family honor. One blood vengeance demanded another so that blood feuds raged through entire families for generations, some whose victims and avengers may even have forgotten the original reason for the blood-letting. The Spaniard was the most susceptible of all the Europeans to the conventions of these chivalric codes.

Because Dominic's brother had submitted to the hereditary Code, Dominic assumes the rearing of his nephew Cesar:

To look at Cesar was not pleasant. His parchment skin, showing dead white on his cranium through the thin whisps of dirty brown hair, seemed to be glued directly and tightly upon his big bones. Without being in any way deformed, he was the nearest approach which I have ever seen or could imagine to what is commonly understood by the word "monster." That the source of the effect produced was really moral I have no doubt. An utterly, hopelessly depraved nature was expressed in physical terms, that taken each separately had nothing positively startling. You imagined him clammily cold to the touch, like a snake. The sligthest reproof, the most mild and justifiable remonstrance, would be met by a resentful glare and an evil shrinking of his thin dry upper lip, a snarl of hate to which he generally added the agreeable sound of grinding teeth. (*The Mirror of the Sea*, "The *Tremolino*," pp. 165-66).

If Conrad in creating a story which deals with the Carlist gun-running expeditions had used the Code of Honor as a mere sub-plot, as well he might, the story would not have depicted the human dimension it does. Conrad, as well as all great artists, takes the framework embodied in the Spanish Code of Honor (*i.e.* vengeance for a real or imagined affront to a family) and *transforms* it so that Dominic becomes a hero who has as his fatal flaw the blind adherence to the hereditary Code. He sees the action he must perform but not vengeance upon a stranger, rather vengeance upon his young nephew Cesar. Had Cesar been basically as noble a character as his uncle, the outcome of the story would have been unbearable, but Conrad uses Cesar as a figure of comic irony, even as a scapegoat. He is "malicious malignity" personified and the arm of justice is literally depicted by the gesture of Domnic's arm:

It was for this venomous performance rather than for his lies, impudence, and laziness that his uncle used to knock him down. It must not be imagined that it was anything in the nature of a brutal assault. Dominic's brawny arm would be seen describing deliberately an ample horizontal gesture, a dignified sweep, and Cesar would go over suddenly like a ninepin—which was funny to see. But, once down, he would writhe on the deck, gnashing his teeth in impotent rage—which was pretty horrible to behold. And it also happened more than once that he would disappear completely—which was startling to observe. This is the exact truth. Before some of these majestic cuffs Cesar would go down and vanish. He would vanish heels overhead into open hatchways, into scuttles, behind up-ended casks, according to the place where he happened to come into contact with his uncle's mighty arm. (*The Mirror of the Sea*, "The *Tremolino*," p. 166).

Everything, in fact, about Cesar is ironic, even his name, that of the illustrious Julius Caesar. Cesar is probably the most amusing of all of Conrad's fictional characters. The significance of the name, always carefully chosen in Conrad's fiction, was not lost on the author. But both he and his uncle did exist as Baines points out, "Now the record of Dominic Cervoni (who played such a vital role in connection with the *Tremolino*) shows that he served as second officer on the Saint-Antoine without interval from 14 June 1875 to 14 October 1877; which means either that he did not take part in the episode or that it happened more than a year and a half after the war was over" (p. 52). Cesar, in reality, was not killed by his uncle. Baines tells us how he lived to serve a long career in the French merchant navy (Inscription Maritime, Bastia).

The blood feud, the blind hereditary adherence to this system of honor, is so ingrained within Dominic that he applies it to the entire behavior, not only of himself, but even of the male members of his own family. It must be remembered that under the Code a husband was obligated to murder his wife if there was even a soupçon of suspicion hovering about her reputation. Browning's great poem "My Last Duchess" illustrates this concept. But Conrad is creating a more human personage of the stoic Dominic, which causes Dominic to apply the Code to all aspects of his life and relations. When Dominic becomes convinced that his ignoble nephew has betrayed the balancelle, his decision of vengeance upon the unlucky youth will follow swiftly. The arm which has meted out judgment and justice to Cesar once more in comic fashion is utilized as the instrument of his death. Dominic stretches out the arm as the *Tremolino* is dashed against the rocks; Cesar falls into the water and is drowned, weighed down by Conrad's (or the narrator's) money belt of gold which he has stolen. Dominic, shaken both by the knowledge that one of his blood has been capable of becoming a dastardly traitor and that he has killed his own flesh and blood, walks off after the sinking of the *Tremolino*. He has succumbed to his tragic flaw; he has blindly adhered to the Code; his "honor" is maintained in his own eyes and in those of the narrator's, but at what human cost? It is this last aspect which Conrad dwells upon because it has come about as a subtle perversion of the Code. The female members of a family, it must be recalled, as well as those men who have insulted other men could have vengeance visited upon them because they were regarded as mere chattel or reprobates. In visiting vengeance demanded by the Code upon his nephew, Dominic has regarded that nephew as less than man, as chattel. *And in that knowledge is Dominic's ignoble end.* Forever must he brood over the knowledge that one of his blood has been less than a man, has in fact been a traitor, and has had to be killed by him. But Dominic we leave walking on the beach:

> He turned and walked away from me along the bank of the stream, flourishing a vengeful arm and repeating to himself slowly, with savage emphasis: "Ah! *Canaille! Canaille! Canaille!* . . ." He left me there trembling with weakness and mute with awe. Unable to make a sound, I gazed after the strangely desolate figure of that seaman carrying an oar on his shoulder up a barren, rock-strewn ravine under the dreary leaden sky of *Tremolino's* last day. Thus, walking deliberately, with his back to the sea, Dominic vanished from my sight.

With the quality of our desires, thoughts, and wonder proportioned to our infinite littleness we measure even time itself by our own stature. Imprisoned in the house of personal illusions thirty centuries in mankind's history seem less to look back upon than thirty years of our own life. And Dominic Cervoni takes his place in my memory by the side of the legendary wanderer on the sea of marvels and terrors, by the side of the fatal and impious adventurer, to whom the evoked shade of the soothsayer predicted a journey inland with an oar on his shoulder, till he met men who had never set eyes on ships and oars. It seems to me I can see them side by side in the twilight of an arid land, the unfortunate possessors of the secret lore of the sea, bearing the emblem of their hard calling on their shoulders, surrounded by silent and curious men: even as I, too, having turned my back upon the sea, am bearing those few pages in the twilight, with the hope of finding in an inland valley the silent welcome of some patient listener. (*The Mirror of the Sea,* "The *Tremolino,*" pp. 182-83).

Cervoni appears again in *The Arrow of Gold.* It is years after Cesar's death. In *The Arrow of Gold* Monsieur George introduces Dominic to Dona Rita and the Carlist cause while in "The *Tremolino"* it had been Dominic who admitted the narrator to the conspiratorial group. He is described by Monsieur George:

He had a great experience of all unlawful things that can be done on the seas and he brought to the practice of them much wisdom and audacity. That I didn't know where he lived was nothing since I knew where he loved. The proprietor of a small, quiet cafe on the quay, a certain Madame Leonore, a woman of thirty-five with an open Roman face and intelligent black eyes, had captivated his heart years ago. . . . Dominic's general scorn for the beliefs, and activities, and abilities of upper-class people covered the Principle of Legitimacy amply; but he could not resist the opportunity to exercise his special faculties in a field he knew of old. He had been a desperate smuggler in his younger days. (*Arrow,* pp. 89-90).

He is an older man in *The Arrow of Gold;* he has a love; but the burden of his self-knowledge will always be upon him. Indeed, Balzac's portrayal of a perverted code of honor in *La Fille des yeux d'or* finds its modern expression in Conrad's embodiment of Dominic Cervoni in "The *Tremolino.*"

GLENN SANDSTROM

THE ROOTS OF ANGUISH IN DOSTOEVSKY AND CONRAD

Conrad consistently expressed his detestation of Dostoevsky, whom he called that "haunted, grimacing creature"[1]; he admired Turgenev, a writer concerned with human beings rather than "damned souls knocking themselves to pieces in the stuffy darkness of mystical contradictions."[2] Yet Conrad's practice belied his denigration. It seems impossible to deny that *The Secret Sharer* runs closely parallel to Dostoevsky's *The Double,* that *Under Western Eyes* directly challenges *Crime and Punishment* on its own psychological ground, or that Conrad throughout his works uses the Dostoevskian devices of foils and doubles to enrich his characterizations. There is a subtle alliance between these two writers in their perception and handling of man's moral and psychological complexity, in particular the agonizing struggles of men confronting the terrible simultaneities of idealism and iniquity.

Like Dostoevsky, Conrad saw man as an amalgam of high purpose and sour degradation. His own humanistic ideals of "fidelity"[3], "immediate duty"[4], "unavoidable solidarity"[5], and "renunciation"[6] glimmer in Jim, Heyst Marlow, Mrs. Gould; the dark and degenerate side of human nature comes out in Donkin, Brown, Jones and Ricardo, Kurtz. But nowhere does Conrad supply a conceptual framework of moral psychology that could envelop the extremes and clarify the tension and interdependence of aspiration and depravity that we often sense in his novels. Dostoevsky, however, did reach a broad synthesis and offers a complete circle of man's moral nature. I think by looking at Dostoevsky's completed concept of man and then reading some of Conrad's major works from that vantage point we can fill in some missing segments and move toward a coherent Conradian view of man's moral anatomy.

---

[1] Albert J. Guerard, *Conrad the Novelist* (Cambridge, Mass., 1958), p. 2.
[2] Frederick Karl, *Reader's Guide to Joseph Conrad* (New York, 1960), p. 30n.
[3] "A Familiar Preface," 1912.
[4] *Ibid.*
[5] Preface to *Nigger of the Narcissus,* 1897.
[6] "Henry James: An Appreciation," 1905.

71

Bypassing *The Secret Sharer* and *Under Western Eyes,* which have received rather full treatment from the Dostoevskian angle,[7] I shall concentrate here on three works that furnish a wide range of protagonists and moral issues: *Lord Jim* most of all, then *Heart of Darkness* and *Victory.*

Dostoevsky's concept of man's moral nature is immensely complicated and comes into full view only in *The Brothers Karamazov,* but it can be sketched out in rather simple terms. Man is hemmed in by his ego—his sensuality, his pride, his intellect—all of which mask higher value. But man contains an element beyond selfishness that bespeaks the solidarity of man, sacrificial love, and total responsibility. It is important to note that this upper sphere of the psyche comprises not an exalted ego-ideal but the annihilation of ego. "After Christ's appearance," Dostoevsky wrote in his notebook in 1864, "it became clear that the highest development of personality must attain to that point where man annihilates his own 'I,' surrenders it completely to all and everyone without division or reserve . . ."[8] This suggests the dynamic nature of the moral process: bogged in ego, man thirsts for egolessness and, in spite of or as a consequence of selfish actions, can force his way across the barriers of greed and lust to take residence in the godly area of self beyond ego. Then he finds a moral standard more demanding than the Golden Rule, yet one that sets him free: give unto others what their welfare and happiness requires, regardless of your own needs or desires. It is not an easy passage. The ego fights bitterly to keep its control. Ugly doubles crawl out of the woodwork to activate or indict one's selfishness. Good can never segregate itself from evil: men hate because they cannot completely love; they do good to spite their own evil propensities.

Looking at *Lord Jim* with this moral psychology in mind, we can see some broad parallels. The novel demonstrates that a shiny ego-image is not enough, as in Brierly's discovery that a "belief in his own splendor" cannot cheat "his life of its legitimate terrors." It shows that every crime has its penance for a decent man and that man has to run from himself to find himself. A Dostoevskian reading can also shed light on two specific, basic issues that have never been quite resolved: what is the motive of Jim's dereliction of duty? and, why are Patusan and the "lordship" of Jim the appropriate consequences of the Patna failure?

The motivation of Jim's leap, as he explains it, seems thin and

---

[7] Notably by Jocelyn Baines, *Joseph Conrad* (New York, 1960), pp. 360-71, and Guerard, pp. 236-46.
[8] Konstantin Mochulsky, *Dostoevsky: His Life and Work,* trans. Michael A. Minihan (Princeton, 1967), p. 261.

incomplete. He abandons the Patna not because he fears for his life or flinches from pain; it is just that acting courageously would have been ordinary, messy, futile, and noisy; it would have involved "making crazy" the doomed passengers, with "added terrors" that would deny him a good and peaceful death. Even in retrospect, the moral criterion he applies is an ego-ideal, rooted in childish visions of heroism and not in any humanitarian instinct. We notice that although he is later "relieved, of course" that the pilgrims survived, he seems uninvolved with their fate. It is the reaction of a shallow and unfeeling man, a moral simpleton. But refracting Jim through Dostoevsky can suggest a richer psychology. Jim, like the other protagonists whom I shall discuss, has an analog among Dostoevsky's heroes—not a physical twin or a complete psychological parallel, but a person with an analogous curve of motivation, act, and consequence. I have in mind Dmitri Karmazov. Dmitri, like Jim, lies under the domination of his sense of honor—"I may be a murderer, but I am not a thief!"—and he too violates that honor and faces with dread the condemnation of his egoistic world. Just as Jim strikes the poor "beggar" with a sick child who needs water, Dmitri abuses the hapless Captain Snegiryov while little Ilusha grips his father in deadly terror and humiliation. Neither gets any sense of brotherhood from his brutal encounter— Jim, for example, only recognizes his own thirst. Jim also fits the pattern of passive crime so common in Dostoevsky: Raskolnikov abandoning the young girl to prostitution, Ivan Karamazov fleeing his father's murder, Dmitri leaving the wounded Grigory in the snow— "If he's dead, he's dead!" Jim, too, feels a "strange illusion of passiveness." He shares something of Dmitri's tendency toward violence and his suicidal urge—"I wish I could die." He too must endure humiliation, trial, and exile, and he must linger on "to wait for another chance." Both men refuse to "shrink"; both accept what Jim calls "execution."

But it is exactly the apparent difference in the curves of Dmitri's life and Jim's that might explain the psychology of Jim and the unity of his novel. Dmitri, through a dream of poor peasants and a dying babe, undergoes a transformation that teaches him the truth of total responsibility. I'm going to Siberia for "the babe," he says, "so the babe will cry no more." In short, he learns a value beyond honor that entails a penance for his "whole life" of egocentricity and violence. It may be that Jim's dereliction springs from the blindness that has twisted Dmitri's life: it was not that Jim could not live up to his golden ideal of heroism, but that that ideal was tainted and invalid from the start. The true criterion is one that had never occurred to him; a selflessness that dictates service to others even when such service gives no grandeur to one's self-image. Lacking this ideal, he lacked a basis for authentic action and thus jumped away from any action whatsoever.

If that truth of selfless service is the truth that comes to Jim during that time that he moves, mostly hidden from us, toward Patusan, it might explain the obscurities of later events. Stein says that Jim wants to be a devil and a saint; there seems to be little evidence of the diabolic in Jim, but he may well want sainthood, in Dostoevsky's sense of self-annihilation. Stein also recommends men to "in the destructive element immerse . . ." Could this mean to submerge oneself in the realm of the psyche that destroys ego and to find therein the true, supportive moral freedom? Is that the saving dream?

If so, then Patusan becomes the logical extension of the *Patna.* Like Dmitri's crimes, Jim's are multidimensional: the classical crime of cowardice, the existential crime of evasion and passivity, the human— or Christian—crimes of brutality and irresponsibility. If only the violations of honor and courage needed atonement, another isolated act such as the charge up the hill would suffice. But Jim's crime most essentially was one against human brotherhood, a violation of Father Zossima's dictate that "all are responsible for all." Thus Jim must atone with a lasting concern and with extended responsibility and service. "He loved to see people go to sleep under his eyes"—that is a chance Dmitri may never get, something closer to the lifelong dedication of Zossima. Marlow first calls it egoism, suggesting that Jim wants both "to do good" and "to keep his position." True, like Dmitri, Jim may never quite escape the toils of ego, just as he needs a woman to support his commitment. But Marlow argues more reliably later that there is a possibility of self-sacrifice beyond the ego-rationale of "ethical progress" and acknowledges that Jim finally "had confessed to a faith higher than the laws of order and progress."

The death of Jim is morally ambiguous. On one hand, Brown—a clear Dostoevskian double, objectifying pure ego—calls Jim back to a white man's world and its siren call of honor, rendering him ashamed to shoot a man who has supposedly been true to his mates. On the other hand, Jim abides by Zossima's idea that we are all criminals and thus cannot judge. "Men act badly," says Jim, "sometimes without being much worse than others." He thus suffers a double paralysis, a fatal softness; but the egoism is cancelled by the ultimate ego-annihilation of death, and Jim's humility survives death as a proof of his "eternal constancy."

Thus, even though *The Brothers Karamazov* seemed to Conrad to be like "fierce mouthings from a prehistoric age,"[9] Dostoevsky's novel can act as a high continuous curve with which *Lord Jim* makes only occasional contact but which allows a psychological wholeness and structural unity to be seen in Conrad's novel—a coherence not so visible from any other point of view.

Kurtz, in *Heart of Darkness*, has been likened to the alienated, isolated hero of *Notes from Underground*, and we might see Raskolnikov in him: the man shaped by poverty, pride, and aspiration into a blood-covered pseudo-superman. But the best analog, I believe, is Nikolai Stavrogin of *The Devils*, that savage, charismatic figure who draws people to him, sucks out their lives for his own use, and then throws aside their empty shells. Even Stavrogin's skull-like face suggests Kurtz, the man of skulls. Stavrogin's exploitation of women is softened in the portrayal of Kurtz's chiaroscuro devotees, and the intensity that produces shrill boredom in Stavrogin is transmuted by Kurtz into frantic action, but there is an essential parallelism in their moral curves. At the center of each man is—or was, at one time—a desire to do good. "I'm still capable of wishing to do something decent," says Stavrogin before his suicide, and his earlier visit to Tikhon reveals a desire to find something better than stagnation or perversity. He never finds that purpose and dies in limbo, attracted equally to evil and good. Kurtz too expresses his benevolent idea of progress for the African blacks: "by the simple exercise of our will we can exert a power for good practiacally unbounded"; but from some other vicious well he draws the counterthought: "Exterminate the brutes!" Marlow's comment on Kurtz could apply equally to Stavrogin: "Whatever he was, he was not common. He had the power to charm or frighten rudimentary souls into an aggravated witch dance in his honour; he could also fill the small souls of the pilgrims with bitter misgivings; he had one devoted friend at least, and he had conquered one soul in the world that was neither rudimentary nor tainted with self-seeking." Most important, evil in both men is a perversion of the will to do good. Because they see higher possibilities, but retreat from the challenge of those possibilities into their diseased egos, both have to confront "the horror." In neither case do we learn fully what that horror is, but we might guess it would be something like the afterlife that Svidrigailov imagines in *Crime and Punishment:* "one little room, something like a bath-house in the country, black with soot, with spiders in every corner . . ."—the eternal confinement in ego. Both men are "whited sepulchres."

That Stavrogin and Kurtz have ideals beyond ego buried within them

---

[9] *Life and Letters,* ed. G. Jean-Aubry (London, 1927), II, 140.

can be posited mainly by the selfless devotion they inspire in other, more worthy people. Kurtz's Russian shares traits of the mad Kirillov, who tries to draw meaning and selfhood from Stavrogin, and the mild, exploited Shatov. Kurtz's English sweetheart has her analog in the self-sacrificial Dasha, just as his Congo woman parallels the wild and dashing Lisa. Then there is Marlow, sucked into Kurtz's aura of mystery, who reverses the usual function of Dostoevsky's doubles and takes into himself not the egoistic monomania of Kurtz but some residue of goodness that Kurtz has rejected. Marlow learns that the ordinary social principles of honor and truth are indeed "chaff in the breeze" and that there are higher principles of the heart.

In *Victory,* the central figure is a man with a penchant for reluctant rescue. Heyst saves Morrison, Lena, finaly the monsters who contrive his destruction, yet he can never justify with his mind the benevolence triggered by his heart. If we look for Dostoevskian analogs, we could say he has the mild and kindly instincts of Prince Myshkin in *The Idiot* but also, because of paternal conditioning, much of the intellectual conviction of Ivan Karamazov that all action is futile and meaningless. So torn, he is pulled like those two into the destructive current of life by pity and unwanted responsibility. The total curve of Conrad's novel is most like that of *The Idiot.* Heyst serves Lena first not out of love but out of pity, in just the way that Myshkin devotes himself to Nastasya. In Dostoevsky's novel, Rogozhin is developed from the beginning as a dark and brooding counterforce to Myshkin; Jones and Ricardo, with Jones especially the "gentleman" double of Heyst, also receive early and elaborate preparation as conveyors of Heyst's doom. In both books, hatred and power and lust roll toward the kindly man and the female victim; both end in tableaux of triple disaster. It must be admitted that Conrad produces at the end an affirmation of individual devotion and the value of life, with an upbeat note alien to *The Idiot.* Heyst commits a final frantic act, but if it is an act of madness, it is not the catatonic madness of Myshkin; and Lena is at the end is more like a Dostoevskian woman-saint—like Sonia in *Crime and Punishment* —than she is like any of the neurotic women of *The Idiot.* In general, the paradox of *Ivan Karamazov* holds for Heyst: man must serve an ideal beyond ego, even when he cannot believe in that ideal, and even when it kills him.

We have, then, three protagonists who can be interpreted, and perhaps more fully understood, in the light of Dostoevsky's vision, three men who contain germs of selflessness and human brotherhood and who suffer because they find the weight of ego pitted against unarticulated ideals. The ego is seen in all its varieties. Jim's ego-ideal is a pretentious heroism; he seems finally to see the vacuity of that ideal and comes close to transcending it. Kurtz channels his capacity for service into a mad, materialistic greed. Heyst acts in accordance with his higher self, but, constrained by intellect, can never really believe it is that which makes life mysteriously valuable. All suffer, like Dostoevsky's people, from the terrible burden of the sacrificial spirit: without that burden they would not have to undergo their dereliction and death, their horror, or their harrowing commitment.

All this is not to say that Conrad consciously imitated Dostoevsky. It may indeed be that the insights of two perceptive geniuses chanced to coincide. But it seems more likely that Dostoevsky's works left deep and basic traces on Conrad's soul despite the vigorous resistence of his mind. That he resisted, and resisted especially the spiritual ideal of Dostoevsky, is underlined by the fact that the analogous works of Conrad almost precisely reverse the order of Dostoevsy's works: *Lord Jim* is closest to the expression of the sacrificial ideal as seen in Dostoevsky's final novel; *Heart of Darkness* retreats into comparisons with *The Devils; Victory* is most like the still earlier *The Idiot,* and *Under Western Eyes* relates to Dostoevsky's first major novel, *Crime and Punishment,* but without the hesitant epiphany of Raskolnikov as we last see him. Why Conrad pulled back in this fashion is not clear. Perhaps his antimysticism ruled out the faith needed to validate an ethical vision like Dosoevsky's; maybe it was a Polish resistance to the intellectual colonialism of a Russian, or a Western retention of the sanctity of the ego. It may have been an aesthetic judgment that drew him toward Flaubert and Turgenev, apostles of control, even though his richest characterizations show few traces of those writers. It could be, as Robert Penn Warren suggests, that he could never fully accept values as anything but "necessary illusions."[10] Whatever the reason, the resistance and retreat were fortunate for us in that they contributed to Conrad's unique accomplishment: works balanced gracefully between the exalted optimism and bleak despair of Dostoevsky, dominated by a vision neither nihilistic nor mystical but steadily humanistic, peopled by characters torn like Dostoevsky's between selflessness and ego but made by Conrad's restraint more like the mysterious humans of our own world.

---

[10] Introduction to *Nostromo,* 1951.

RIDLEY BEETON

JOSEPH CONRAD AND GEORGE ELIOT:
An Indication of the Possibilities

This paper will not attempt to prove a direct influence of George Eliot on Joseph Conrad, if only because I can find no evidence to support such a proposition.

Indeed, there seems to be sparse mention of George Eliot in Conrad's statements. The following, taken from a letter to William Blackwood, is no more than a glancing (and mis-spelt) reference:

> I am long in my development. What of that? Is not Thackeray's penny-worth of mediocre fact drowned in an ocean of twaddle? And yet he lives. And Sir Walter, himself, was not the writer of concise anecdotes I fancy. And G. Elliot [*sic*] — is she as swift as the present public (incapable of fixing its attention for five consecutive minutes) requires us to be at the cost of all honesty, of all truth, and even the most elementary conception of art? But these are great names. I don't compare myself with them.[1]

In greater understanding of what Conrad is saying here, and to achieve sufficient illumination for his remark about George Eliot, the back-ground to this statement should briefly be sketched. Conrad had called on his publisher William Blackwood for a loan of several hundred pounds, in advance for work he proposed carrying out: Blackwood had found Conrad to be a bad financial proposition, and he unfortunately let this slip in conversation. Conrad once he had time to brood over the allegation, was stung to a retort. He rejected (not that this was alleged) the notion that his work was worthless; he asserted that he knew exactly what he was aiming at, and stated that he could not depart from his chosen method. He felt that he would, as other notable writers had done before him, enjoy ultimate recognition.

His references to Thackeray and (to a lesser extent) Walter Scott are not flattering, although, somewhat hollowly, he finally calls them "great names." But the reference to George Eliot *is* flattering: he points, voguishly, to the prevailing view of her ponderousness, but contrasts

[1] Jocelyn Baines, *Joseph Conrad: A Critical Biography*. London, Weidenfeld and Nicolson, 1959, p. 284.

her approach with the frothy superficiality of the reading public, and in an oblique reference he indicates her honesty, her pursuit of truth, her concept of art.

Before leaving this letter perhaps one should suggest that there was an immediate reason for his consciousness of George Eliot and her achievement: the Blackwoods were at this stage his publishers; before him they were George Eliot's publishers. George Eliot was one of their outstanding and astounding successes, astounding because her art has not that easy quickness to which Conrad alludes.

Nor, for that matter has Conrad's: though particular episodes can move at the swift pace they would seem to demand, the total architecture (to change the metaphor rather awkwardly) of both Conrad and George Eliot's work militates against quick building and easy surfaces. I must now confessedly stand before you as yet another seeker of affinities, though I dare to hope that the examples I provide will give light to the method of both writers.

What I trust I am not going to do is simply to regurgitate Leavis; but it would be foolish not to recognize that it was Leavis in *The Great Tradition* who first brought the names together in meaningful conjunction. It was Leavis who linked them in the tradition he perceived, though he also linked them by virtue of their astonishing modernity. He made one of the most forthright of his many forthright assertions in the introduction:

. . . it would certainly be reasonable to say that "the laws conditioning the form of Jane Austen's novels are the same laws that condition those of George Eliot and Henry James and Conrad."[2]

The intermediary position of James, and the direct impact of George Eliot on him, carry a pronounced insistence further on in the introduction: "It is more than a guess that, in the development of James, George Eliot had some part." (p. 16) This is, I think, completely valid, as I shall indicate later on. Even Leavis's description of the method of Henry James seems to have upon it the shadow of George Eliot:

He creates an ideal civilised sensibility; a humanity capable of communicating by the finest shades of inflection and implication: a nuance may engage a whole complex moral economy and the perceptive response be the index of a major valuation or choice. (p. 16)

Between George Eliot and James there is a direct connection. Between Conrad and George Eliot (and with her, the rest of the great tradition)

---

[2] London, Chatto and Windus, 1955, p. 7.

there is no such connection:

> When we come to Conrad we can't, by way of insisting that he is indeed significantly "in" the tradition — in and of it, neatly and conclusively relate him to any one English novelist. Rather, we have to stress his foreignness . . . (p. 17)

In other words, the affinity between James and George Eliot is well perceived. That between George Eliot and Conrad is scarcely admitted: the purpose of my contribution is to suggest the strength of the second affinity.

Only in one sense, that of modernity, does Leavis allow this connection (apart, that is, from the ever-vigilant enclosures of his tradition): "Conrad is incomparably closer to us to-day than Hardy and Meredith are. So, for that matter, is George Eliot." (p. 22)

Apart from Leavis's perhaps one of the few important notes of identification is that made by Avrom Fleishman in his work *Conrad's Politics:*

> There is . . . an inveterate scientism in George Eliot's accounts of the individual's relation to society that is far from Conrad's studied belletristic tone. But he shares with her a firmly rooted distrust of abstract laws as applied to human things — shares, too, her avowed casuistry in morals and politics. And her tragic individuals sundered from their societies (Maggie Tulliver, Tito Melema, Gwendolen Harleth, and others) are closer to Conrad's isolated individuals than are those of any other of his predecessors.[3]

This last comment, in particular, is, I believe, a telling one, to which I shall briefly return in placing two short works in juxtaposition. (The conclusions of these two works will, however, be notably different.)

I wish to push the affinity with Henry James a little further, in order firmly to establish that what we are here trying to explore is George Eliot's far less obvious kinship with Conrad. That James closely examined George Eliot's approach and method is clearly evidenced by his several brilliant essays on her work: his particularly close interest in *Daniel Deronda* is vividly indicated by the "Conversation" he wrote about it, reproduced by Leavis in *The Great Tradition.*

His debt to George Eliot, and in particular to *Daniel Deronda,* is most strongly evidenced by the many close parallels between the latter work and *The Portrait of a Lady.* These parallels are so well-known that I do not intend pointing to them here. The affinities of other works such as *The Wings of a Dove,* and even *The Ambassadors,* would bear scrutiny at a conference different from the present one.

---

[3] Baltimore, Johns Hopkins Press, 1967, p. 66.

With Conrad and George Eliot we are to have no such reassurances, and yet we are to have a sense of affinity far closer than Leavis's tradition allows. In what follows I shall be able to touch only on some points of comparison and identification, and only on a very few books. But this study can, meaningfully I believe, be extended. I shall largely be concerned with the matter of structure; I shall to a lesser extent be concerned with matters of style and characterization—but I believe that here too there are worthy parallels.

The affinity of style is the most inconceivable, because the most difficult to prove. But possibly I could hint at its presence by producing a few brief, comparable passages.

The first comes from *Nostromo*. Captain Mitchell is being delineated:

He did some hard but not very extensive thinking. It was not of a gloomy cast. The old sailor, with all his small weaknesses and absurdities, was constitutionally incapable of entertaining for any length of time a fear of his personal safety. It was not so much firmness of soul as the lack of a certain kind of imagination — the kind whose undue development caused intense suffering to Senor Hirsch; that sort of imagination which adds the blind terror of bodily suffering and of death, envisaged as an accident to the body alone, strictly — to all the other apprehensions on which the sense of one's existence is based.[4]

One might, to perceive the proximity, turn immediately to a description of Savonarola in George Eliot's Florentine novel *Romola:*

Savonarola's nature was one of those in which opposing tendencies coexist in almost equal strength: the passionate sensibility which, impatient of definite thought, floods every idea with emotion and tends towards contemplative ecstasy, alternated in him with a keen perception of outward facts and a vigorous practical judgment of men and things. And in this case of the Trial by Fire, the latter characteristics were stimulated into unusual activity by an acute physical sensitiveness which gives overpowering force to the conception of pain and destruction as a necessary sequence of facts which have already been causes of pain in our experience. ... with the Frate's constitution, when the Trial by Fire was urged on his imagination as an immediate demand, it was impossible for him to believe that he or any other man could walk through the flames unhurt — impossible for him to believe that even if he resolved to offer himself he would not shrink at the last moment.[5]

Although radically dissimilar types are here being depicted, the proposals of the writers are not unlike. One senses in parallels such as these, the tradition not only of a great moral subject, but of a manner in which thoughts and opinions are urged on in the combination of

---

[4] London, Dent, 1947 (Collected edition), p. 338.
[5] Edinburgh, Blackwood, 1901 (Library edition, pp. 543-4).

certain words and sentences. Place passages about Lord Jim in the context of George Eliot's remarks and the resemblances become even more striking.

Or observe a series of intimations from *Middlemarch:* they can firmly be referred forward to statements on morality, combined with the shrewd assessment of character, to be found in *Nostromo* or *Lord Jim.* Here, for example, is the briefest of glimpses at Bulstrode:

> In his closest meditations the lifelong habit of Mr. Bulstrode's mind clad his most egoistic terrors in doctrinal references to superhuman ends. But even while we are talking and meditating about the earth's orbit and the solar system, what we feel and adjust our movements to is the stable earth and the changing day. And now within all the automatic succession of theoretic phrases — distinct and inmost as the shiver and the ache of oncoming fever when we are discussing abstract pain, was the forecast of disgrace in the presence of his neighbours and of his own wife.[6]

Consider the character and the struggle of Razumov within the reference of this passage; I believe that not only will similarities of story emerge, but the more subtle affinities of stylistic impetus.

But, perhaps, most such comparisons are finally chance things, and I pass on to the larger structures within which the two novelists work. I shall begin by taking two of the works that are smaller in scope.

In *Heart of Darkness* Marlow records one of the many observations that accompanied his journey to Kurtz:

> I saw him extend his short flipper of an arm for a gesture that took in the forest, the creek, the mud, the river, — seemed to beckon with a dishonouring flourish before the sunlit face of the land a treacherous appeal to the lurking death, to the hidden evil, to the profound darkness of its heart.[7]

In terms of the present study, it is important that the feeble flipper gesturing at the dark surrounding forest should be kept in mind.

The following occurs at what is possibly the central point of *Silas Marner:*

> He felt his heart begin to beat violently, and for a few moments he was unable to stretch out his hand and grasp the restored treasure. The heap of gold seemed to glow and get larger beneath his agitated gaze. He leaned forward at last, and stretched forth his hand; but instead of the hard coin with the familiar resisting outline, his fingers encountered soft warm curls.[8]

There you have the two parables, and the comparison: the gesturing

---

[6] Library edition, 1901, p. 381.
[7] Dent Collected edition, 1946, p. 92.
[8] Library edition, 1901, p.149.

at darkness; the reaching into light. Man is defeated by the universe; man is saved by his awareness of humanity. I do not seek to suggest which parable is the greater: what I do wish to indicate is that they have the comparable, though opposite, effects that are the hallmarks of a superb literary knowledge. Both have undeniable claims on greatness: they are both different and similar in their significant use of structure.

Time will not permit a detailed analysis of this structure, and I shall attempt only the crudest of outlines. *Silas Marner* is a journey in time as we follow the miser through his dark world to his emergence into fulfilment and understanding. *Heart of Darkness* is a journey in space as we follow Marlow up the Congo river, through the jungle, to his confrontation with defeat and puzzlement. The one a journey into light; the other into darkness. The one proposes the meaningful light of faith; the other the meaningless darkness of the universe. The one stresses what is human and effortful; the other what is mechanistic and unavailing. Both are major propositions: it would be a reduction, I think, to read into the one simply a Victorian optimism, and into the other a *fin de siècle* pessimism. Perhaps this had a little to do with it — but the works are much more than this; they are the explorations of two minds significantly, if insufficiently, linked by Leavis, and I believe each would have recognized, indeed discovered an identity in, the other's method.

I wish for the moment to stay with *Silas Marner,* but, in the case of Conrad, to expand into a much more extensive, much greater, work in *Nostromo.* In this case I want to discuss the function of what I have crudely identified as the structural symbol. What I am focussing on here are the unifying roles played in the novels by gold and silver respectively, though the silver of San Tomé becomes a much more extended thing, both in terms of setting and exposition, than does the gold of *Silas Marner.* We should, to qualify the assertion, look at the place and function of each.

In an essay I wrote several years ago entitled "The Silver of San Tomé" I dealt with the effect of the structurally unifying silver on the lives of each of the protagonists. To each it looks different, and each describes it in a different way. To Charles Gould it is the source of his influence and power; he suitably jackets it with the respectable name of "material interests," and is enmeshed in the administrative problems it engenders for him. Nostromo becomes the "master and slave" of the silver, which, initially, when he must save it from the insurgent Monterists, seems a clarion call to his heroism, and then later becomes a token of his rejection, and finally, to mirror Charles

Gould, a signal of his greedy lust for influence. For Decoud, symbolically, it becomes a reflection of his wasted life when he goes overboard weighted by four bars of the precious metal. Most movingly to Mrs Gould it is a signal of her defeat by her milieu. For each the aspect of the silver is different, yet made comparable by the book's structure. In the wider world of the novel it is also at the centre: it is the pivot on which the fate of the Occidental Republic rests; it is the source of Costaguana's wealth; it becomes the object of the armies and political manipulators who descend on the seaboard city. It is a remarkably simple structural force in a complicated novel.

When we come to *Silas Marner* the scale seems to have diminished, and yet the remarkable force remains. Silas Marner has lost the gold that has narrowed his life into a mere mechanical existence. In the uncertain firelight he rediscovers his wealth, and reaches out to touch the soft curls of Eppie, and in this act to broaden out into a wonderful, though restrained, vitality. There is a play here on unyielding and dead, and pliant and living; but I don't want to labor this. What I do want to emphasize is that this gold of Silas Marner's, like the silver of San Tomé, is continually changing its color and its quality. The novel is indeed a highly subtle (and yet simple—great art can assert the paradox) parable on the word "gold" and on the realities suggested by words and things.

Despite these subtleties and complexities, both gold and silver always remain unforgettably at the centre of their respective novels. They deserve detailed exploration.

In what follows I shall have to curtail my utterances drastically and confine myself to some fairly stark contentions.

Middlemarch and *Nostromo,* of all the two writers' novels, are, I think, those most frequently prescribed for senior undergraduates, who, on occasion, have made much of the exotic, grand setting of the one, and the provincial, confined setting of the other, settings which have often been carried forward to statements on their different structural dimensions. I have resisted this alienation of scale and concern, and indeed have tried to relate them — because I believe that *Nostromo* is not all that strange and rare a literary bird, and that its affinities with *Middlemarch* are many and helpful. Both are works of great structural consequence.

I am one of those people who believes that it is not idle to compare George Eliot with Tolstoy (from his own statements it seems that Tolstoy would not have thought this either), although the work of the one is provincially confined, and that of the other continentally expansive. Conrad learnt from Tolstoy, as I think he did from Dostoyevsky in *Under Western Eyes* — although in both cases he would radically change the perspective of his own work. In their sense of a series of parallel and comparable stories, in the way in which they allow one to reflect and to work upon another, in their sense of building up to a major unifying conclusion, I believe *Middlemarch* and *Nostromo* not to be strangely alien phenomena, but to be wonderfully comparable. But I must, I am afraid, leave this at mere assertion.

Having touched on *Middlemarch,* and having touched on the structural symbol, I wish to suggest another aspect of the art of each novelist that would bear illuminating comparison into the manner of great method. This quality I have loosely distinguished as the structural *image:* not the symbol that dominates the book, and draws the plot into itself, but the image that unifies structurally in a far more delicate manner, either by unobtrusively predicting ahead, by encouraging apprehension; or by signalling back, and allowing retrospection. I confine myself to two short examples.

The first is the furniture of Mr. Casaubon's home in *Middlemarch:*

> . . . the furniture was all of a faded blue, and there were miniatures of ladies and gentlemen . . . A piece of tapestry over a door . . . showed a blue-green world with a pale stag in it. The chairs and tables were thin-legged and easy to upset. It was a room where one might fancy the ghost of a tight-laced lady revisiting the scene of her embroidery. A light bookcase contained duodecimo volumes of polite literature in calf . . .[9]

Beside this the map (also in an early scene) of *Heart of Darkness* might seem more structurally obvious, and yet the method is illuminatingly comparable. In this well-known scene Marlow visits the office where he receives his Congo commission:

> Deal table in the middle, plain chairs all round the walls, on one end a large shining map, marked with all the colors of a rainbow. There was a vast amount of red — good to see . . . a deuce of a lot of blue, a little green, smears of orange, and, on the East Coast, a purple patch ... However, I wasn't going into any of these. I was going into the yellow. Dead in the centre. And the river was there — fascinating — deadly — like a snake.[10]

And now for my last, and most rapid, essay into the effect of structural force: the impact of events on character and its development. My models are Gwendolen Harleth in *Daniel Deronda,* and Razumov in *Under Western Eyes* (though Jim of *Lord Jim* would serve almost as well — for the comparisons are rich and infinite). In these cha-

---

[9] Library edition, 1901, p. 53.
[10] Dent Collected edition, 1946, pp. 55-6.

racters we perceive people of undoubted limitation, practising the dubious social art of blinkering and delusion, until by one of those hard miraculous accidents (?) of the universe or society, the limited character is brought short, tries to escape, and eventually accepts confrontation, and discovery. In exploring structures such as these one understands the complexities of one's own choices — for I believe that literature *does* have a reference back to life. Certainly both George Eliot and Joseph Conrad believed that literature was a means to moral literacy.

I should have liked to follow Gwendolen Harleth, and Razumov, and Jim — for they are among my favorites in fiction. But the curtain has all but fallen on my contribution to this conference. My hope is that the limited suggestions of so short a paper have permitted a glimpse past that curtain onto the wide stage of Conrad's work, and the even wider stage that is the community of great art.

PRZEMYSŁAW MROCZKOWSKI

CONRAD THE EUROPEAN

To describe a writer's position in the history of ideas even one chiefly noted for his poetry, is now a legitimate line of inquiry. More specifically, if an author's themes include a picture of man's social as well as individual being, it is useful to know something of his outlook on the relative problems. Thus, the present article continues to some degree, the approach already made familiar by some comparably recent studies, e.g., by Eloise Knapp-Hay[1] and Avrom Fleishman[2]. This line of inquiry also includes studies by Andrzej Busza,[3] Zdzisław Najder[4] and myself.[5]

I will try to suggest accordingly that Conrad thought of the notion and the reality of the Europe of his time.[6] The focus is located somewhat at a distance from the focus of the studies already referred to which deal with "Conrad's politics" or political novels proper, since I shall want to consider the cultural and moral implications of the political views or topics, while restricting slightly the problems, universal by their nature, to the perspectives and traditions of Europe.

The restricting of the scope may appear somewhat arbitrary but is unavoidable in the introductory part of any reasoning where one defines the terms, in agreement with the Frenchman's declaration: "Les définitions sont libres" (new definition of terms). Having implied how varied or controversial the definition of Europe has been[7] and how unlikely an agreement on its content, I proceed to my own choice of the determining elements.

---

[1] Eloise Knapp Hay, *The Political Novels of Joseph Conrad: A Critical Study*, Chicago University Press, 1963.
[2] Avrom Fleishman, *Conrad's Politics: Community and Anarchy in the Fiction of Joseph Conrad*, Johns Hopkins, 1967.
[3] Andrzej Busza, "Rhetoric and Ideology," read at the International Conference on Conrad, 1974 at Cantenbury, England.
[4] Zdzisław Najder, "Conrad and Rousseau: Concepts of Man and Society," *ibid.*
[5] Przemysław Mroczkowski, "Joseph Conrad's International World of Men", first read in a shorter version at the Birkbeck College Conference on Conrad in 1972 and printed in *Kwartalnik Neofilologiczny, II,* 1974.
[6] Cf. e.g. E. Knapp Hay's statement: "Politics turned from action to art: this was Conrad's achievement". (*op. cit.,* p. 79).
[7] Cf. for a discussion of this point *Europe and the Europeans An International Discussion* by Max Beloff with an Introduction by Denis de Rougemont. A report prepared at the request of the Council of Europe, London, 1957.

I begin by shirking the geographical or territorial puzzle, and so by ignoring for example the question of how many miles east from the 1974, or for that matter from the 1939 or 1773 Polish frontier should here be counted or which countries drawing on the heritage common to Spain, France and England (such as the Americas) should be included and to what extent and even how many centuries back we ought to go.[8]

The crucial point or value is the human person, conceived both individually and socially, i.e., in the latter aspect as the builder of fully human communities. Furthermore the basic concept of personality necessarily implies such faculties as reason and will: moral responsibility (riveted to freedom) must follow. Implied, too, is the need and right of self-expression, notably through art. Derived from the above are the cognitive urge and the critical spirit with the latter controlling the former, while set into action by it.

In the social and public field the awareness of the importance of personality must mean that whatever communities are created, they must provide scope for personality or have personalities themselves. In this way, European communities, national or smaller (or larger) must in some way be democratic.

Before proceeding to a survey of the points which relate Conrad to the Euroepan heritage as characterized above, a few of the relevant formative influences on him must be indicated. In national terms these influences were mainly: Polish, French and English, in chronological order. All three have by now been fairly well explored in Conrad criticism. However, a certain range of problems of which European people had become aware in all three countries involved at the time of Conrad's boyhood and early maturity (circa 1866-1896) must be emphasized. These problems frequently took the form of challenges to the accepted thinking and behavior. Thus, the last three decades of the nineteenth century witnessed, in several European countries, together with a continuation of individualism, a deepening or a further expansion of the self-questioning attitude which European thinkers had developed since the Enlightenment (or Renaissance, or the later Middle Ages, depending on one's school of historical thinking). This meant such components of the Victorian and Edwardian atmosphere (with their continental equivalents) as skepticism, pessimism and cosmopolitanism. These by their nature tended to dissolve the values inherent in the notions of organic personality endowed with reason used so as to make

---

8 " . . . un espace spirituel que les contingences de la politique ne sauraient entamer". *La Grande Encyclopédie Larousse,* 1973, s.v. Europe.

life worth living or of *polis,* the organic community. They were also, however, extensions of the developed personality of the inquiring mind, of the sensitiveness to the general human predicament and to the excesses of national self-assertion. In a somewhat more positive way, what came to be added to the already current ideas were humanitarianism and pacifism, with emphasis on averting pain and war with its cruelties.

It may have been as a result of these ideas that a writer, in particular a novelist, was inclined to probe with "artistic compassion" into the souls of human beings in various predicaments, including very trying ones, imagining extenuating circumstances for law-breakers etc. (cf. *The Secret Sharer*).

All the above are well-known, indeed, well-worn ideas, but without them it would be difficult to specify the relevant components of Conrad's formation.

Paradoxically, Conrad the renownedly exotic writer shows in a masterly way the dangers of exoticism for people relinquishing their native shores (whether these be taken literally or figuratively) which means veering out of their primary personalists frame. Part of the folly of Almayer consists in uniting himself in marriage with a woman so differently made from himself as to make mutual understanding impossible. As a sequel of this folly he hankers later for the sake of his daughter after the world he has in a way betrayed, although he fails to see what the real values of that world were.

The problem is restated in *An Outcast of the Islands* whose titular protagonist, Willems, defects from an (already politically artificial) establishment of the Dutch in the Malay surroundings to make his position even less acceptable by becoming a lover of the Malay beauty Aissa, repudiated by her tribe.

But the problem becomes truly poignant with Kurtz in *Heart of Darkness* who allowed wilderness to seize complete control of him. In Kurtz's case the experiment is totally destructive of personality and shows his being in the oft-quoted phrase "hollow at the core." Almost the same is true, of course, of the two protagonists of "An Outpost of Progress."

If the above are cases of European people out of their framework, there are other ways in which the novelist's attention centers on the individual. It may be the famous Conradian theme of man's solitude, inherited, in all likelihood, from the Romantics. Even in this case the problem is also concerned with the relationship to the community already forsaken or to the new one in which the estranged man leads his altered situation: Jim after the fatal jump, particularly in Patusan,

Nostromo, especially in the later part of the novel entitled after his nickname, or Heyst in *Victory* etc.

Then it may be an individual solving the problem of his relationship to his human surroundings in another sense, such as James Wait on board the *Narcissus*, asserting his wishes or dislikes in the teeth of the stupefied crew.

One way or another, the individual human being receives full artistic and/or intellectual consideration. This becomes conspicuous when one bears in mind Jim's crucial experience in his and Marlow's account. Much has been said of Conrad's insistence on moral imperatives, but a little less, perhaps, of his sensitive probing of the psychology of those who become delinquent by breaking the moral imperatives. Now there have been many narratives in world literature in which a fatal step or transgression is part of the tale, but it is the perspicacity in imagining the transgressing individual's thoughts and feelings and subsequent reactions that constitutes one of the great achievements of Conrad. And if we recall that the European novel has displayed some precedents of that kind of insight, it would only promote our argument. The European novel focuses if not fully, then to a large extent, on the personality. This particular forms in literary art, I suggest, is a European "invention" or contribution to humanity's culture.

One could describe the basic content of much of Conrad's fiction by saying that it deals with the integrity of a human being, or, negatively, with the ways in which it may be jeopardized.

One of these ways, in partly philosophical terms, is fatalism. A standard opinion in earlier Conrad criticism is that the protagonists of *Lord Jim, Nostromo,* or *Victory* fail to conquer their destiny (the qualified formula might be that they fail to use the conquest). It is immaterial here whether the vision of that shadow of destiny comes chiefly from pagan antiquity or from the tragic poetry of Polish Romanticism. What matters is the implication: the descent into darkness can only be sad and depressing, because it is the human being who goes down.

The same is applicable to the political fiction which has attracted, as already mentioned, so much critical attention over the last decade. Charles and Emilia Gould find their existence with its spiritual potentialities sucked up by the enormous, inhuman abyss of the San Tomé silver mine. In their case it is more direct, but it is also perceptible in the life course of Nostromo himself or Viola and others. The acquisitional urge — even the hope of using it profitably for the welfare of a human community — is a disaster for the person and the society in which he operates. In simpler terms, adapted to our initial assumptions, one of the great betrayals of European ideals was bowing to money — both as end and as means.

I agree here with Prof. Fleishman that for all the impression to the contrary, Conrad, whether or not with full consciousness, seems to declare or imply his adherence to an "organicist" program of society. This means assuming that human beings can think out and work out a viable body politic in which their common good and good as individuals shall be assured in a natural and organic way with minimal coercion. It is another matter that the belief was never fully articulated by Conrad or made to prevail over its tragic opposite.

If we thought of the works considered here as a sequence, its climax would be found in *The Secret Agent.* It is fair to say that here the very foundations of organized civic existence are most dramatically menaced by actual physical destruction. What has been admired in the novel, and deservedly so, is the well-knit series of psychological portraits and situations; once more the writer can "throw himself into the minds" of most varied people: those out to avert destruction; those eager to bring it about; and, last but not least, those who manipulate either of the previous groups.

But the point is different here. It is he extreme character of the confrontation that matters. In 1935, a German critic of the Marburg philosophical school, Johanna Burkhardt, made the point that Conrad tends to present human beings in what she called *Grenzsituationen,* situations, as I understand it, which set off the deepest or the most decisive qualities of a man (and of a problem) by stripping off the accidental and the superficial.[9] As far as individuals are concerned, it may be called testing a person's mettle. Obviously Kurtz in *Heart of Darkness* is a classical instance of the outwardly civilized man whose inward worthlessness is revealed under the "extreme pressure" of exotic life; to him such life means an abyss of social formlessness — such as in Europe might yawn under a hole burst open by an anarchist's bomb. Now in the European context proper it seems, indeed, that the threat of anarchism is a *Grenzsituation,* a border line situation for a community. Whatever the doubts about modifications or transformations of the model of a good community which European thinkers may have formulated in the course of centuries, the basic notion of a community with some guarantee of safety and order is reaffirmed as something primary and indispensable when all may be swallowed up by the blast of an explosion.

---

[9] Johanna Burkhardt, *Das Erlebnis der Wirklichkeit und seine künstlerische Gestaltung in Joseph Conrads Werk,* Marburg, 1935, pp. 26-41.

It is true that one may trace in Conrad something like a passing sympathy with or at least understanding for the anarchist hope of "making a clean breast" of the things soiled or spoiled by crimes and mistakes of humanity[10]; such understanding may be a small fruit of Conrad's being acquainted with the revolutionary thought of nineteenth century Europe; it may be a wish, legitimate in a writer, to show both sides of a problem; or even a temptation, sometimes perverse, to voice the feeling of a void beneath any reality or any conviction. Yet the reader feels like asking: "But goes thy heart with this?" and concluding that when a genuine threat of radical destruction like that which shook European capitals near the turn of the century loomed on the horizon, the writer was rather likely to revert to his belief in a stable, indeed, an "organicist" community and present those threatening it as pathological.

I have so far been drawing my material from Conrad's fiction, hoping to keep within legitimate bounds of the exercise, always risky, of culling ideas from images. But we know that there are also direct and in a sense more reliable expressions of the writer's views in his essays and various letters.

In the latter they are more scattered and occasional, though sometimes illuminating: among the former we note above all the fairly lengthy rhetorical essay in political science and history "Autocracy and War"; the somewhat similar "The Crime of Partition" holds the second place, being more historical.

In "Autocracy and War", although the trend is to a large extent on the negative and polemical, an echo of Russia's defeat in the Far East and a diatribe against her role in modern history, the positive implications or even actual statements are sufficiently clear and numerous to provide premises towards a conclusion bearing on what we may call the deeply held positive convictions of Conrad.

Now I submit that it is easy to focus the guiding principle of those convictions on the notion of human personality which we accepted as basic; as to the next step, setting up the social-and-political framework for the personality, it will have the right features if built by developed persons worthy of the name; and it is Europe that provides here the scope and the example.

To take up this basic notion and rivet it to a specific text, Conrad

---

10 "La sociétè est essentiellement criminelle — ou elle n'existerait pas. C'est l'égoisme qui sauve tout — absolument tout, tout ce que nous abhorrons, tout ce que nous aimons. Et tout se tient. Voilà pourquoi je respecte les extrêmes anarchistes." Letter to R. Cunninghame Graham of 8 February 1899, p. 117 of C.T. Watts' ed. References to this collection of letters hereafter will be marked "To RCG" and the date.

bitterly scolds Russia for "swallowing up" any "aspiration towards personal dignity, towards freedom, towards knowledge".[11] We do have, therefore, every right to assume that for Conrad human dignity, freedom and knowledge are essential to human existence. We might in fact add a slightly more latent implication, yet one that cannot be eliminated. If the ideals listed are presented in the essay as so important and their violation as so dreadful, then what we are also bound to assume is their attainability, at least within reasonable bounds; for otherwise how could anybody be blamed for suppressing that which nobody could achieve?

Elsewhere in the same essay we find specified the conditions of "the true greatness of a State" which ". . . is a matter of logical growth, of faith and courage". The qualities involved are again those of a human being worthy of the name and creating a social frame worthy of him. The communities should be "close-knit" (another confirmation of Professor Fleishman's discovery of the organicist ideal in Conrad's thinking,) "possessing the ability, the will and the power to pursue a common ideal".

The next important step is a consideration of the multiple qualities adumbrated in Europe's history which the author of "Autocracy and War" read into it.

Nations of the Continent and England should live as members of a higher unity and in fact have thought of doing so for a long time. Such is one more clear assumption behind "Autocracy and War." We find there such expressions as "The Policy of Nations"[12] which would have the right to expect "service rendered" to itself by the particular members or "the solidarity of Europeanism, which must be the next step towards the advent of Concord and Justice."[13]

The opposites denounced in the essay which help the reader to grasp the positive content are chiefly three: greed, war and despotism.

Whatever Conrad's links with the conservative attitude, they do not appear to include a wish to preserve the domination of commerce. Partisans of biographical criticism might point out at this juncture that the Polish gentry of which Conrad was a scion traditionally (and often thoughtlessly looked down on the trading class or that the writer himself had to depend for his living on hired labor (i.e. his own) as seaman; others of the same school might wonder that his uncle Tadeusz Bobrowski's realistic advice about the necessity of making good did

---

[11] Cf. "Autocracy and War" in *Notes on Life and Letters* (hereafter referred to as NLL), Dent ed. p. 100.
[12] NLL, p. 92.
[13] NLL, p. 96/97.

not color his nephew's outlook in this respect.[14] But that need not be considered relevant here.

What does matter is an unmistakable awareness of the danger of riches, perceptible throughout *Nostromo* and, in discursive terms, in essays and letters.[15] The danger affects, of course, the human personality, but also the polity (as symbolized by Costaguana) including a fraternity of nations, whether potential or actual. Idealistic motivation behind commercial expansion, as in the case of the California millionaire Holroyd, would not qualify Conrad's condemnation: in the writer's opinion, Americans are bound to betray whatever they may have inherited of the best European tradition, if they rely on sheer commercial expansion.

However disastrous their shortcomings in point of fact, the European nations, or at least a sufficient percentage of them, appear, as Conrad felt it, to have worked out a sketch, or at least the psychological premises, for a code to settle their disputes peacefully or by negotiations, with a certain determination to keep armed conflict to a minimum. Breaches of this understanding were the war venture of a Napoleon;[16] and the Germans' way of conducting war against France in 1870[17] brought shock, and shock could only be felt since particular expectations had been frustrated.

Extreme nationalism of any single state, (as such detrimental to other nations' rights) was also ruled out from the supposed charter for Europe; national allegiance proper would be considered a natural part of human loyalties: thus the Europe envisaged was, to use de Gaulle's formula, "une Europe des patries."

The famous explanation echoed by Conrad just in this context: "Il n'y a plus d'Europe!" is relevant just here. If the words "there is no more Europe" are a cry of despair and if they contain a truth on account, as he points out, of rampant commercialism and war increasingly more barbaric than usual, then what is clearly postulated is again the notion, however theoretical, of a civilized family trying to share peacefully the same continent.

That a civilized international community excludes tyranny would go without saying, but Conrad does say it when characterizing the contrary: "this despotism has been utterly un-European".[18]

---

14 "I have seen commerce pretty close. I know what it is worth, and I have no particular regard for commercial magnates... "NLL, p. 214 (NB: other magnates might appear to escape censure).
15 To RCG 1 May 1898.
16 NLL, p. 86.
17 NLL, p. 105.
18 NLL, p. 97.

The question about the scope of Europe in Conrad's thinking cannot be answered with precision. In a broad sense, a considerable range of European nationals have claimed his attention: obviously the English and the Polish as people of his two countries, of adoption and birth respectively, notably also the French and the Italians, the Dutch and the Scandinavians.[19] Special sympathy was directly expressed in the case of the French[20] and the Spaniards.[21]

Conversely, through their conduct the Germans and through the spirit — or the lack of it — the Russians were excluded from the code of an European community.

The important thing is that in no case would there be a narrowing down to one nation or region. Neither the nation of Conrad's birth nor that of his adoption would thus be considered a sufficient model. And yet he was not indiscriminately global. He was aware of the multinational continent of Europe, finding it unique in the history of humanity, and was committed to what he considered its best qualities.

Despite Conrad's creed about Europe one is bound to recall the many expressions of the writer's skepticism about humanity, its capacities and its achievements, and is bound to ask which side, the quasi-affirmative or the quasi-questioning should be thought to be decisive.

"L'homme est né poltron", opines the oft-quoted French lieutenant in *Lord Jim*[22]; reason is an impediment[23]; man's very birth is conceived, with poetic bitterness, after Calderón's line as his "delito mayor"[24]; his efforts to shape his life are futile, and he can only "to the destructive element submit himself"[25]. At the same time not only his instinct of self-preservation but his egoism is something to be praised,[26] though even a child can see that unrestrained it must lead to a *bellum omnium contra omnes* in which the appetite of a universal wolf must make perforce for a universal prey. In view of such accents who would be surprised by a reminder of Conrad's resistance to the notion of international fraternity and the like?[27]

However for all his remarkable aphoristic workmanship, his intelligence, his perceptiveness, Conrad remains a unique teller of stories,

[19] Cf. P. Mroczkowski, *op. cit.*, p. 177, 180, 185.
[20] NLL, p. 104.
[21] To RCG 1 May 1898.
[22] *Op. cit.*, Dent 1946 ed., p. 147. Cf. too, the Letter to RCG (C.T. Watts suggests the date of 23 Jan. 1898): "Not that I think mankind intrinsically bad. It is only silly and cowardly."
[23] "Thinking is the great enemy of perfection. "Author's Note to *Victory*. Cf. also to RCG 14 Dec. 1897 with an unmistakable eulogy of the instinct-based fitness for life of the uneducated man.
[24] Motto to *An Outcast of the Islands*.
[25] *Lord Jim, ed. cit.*, p. 214.
[26] *Cf.* supra, n.[10].
[27] To RCG 8 Feb. 1899.

the verbal painter of fleeting surfaces to things and people and even problems.

Things being so, it would be downright foolish to take Conrad unreservedly for a guide or oracle or to expect consistent, let alone systematic lessons on matters of political or other philosophy. A novelist is there to describe things, and people, conjure up their visions, not chain up notions about them.

Nevertheless a kind of instinct which we noted him as approving did enable him to avoid pitfalls, intellectual or emotional, and to react from the heart and with sound logic, in one political case in particular. It is once more the matter of a *Grenzsituation,* a borderline case, this time in the field of ideas on Europe. The notion of Europe, too, like human beings, needs a mortal test for doubtful points to become blindingly clear: and Conrad seems to have decided later in his life[28] that the test for Europe's fidelity to its *raison d'être,* to its quiddity, is the lot of the counry of his birth, Poland. Whatever may have been doubtful or ambivalent, the Crime of Partition *was* undoubtedly a crime and a uniquely unequivocal violation of the European spirit.

From his childhood the writer had been taught to look at the culture of the country of his birth as embodying the notions associated with Europe; topmost among them, democracy and freedom with the federation principle being derived therefrom. Thus the crime was not only one committed with phenomenal unfairness by three states against one neighbor, but one that stood in a special way for an idea.

On that ground whatever was wavering or changeable in Conrad's opinions on Europe as intentional example of civilized international equality acquired temporary firmness and clarity. The whimsicality and skepticism noticeable elsewhere remain.

One may accordingly leave things at that, accepting a great writer with his inconsistencies in the field of ideas, still feeling grateful for what he has left.

---

28 Earlier he seems to have allowed his bitterness and skepticism to cast a doubt over the possibility of his country's resurgence. This of course is not identical with a repudiation of the principle or the idea involved, but he had been reticent about his country's affairs. The attitude changed during World War I.

SOME PARTICIPANTS IN THE INTERNATIONAL CONFERENCE OF CONRAD SCHOLARS

First row: Julia Packard, Ludwik Krzyżanowski, Adam Gillon, Suzanne Henig, Virginia Teets, Bruce E. Teets, Elaine Boney, Helen Farr, Ruth C. Brown. *Second row:* Florence Talamantes, Tood K. Bender, Isabella Gillon, Donald W. Rude, Harry T. Moore, Arnold E. Davidson, Paul I. Gaston, Leland Fetzer, ————, Alyce Benson. *Third row:* Herbert Francis, Mrs. Owen Knowles, Leon Guilhamer, D. Ridley Beeton, ————, Vera F. Beck. *Fourth row:* Victor Kyrasy, Kenneth Lincoln, Owen Knowles, Glenn Sandstrom, Paul Bruss, Jack I. Biles, John S. Lewis.

II Conrad's Text and Criticism

DAVID LEON HIGDON

THE TEXT AND CONTEXT OF CONRAD'S FIRST CRITICAL ESSAY

"If we want insight into the major Conrad, we must return to the critical comments thrown out when he was an apprentice writer still excited by the ideas he and Ford had agreed upon . . ." — so wrote Frederick R. Karl fifteen years ago in what remains the fullest and perhaps the most perceptive discussion of Joseph Conrad's literary theory.[1] Later scholarship has revised our understanding of Ford Madox Ford's influence on Conrad,[2] but the basic truism of Karl's statement still stands. The search for the apprentice writer has concentrated on Conrad's letters, especially those to Marguerite Poradowska and Edward Garnett,[3] and on the "Preface" to *The Nigger of the "Narcissus"*.[4] More recently, collation of the Leeds Typescript of *Almayer's Folly* has identified the apprentice writer's careful revisions in this first work.[5] Overlooked in all of these studies, however, is Conrad's first critical essay written in late 1894 before the publication of his first novel, before any extant letters to Garnett, and two-and-a-half years before the famous

[1] "Joseph Conrad's Literary Theory," *Criticism*, 2(1960), 317
[2] See Frederick R. Karl, "Conrad, Ford, and the Novel," *Midway*, 10(1969), 17-34, and Arthur Mizener, *The Saddest Story: A Biography of Ford Madox Ford* (New York and Cleveland: World Publishing, 1971), pp. 71-83 in particular.
[3] See *Letters of Joseph Conrad to Marguerite Poradowska: 1890-1920*, ed. John A. Gee and Paul J. Strum (New Haven: Yale University Press, 1940), and Joseph J. Martin, "Edward Garnett and Conrad's Reshaping of Time,' *Conradiana*, 6:2 (1974), 89-105.
[4] The most recent discussions of the "Preface" are *Conrad's Manifesto: Preface to a Career*, ed. David R. Smith (Philadelphia: Rosenbach Foundation, 1966); David Goldknopf, "What's Wrong with Conrad: Conrad on Conrad," *Criticism*, 10(1968), 56-64, reprinted with revisions in *The Life of the Novel* (Chicago: University of Chicago Press, 1972); Ian Watt, "Conrad's Preface to *The Nigger of the 'Narcissus,'* " *Novel*, 7(1974), 101-15; and David Thorburn, *Conrad's Romanticism* (New Haven: Yale University Press, 1974), pp. 149-52.
[5] See Floyd Eugene Eddleman, David Leon Higdon, and Robert W. Hobson, "The First Editions of Conrad's *Almayer's Folly*," *Proof*, 4 (1974), 65-90.

97

"Preface." This essay is the long suppressed "Author's Note" to *Almayer's Folly.*

Because it was not published until 1920 when it appeared in the Doubleday Sun-Dial Edition, the note has been lumped with the other retrospective notes written when "Conrad was looking back and defining himself to his newly-acquired reading public"[6] and also defending his works in tones of "querulous selfvindication."[7] However, the "Author's Note" had been written by 4 January 1895, for on that date Conrad mentioned it in a letter to Edward Garnett.[8] Before 9 January 1895, Wilfrid Hugh Chesson, the T. Fisher Unwin reader who first recommended acceptance of *Almayer's Folly,* had read and critiqued the note, obviously suggesting some changes, because on that date Conrad responded to a now lost letter: "As to that preface (which I have shown you) I trust it may be dispensed with, but if it must appear you are quite right—*Aversion from* not 'aversion for' as I wrote—and stuck to like a lunatic. You will correct?"[9] Ugo Mursia, who now owns this letter, surmises that Conrad must have revised the note even further for "in the definitive text no trace was left of that word ('aversion') which was the cause of the mistake pointed out by Chesson."[10]

The preface was put aside until Conrad began selling manuscripts to John Quinn. In 1913, Conrad sent the manuscript of *Almayer's Folly* (except for the missing Chapter IX) and the preface to Quinn. He included a note which reads: "This is my first novel and indeed the *first thing of any sort* which I ever wrote for publication. I shall join to it the MS (2½ pp) of the suppressed preface I wrote for it at the time. Thus you shall have the MSS of all the prefaces (and all unpublished) I ever wrote up to last year when the Familiar Preface to my Reminiscences managed to get itself printed at last."[11] On 10 April 1919, Conrad again wrote Quinn concerning the preface, this time to retrieve it for use in the Collected Edition shortly to be issued by Doubleday, Page.[12] Quinn responded by having two copies typed and proofed in his office before sending them to Doubleday.[13] Although Conrad

---

[6] Karl, p. 333.

[7] Goldknopf, p. 81.

[8] *Letters from Joseph Conrad: 1895-1924,* ed. Edward Garnett (Indianapolis: Bobbs-Merrill, 1928), p. 31.

[9] Ugo Mursia, "The True 'Discoverer' of Joseph Conrad's Literary Talent and Other Notes on Conradian Biography with Three Unpublished Letters," *Conradiana,* 4:2 (1973), 10.

[10] Mursia, p. 10.

[11] This note is written on the third page of the prefatory matter to the manuscript. It is quoted in *Complete Catalogue of the Library of John Quinn* (New York: Anderson Galleries, 1924), 1:166.

[12] B. L. Reid, *The Man from New York: John Quinn and his Friends* (New York: Oxford University Press, 1968), p. 378.

[13] Reid, p. 379.

supposedly allowed the preface to be printed "unaltered and uncorrected, as [his] first attempt at writing a preface and an early record of exaggerated but genuine feeling,"[14] the English and American editions of the preface differ, and several changes were made in the typed copy.

The manuscript (purchased in the *Almayer's Folly* lot for $5,300 by A. S. W. Rosenbach at the Quinn sale) illustrates Conrad's usual manner of writing his first drafts. Words and phrases, sometimes half completed, are crossed out only to reappear later in the sentence. More interesting are the additions and revisions. Conrad changed the phrase "our glorious civilization" to read "our glorious virtues," expanded the single word "judged" into the phrase "condemned in a verdict of contemptuous dislike," added "misses the delicate detail" to describe the effect of exotic settings on "the dazzled eye," and, perhaps the most interesting revision, crossed out "my brothers and sisters" and replaced it with "common mortals."[15]

Despite Quinn's care in preparing the two typescript copies, he and his secretary made a number of changes. They Americanized the spelling of some words and lowered the capitalization on two others. They misread "shadows" as "shadow," "huts" as "tents" — thus destroying the fine alliteration of "houses and huts" and giving a strange idea of housing in Borneo—, and failed to set off the last sentence as a separate paragraph. These changes appear in both the Sun-Dial and the Heinemann; however, the Collected Editions add fifteen additional variants, mostly accidentals. The Heinemann reads "judgment that:", "seem," and "But," where the Sun-Dial reads "judgment:", "seems", and "Only".[16] Also, the Heinemann reads "aversion from it" where the Sun-Dial reads "disapproval of it." The variants are puzzling, because the Sun-Dial, using the Quinn typescript for copy-text, makes three major substantive changes, one a discarded manuscript reading, whereas the Heinemann is much closer to the typescript. Though Conrad intended for the "Author's Note" to stand "unaltered and uncorrected," it did not.

Why did Conrad write a preface in the first place? Traditionally, novelists have written prefaces to state an artistic creed, to define, explain, or justify a subject, to engage in a literary quarrel, or, from the the vantage of several years, to reminisce about the creation of the work. The more memorable prefaces tend to join all four categories,

---

[14] *Almayer's Folly*, Collected Edition (London: W. W. Heinemann, 1921), p. x. All quotations from the "Author's Note," unless otherwise indicated, are from this edition.

[15] The quotations from the manuscript and the typescript are printed with the permission of the Philip H. and A. S. Rosenbach Foundation and J. M. Dent & Sons, trustees of the Conrad Estate.

[16] *Almayer's Folly*, Sun-Dial Edition (Garden City: Doubleday, Page, 1920), pp. ix-x.

and one has only to recall the prefaces to Daniel Defoe's *Moll Flanders,*
Henry Fielding's *Joseph Andrews,* Charles Dickens' *Oliver Twist,* and
the seventeenth chapter of George Eliot's *Adam Bede* (the first chapter
of Volume Two and thus a preface of sorts) to realize what a rich
harvest exists in all four categories. Often the quarrel has led to the
most important theoretical statements. Henry James' "The Art of
Fiction," for example, would probably not have been written had it
not been for Walter Besant's earlier essay which provoked James. The
"Author's Note" to *Almayer's Folly* belongs to this category as well,
for in it Conrad quarrels directly with one of his noted contemporatries.

The opening paragraph of the "Author's Note" clearly identifies both
the target and the grounds of the quarrel:

> I am informed that in criticizing that literature which preys on strange
> people and prowls in far-off countries, under the shade of palms, in
> the unsheltered glare of sunbeaten beaches, amongst honest cannibals
> and the more sophisticated pioneers of our glorious virtues, a lady—
> distinguished in the world of letters—summed up her aversion from it
> by saying that the tales it produced were "decivilised." And in that sentence
> not only the tales but, I apprehend, the strange people and the far-off
> countries also, are finally condemned in a verdict of contemptuous dislike.
> (p. ix)

The paragraph leaps to the defense of the soon-to-be-published *Almayer's
Folly.* Its Bornean setting, its exotic characters, and its colonials had,
by implication, been included in the "verdict of contemptuous dislike."
We glimpse a nervous author uneasy as to the effect such dismissals
might have on the reception of his work.

And who was this lady—"distinguished in the world of letters"—of
intuitive, clear, felicitious, and infallible judgment? Fortunately, Conrad
identified her in a brief paragraph written for the Heinemann Collected
Edition.[17] She was Alice Meynell (1847-1922). Today, Alice Meynell
has almost been forgotten; in 1895, she was a prominent literary figure.
Ruskin, Dante Rossetti, and George Eliot had praised *Preludes,* her first
collection of poems, published in 1875, and, in the 1890's, she was
frequently mentioned as a possible successor to the poet-laureateship.
Following *Preludes,* she continued to write poetry, essays, and reviews,
and assisted her husband in editing *The Pen, The Weekly Register,* and
Merry England. Her interests in poetry brought friendship with Coventry

---

17 The paragraph reads: "I wrote the above in 1895 by way of preface for my first
novel. An essay by Mrs. Meynell furnished the impulse for this artless outpouring.
I let it now be printed for the first time, unaltered and uncorrected, as my first
attempt at writing a preface and an early record of exaggerated but genuine feeling"
(p. x). Conrad sent this short paragraph to Heinemann 3 September 1920: see,
Georges Jean-Aubry, *Joseph Conrad: Life and Letters* (Garden City: Doubleday,
Page, 1927), 2:248.

Patmore and Francis Thompson. Her incisive, often outspoken, reviews brought first attention and then friendship with George Meredith who in 1895 pronounced her article on Eleanora Duse "the high-water mark of literary criticism of our time."[18]

Meynell's essays on other poets, especially seventeenth century poets such as Lovelace, Crashaw, Marvell, Campion, Vaughn, and Waller, show her at her most perceptive. Her views were seldom shapped by mere popularity, and she did not hesitate to reprove Charlotte Bronte, Tennyson, and Swinburne and to dismiss Gray's "Elegy Written in a Country Churchyard" as "the high point of mediocrity."[19] However, her comments on novelists single out weaknesses and strengths with equal accuracy. Her talent for the epigram is called forth by novelists who held the public's attention for a short time: Ouida (1839-1908) has "a talent, an impulse, but a perfect mastery of mediocrity therewith"; works of the enormously popular Ellen Wood (1814-1887) can be read without fatigue "for she does not fatigue herself"; and Fanny Burney's *Evelina* is "an unabashed manifestation of waste thoughts."[20] Her critical standards never falter: she admires vivacity of portrait, dramatic scene, accuracy and economy in dialogue, a sense of structure, and, above all, style. Dickens elicited praise for his "conspicuous genius of words." "I never read him," she wrote, "but I undergo a new conviction of his authorship, of the vitality of his diction, springing, striking, making a way through the bonds of custom."[21] Her concern for style permeated all her works. In introducing the Centenary Volume of her prose and verse, Vita Sackville-West admiringly commented: "The roughest reader could not disregard its elaborate finish, whether in prose or verse. Reading her essays, one is reminded of old jewellers sometimes perceived seated at a cluttered table in the back room of a little shop, a cylindrical magnifying-glass fixed in one eye, bent over a skeleton framework, and with infinite delicacy dripping rather than dropping the tiny glittering stones into the setting from the tip of a pair of pincers. Such precision was Alice Meynell's in her choice of words."[22]

"Decivilised," the essay which provoked Conrad's "Author's Note," appeared in the 24 January 1891 issue of *National Observer* and was

---

[18] *The Letters of George Meredith*, ed. C. L. Cline (Oxford: Clarendon Press, 1970), 3:1220. Meredith's comment appeared in the *Illustrated London News*, August 1895.

[19] *The Wares of Autolycus: Selected Literary Essays of Alice Meynell*, chosen and introduced by P.M. Fraser (London: Oxford University Press, 1965), p. 29. The essay appeared in *Pall Mall Gazette*, 21 April 1897.

[20] *Wares*, pp. 7, 14, and 169. The essays on Ouida ("Oblivion"), Ellen Wood ("Forty-fifth Thousand"), and Fanney Burney ("Evelina") appeared in *PMG*, 16 August 1895, 16 September 1896, and 31 January 1896 respectively.

[21] *Wares*, p. 93. "Charles Dickens as a Writer" appeared in *PMG*, 11 January 1899.

[22] *Prose and Poetry: Centenary Volume*, ed. F. P., V. M., O. S., and F. M. (London: Jonathan Cape, 1947), p. 17.

reprinted as the second essay in Meynell's *The Rhythm of Life* in 1893.[23] It was undoubtedly in this latter form that Conrad encountered the essay for the first time. The short essay—not one of her better works—directly attacks colonial literature and discusses man divested of or degraded from a civilized condition. "Decivilised," its key term, seems to have enjoyed some popularity in reviews and journals, possibly because of its use by Herbert Spencer in *Principles of Sociology.*[24]

Ironically, the views of Conrad and Meynell are quite close on two major points; however, the generalities and nebulous thesis of Meynell's essay invite misunderstanding because of the uncertainty of subject. It is difficult to tell whether she is attacking colonial literature or reacting to the primitivism surfacing in European painting, sculpture, music, and literature. Basically, she objects to colonial literature because in its claims to newness it ignores the value of continuity. Of American literature, she comments: "Even now English voices, with violent commonplace, are constantly calling upon America to begin—to begin, for the world is expectant. Whereas there is no beginning for her, but instead a continuity which only a constant care can guide into sustained refinement and can save from decivilisation" (p. 8). She particularly values continuity because she finds in it a measure of the best and a keeper of civilized values. She argues that though we cannot select our posterity, "we may give our thoughts noble forefathers . . . Our minds may trace upwards and follow their ways to the best well-heads of the arts" (p. 9). Although this has an Arnoldian ring, we should remember that Meynell later rejected much of Arnold's thought, claiming "he did himself injustice when . . . he prescribed poetry as a kind of regent over mankind—mankind in need of law, fundamental law and a code" to console and soothe it.[25] However, these words came fifteen years after "Decivilised."

Nine months before Meynell's essay appeared, James G. Frazer wrote a brief preface to the first edition of *The Golden Bough* which helps place Meynell's essay in the context of late Victorian thought. In the preface, he made certain sweeping claims for literature: "For literature accelerates the advance of thought at a rate which leaves the slow progress of opinion by word of mouth at an immeasurable distance

---

[23] "Decivilised," *National Observer*, 24 January 1891, pp. 250-51, and *The Rhythm of Life and Other Essays* (London: John Lane, 1893), pp. 7-11. I have used a Third Edition (Boston: Copeland and Day, 1896).

[24] See Volume One, Section 71. The term appears in discussions of public health, law, war, and social decline in *North American Review*, 127 (November-December, 1878), 447; *Law Times*, 78 (1885), 338; and *Saturday Review*, 27 August 1892, p. 246.

[25] *Wares*, p. 158. The essay on Arnold appeared as the "Introduction" to the Selection of Arnold, *Red Letter Library* (London: Blackie and Company, 1906).

behind. Two or three generations of literature may do more to change thought than two or three thousand years of traditional life."[26] This view of literature assisting melioristic evolution with man progressing to a state of superior civilization informs Meynell's essay, for the subject of her attack is retrograde art: "To the eye that has reluctantly discovered this truth—that the vulgarised are not *un*civilised, and that there is no growth for them—it does not look like a future at all" (p. 11). Continuity measures the survival of the fittest art; decivilized art, on the other hand, presents the "mentally inexpensive." She stresses that decivilized works "are designed to betray the recklessness of [their authors'] nature and to reveal the good that lurks in the lawless ways of a young society" (p. 7). In arguing that the world does not need "more ballad-concerts, more quaint English, more robustious barytone songs, more piecemeal pictures, more young decoration, more colonial poetry, more young nations with withered traditions" (p. 11), she writes of decivilized art as though it were vestigial remains. In a review of *Charades Written a Hundred Years Ago by Jane Austen and Her Family,* she recounts an attempt by "certain English people" to introduce charades to an Italian country town and then generalizes: "It should have been a lesson against interfering with nations and periods. . . You cannot abridge the stages of intellectual progress."[27]

Conrad's attitude toward such thoughts is succinctly indicated in his suggestions concerning literary notices for his novel. "I am quite content," he wrote Chesson, "to be in your hands but it struck me that perhaps a suggestion from me would meet with your approval. Could you not say something about it being a 'Civilized story in savage surroundings?' Something in that sense if not in these words."[28] The "Author's Note" focuses almost exclusively on the idea that the "savage surroundings" serve only to throw the basic similarities of man in sharp relief. According to Richard Curle, Conrad once told the Dean of Canterbury that he was not "a topographical writer,"[29] and, in line with this, the Borneo of *Almayer's Folly* mirrors man's metaphysical, not his physical, condition. Conrad juxtaposes Borneo and London in the third paragraph of the "Author's Note" and asserts that man is one everywhere:

The picture of life there as here is drawn with the same elaboration of detail, coloured with the same tints. But in the cruel serenity of the sky, under

---

[26] "Preface," *The Golden Bough,* Second edition (London: Macmillan, 1900), 1:viii. The preface is dated 8 March 1890.

[27] *Wares,* p. 4. The essay, "The Wares of Autolycus," appeared in *PMG,* 26 July 1895.

[28] Mursia, p. 9.

[29] Quoted in *The Last Twelve Years of Joseph Conrad* (London: Sampson Low, Marston, 1928), p. 195.

the merciless brilliance of the sun, the dazzled eye misses the delicate detail, sees only the strong outlines, while the steady light, seem crude and without shadow. Nevertheless it is the same picture. (pp. ix—x)

The fourth paragraph restates this assumption:
And there is a bond between us and that humanity so far away. (p. x)

And he returns to the concept in the final paragraph:

I am content to sympathize with common mortals, no matter where they live—in houses or in tents, in the streets under a fog, or in the forests behind the dark line of dismal mangroves that fringes the vasts solitude of the sea . . . Their hearts—like ours—must endure the load of the gifts from Heaven: the curse of facts and the blessing of illusion; the bitterness of our wisdom and the deceptive consolation of our folly. (p. x)

In 1920, Conrad dismissed these comments as an "artless outpouring" but admitted that they were "an early record of exaggerated but genuine feeling" (p. x). How genuine they were may be judged by their recurrence in "Heart of Darkness" where recognition of his "remote kinship" with the natives forms part of Marlow's disturbing discovery,[30] and in "A Familiar Preface," where Conrad explains the initial attraction the characters in *Almayer's Folly* had for him: "why should the memory of these beings, seen in their obscure sun-bathed existence, demand to express itself in the shape of a novel, except on the grounds of that mysterious fellowship which unites in a community of hopes and fears all the dwellers on this earth?"[31] The insistence on the general nature which unites mankind and the belief, implicit in his metaphors, that the artist, like the painter, presents a picture for his audience may find fuller expression in the "Preface" to *The Nigger of the "Narcissus"*, but they do not find clearer expression.

Gradually a less existential and a more romantic Conrad, whose critical roots derive more nourishment from Wordsworth and Schopenhauer than from Flaubert and Maupassant, has begun to emerge in Conrad criticism. By carefully exploring the implications of each sentence in *The Nigger of the "Narcissus"* "Preface," Ian Watt has grounded Conrad's "critical bearings" firmly in the Romantic traditions,[32] and David Thorburn has even more emphatically asserted that Conrad stands to one side of the Daedalian craftsman. Commenting on the same preface, he pointed out that "Conrad's comparison of the writer to a worker in a field, his identification of ordering human work with the enterprise of art, runs counter to symbolist and postsymbolist notions of the

[30] "The Heart of Darkness," in *Youth*, Kent Edition (Garden City: Doubleday, Page, 1926), 16:96.
[31] *A Personal Record*, Kent Edition (Garden City: Doubleday, Page, 1926), 6:9.
[32] Watt, pp. 103-05 in particular.

artist as a man isolated from his fellow men, relying (like Joyce's artist-hero) on silence, exile, and cunning to get his work done."[33] Conrad's interest in the relationship between the particular and the general, in the community of man, and in the artist's mediation between audience and reality, working primarily through sympathy and hearts, bares the Romantic assumptions in the *Almayer's Folly* "Author's Note" as well. Indeed, Wordsworth's description of the poet's activities could easily stand as a gloss to both the "Preface" and the "Author's Note." Wordsworth describes the poet as "the rock of defence for human nature; an upholder and preserver, carrying everywhere with him relationship and love. In spite of difference of soil and climate, of language, and manners, of laws and customs . . . the Poet binds together by passion and knowledge the vast empire of human society as it is spread over the whole earth, and over all time. The objects of the Poet's thoughts are everywhere . . . "[34] It is quite easy to see why an artist holding these views would have been annoyed by Alice Meynell's essay. She spoke for change, progress, and evolving man; Conrad and Wordsworth speak for what is permanent, common, and enduring.

Why this first critical essay by Conrad was not published as the preface to *Almayer's Folly* remains a mystery. Conrad's letter to Chesson hints that he wished to see it published, and he later spoke of it as being "suppressed," but did not indicate who suppressed it or why. In terms of general literary theory, the loss was not significant. The "Author's Note" is not a closely reasoned creed, it is not an outrageous manifesto, it is not even a very direct rebuttal of Alice Meynell's essay. Nevertheless, it is our first clear view of the critical, theoretical, and literary Conrad. It establishes the critical assumptions with which Conrad began writing and allows us to measure more exactly the aesthetic distance he travelled by the time of the later essays. It displays a novelist concerned from the beginning of his career with the relationship between subject matter, vision, and the role of the artist, and thus strikingly anticipates his later and more famous pronouncements. More than that, by implication the preface partakes of one of the most important continuing battles fought by Conrad's contemporaries. In Henry James' words, "All life belongs to you, and do not listen either to those who would shut you up into corners of it and tell you that it is only here and there that art inhabits. . ."[35]

---

[33] *Conrad's Romanticism*, p. 150.
[34] *Lyrical Ballads: The Text of the 1798 Edition with the Additional 1800 Poems and the Prefaces*, ed. R. L. Brett and A. R. Jones (London: Methuen and Company, 1963), p. 253.
[35] "The Art of Fiction," *Selected Literary Criticism*, ed. Morris Shapira (London: Heinemann, 1963), p. 67.

DONALD W. RUDE

CONRAD'S REVISION OF THE FIRST AMERICAN EDITION OF "THE ARROW OF GOLD"

Joseph Conrad's bibliographers noted the existence of two distinct issues of the first American edition of *The Arrow of Gold* as early as 1929. The short description of the first edition of this novel in George T. Keating's *A Conrad Memorial Library* states:

This is the first issue, which differs from the second issue in the wording on pages 5 and 15. On page 5, line 16, the first issue reads "with proper credentials apparently" and the second issue, "with proper credentials and who." On page 15, line 24, the first issue reads "almost absolute strangers" and the second issue reads "almost complete strangers." There is also a mistake on page 248, the sixth and seventh lines reading: "in her whole attitude—as though she had never been kissed before." In subsequent issues this was changed to: "in her whole attitude—as though she had never even heard of such a thing as a kiss in her life." These errors were discovered by the author while the book was in press.[1]

This description of the two issues of *The Arrow*, while sufficient for bibliographical identification, is incomplete, and the explanation that the variants result from the discovery of printer's mistakes is incorrect. A comparison of the two volumes on the Hinman collator reveals that these two issues of *The Arrow of Gold* are set apart by nearly 50 variants. The nature of the changes separating the two texts, (these are set out in Table A) indicates more than the chance discovery of mistakes "while the book was in press." Rather, the variants resulted from Joseph Conrad's having made a final revision of the edition after Doubleday, Page and Company had printed it.

A consideration of the circumstances surrounding the novel's publication in America provides a partial explanation of the existence of variants in the two states Conrad began work on *The Arrow* in 1917. His enthusiasm for the project, which he had contemplated for many years, ran high, and after nine months, sometimes writing and sometimes, when plagued by gout, dictating, he completed a draft of the text. Typescripts of the novel must have been prepared and circulated

---

[1] Garden City, New York: Doubleday, Doran, 1929, p. 278.

106

in short order, for the serial version of *The Arrow* began to appear in *Lloyd's Magazine* in December, 1918. In America, F. N. Doubleday's interest in the novel remained intense, even though he had been unable to secure a serial publisher. In fact, Doubleday wished to rush the novel into print in January, 1919, perhaps in an effort to capitalize on the author's popularity, then at its very peak. Conrad evidently rejected this proposal prior to December 21, 1918, when, in a letter to the publisher, he reiterates his objections to early publication of *The Arrow* and explains his reservations. After expressing disappointment at Doubleday's failure in locating a serial publisher in the United States, he writes:

I was right in the objections I raised against the proposal to publish *The Arrow of Gold* in book form in January. First of all, it seemed to me that, at the date the proposal reached me, there was not enough time left to make the business and publicity arrangements for a novel by J. C., whose merit is not of that kind that could secure a response without all the help that the standing, influence and organization of Doubleday, Page & Co. can give him. I also doubted the advisability of publishing a book at a time when, . . . the public mind is bound to be absorbed by the problems of peace and the settling of political questions all over the world. Besides, I felt that in justice to myself, and also to your efforts on my behalf, I must see the proof sheets; not for material alterations, but for the exact setting of the text. I felt this the more because your printers would be setting up from a typewritten copy which I myself had not seen, but which, I am sure, contains the usual amount of errors and mistakes of a kind that cannot be easily discovered by the most conscientious of proof readers. I am perfectly aware that I had no book proofs from you for the previous books, but this was only because then the setting up at Garden City was done from printed texts which were already carefully revised by me.[2]

The letter suggests a great deal about the preparation of the American text of *The Arrow*. Doubleday intended to use as a copy-text a type-written draft of the novel prepared for use by the American serial publisher. Conrad's early biographer, Richard Curle, has noted that the author took little interest in the preparation of his serial texts,[3] and one can understand his reluctance to have the American firm publish an edition of *The Arrow* set from an imperfect copy. One might go on to make the easy assumption that the variants in the two texts published in America in the spring of 1919 simply reflect the fact that Doubleday used an uncorrected typescript or that Conrad did not see the proofs he requested in December. However, unpublished letters in the Berg Collection of the New York Public Library, disprove such conjectures. In the extensive file of correspondence between Doubleday, Page and

---

[2] Georges Jean-Aubry, *Life and Letters* II, Garden City, New York: Doubleday, Page and Company, 1927, 214.
[3] *The Last Twelve Years of Joseph Conrad*, London: Sampson, Low & Marston, 1928, 71; hereafter cited as *Last Twelve Years*.

Co., and J. B. Pinker, one finds two memos from L. A. Comstock, F. N. Doubleday's personal secretary, to J. B. Pinker. Both are dated February 5, 1919, and both acknowledge the arrival of Conrad's corrected galley proofs of *The Arrow of Gold*. "These," Miss Comstock notes, "will be very carefully read," and the firm "will send two sets of corrected proofs to you at the earliest possible moment."[4]

As they continued their publication plans, editors at Doubleday, Page & Co. must have assumed, with every justification, that Conrad had made those corrections which he wished to introduce into *The Arrow* when he returned corrected proofs to the company in early February. Sometime in late March, 1918, Doubleday, Page forwarded Conrad the corrected proofs promised by Miss Comstock, before issuing the first American edition of the novel on April 12 in a press run of 15,000 copies.[5]

To what must have been the great surprise of all concerned, Conrad replied to the receipt of "corrected" proofs with a request for additional changes in the text and headmatter of *The Arrow of Gold,* making numerous revisions of the text and asking that the dedication be changed from Richard Curle to John Quinn, the manuscript collector who then frequently acted as Conrad's intermediary with Doubleday, Page. An unpublished letter from John Quinn to Conrad offers a full account of the episode. Quinn, who had been notified by Conrad of his request that the dedication be changed,[6] cabled for the author's instructions, after urging the firm to delay publication of the second issue of the novel. Immediately, he wrote to Conrad of the matter:

I was delighted at your intention of dedicating the *Arrow of Gold* to me, but the first edition stands dedicated to Richard Curle, who I thought, was entitled to that honor. Knowing the stupidity of publishers, I was afraid that they might act upon the "corrected proofs" with the dedication to me which you wrote "had already been mailed to Garden City", and I called them on the telephone and after two talks found the following:

The first edition of 15,000 copies was published on Saturday, April 12th, and was dedicated to "Richard Curle". A few days after that Doubleday-Page received the corrected proofs with the dedication "to

---

[4] TLS, dated February 5, 1919, in The Berg Collection, New York Public Library. I am indebted to Mrs. Lola Szladitz, curator of The Berg Collection, and her staff for allowing me to consult the Doubleday-Pinker correspondence, and I am deeply grateful to Mr. Ken McCormick, vice-president of The Doubleday Company, for granting me permission to quote from that firm's official correspondence.

[5] Theodore G. Ehrsam, *A Bibliography of Joseph Conrad*, Metuchen, N.J.: The Scarecrow Press, 1969, p. 261.

[6] Joseph Conrad to John Quinn, TLS dated 10 April, 1919 in the Quinn Collection, Manuscript Division, New York Public Library.

John Quinn". This was "just a few days after the publication of the first edition". Of course the printing of the first edition was finished before April 12th, for it was technically published on April 12th, and after the printing there came, as you know, the binding and so on. . . . They told me in my second talk with them on the telephone today that the second edition is ready for the press. Apparently the steam engines at Garden City are panting steam pants and the jaws of the press are fairly aching to print the second edition of 5,000. Stupid asses! They were going to follow the "corrected proofs" and therefore have the second edition dedicated "to John Quinn". I am sure you would not want that, for your sake or for Curle's sake or for Quinn's sake. It would be like literary Mormonism, you being the Mormon and the two dedications of the one book the plural wives; or perhaps polyandry might be the symbol. So I told Doubleday's people to reduce the pressure on the presses and to hold their presses, if they hadn't any horses to hold, for a few days and that I was cabling you. Apparently the steam presses at Garden City are very hard to hold . . . It would have been a devil of a thing to have changed the dedication of the second edition from Curle to Quinn.[7]

Conrad cabled his concurrence with Quinn in the matter of the dedication, and Quinn resolved the matter with F. N. Doubleday, writing to Conrad two days later that he had instructed Doubleday's secretary to continue with the publication of the second edition without the new dedication and sending a copy of Conrad's cable to the publisher. Writing to Conrad, Quinn states:

He got that yesterday and replied at once and said:

About the dedication for *The Arrow of Gold* — of course we never knew about this until our book had been printed, and Conrad did not tell me anything about it when I was in England. We think it would be a poor compliment to you to change the dedication in the middle of an edition. We should strongly advise that the dedication be substituted, perhaps in *The Rescue,* which is a very fine book and which is coming perhaps a year from now.

So you will see that Doubleday thought the same as I. It was only his subordinates who were banging ahead and who would have printed the second edition with the dedication to me but for the fortunate receipt by me of your letter . . .[8]

---

[7] TL, dated April 28, 1919. The letter is a carbon copy of one mailed to Conrad on this date; copies of all of Quinn's correspondence to the author are housed in the Manuscript Division of the New York Public Library; I am indebted to the curators for granting me permission to utilize material in the John Quinn Collection, Manuscript and Archives Division, the New York Public Library, Astor, Lenox and Tilden Foundations.

[8] TL, dated April 30, 1919, Manuscript Division, New York Public Library.

Two additional pieces of correspondence in the Quinn archives clarify our knowledge of the revision of *The Arrow of Gold*. The first is a neatly typed 'copy' of a memorandum from Conrad to Doubleday, Page and Company. It begins with the notation: "Mr. Joseph Conrad thanks the proof-reader entrusted with the text of *The Arrow of Gold* for the almost complete absence of printer's errors, and will be very grateful to him for the same good care in carrying out the following author's corrections."[9] There follows an enumeration of the changes Conrad wished to make in the text and dedication, which confirms that the variants detected in a collation of the two texts originated with the author. The second relevant piece of correspondence is a brief letter from Conrad to Quinn in which the author writes:

It was a curious imbroglio of which the fault was entirely mine, though I think the Doubledays might have sent me revised slips of *Arrow* early enough to have them returned in time for correction.

The fact is that the dedication to you was a sudden thought insofar that for a long time I had determined to dedicate to you my Napoleonic novel, which is the next work I am to write . . . Then, while passing the first proofs of *Arrow* it occurred to me that I would not keep you waiting . . .[10]

With Conrad assuring Quinn that he would be the dedicatee of *Suspense*, the "curious imbroglio" came to its conclusion. The original dedication was left standing, and Conrad's revisions were introduced in the second American issue of *The Arrow of Gold*. The whole affair, I think, in addition to explaining the existence of two distinct issues of the novel, reveals much about Conrad's working relationship with Doubleday, Page and Company. First, the author had provided Doubleday with a typescript that he had not scrutinized carefully. Although the firm gave the author an opportunity to make corrections in galley proofs, he apparently could not resist the temptation to make additional "material" changes in the text, a task which he had assured the publisher would be unnecessary when he wrote to him in December, 1918. Certainly, the affair confirms Curle's suggestion that

Conrad did an enormous amount of re-writing. Page after page of his type-scripts has the appearance of original manuscript, just as page after page of his proof sheets resembles a battle-field. . . . I doubt, indeed, whether any author's work shows more variations than does that of Conrad.[11]

---

[9] TL, dated 30 March, 1919, in the Quinn Collection, Manuscript Division, New York Public Library. I am indebted to the trustees of the Joseph Conrad estate for granting me permission to quote from the author's unpublished correspondence.
[10] TLS, dated 3 May, 1919, in the Quinn Collection, Manuscript Division, New York Public Library.
[11] *Last Twelve Years*, p. 71.

The variants separating the two issues of the first American edition of *The Arrow of Gold* clarify the nature of the particular war Conrad waged when he revised page proofs of the novel in the spring of 1919.

Three distinct types of changes appear in the text. First, there are changes involving accidentals. These changes may have resulted from Conrad's having sent Doubleday, Page and Company an imperfect typescript of *The Arrow of Gold*. Secondly, there are a number of changes which reflect the author's concern with rhetoric and idiom, — changes affecting the texture of Conrad's prose withould drastically modifying its sense. Finally, there are numerous instances of revision in which Conrad's alterations of diction or syntax, his cancellations and his additions produce a heightened stylistic effect or introduce a subtle nuance. Such modifications reflect what Curle described as Conrad's torturous effort "to make his full vision materialize," gazing all the while at his book "as a chess master gazes at the board before him in a complicated game."[12]

The first group of changes, primarily involving accidentals, may have resulted from Conrad's being forced to rely heavily on dictation while writing *The Arrow*.[13] It is probable that the various changes of a typographical nature, such as the introduction of italic type in a number of passages and an occasional change in capitalization resulted from authorial oversight while dictating or from the carelessness of a typist. That Conrad concerned himself with such matters indicates that over the course of his career, the author had acquired a comprehension of typographical conventions not always evident in his earlier texts. Other minor substantive changes might also reflect the difficulties posed by dictation. Could not, for instance, the reading "Some personage from the Foreign department and the headquarters" (p. 55) which is altered to read "at headquarters", have crept into the text to begin with due to the difficulty that a stenographer might have had in transcribing the spoken English of the author, which was at best, difficult to understand?

A comparison of the variants separating the two issues of *The Arrow* also shows us the author working to perfect his rhetoric and to impose a more idiomatic usage on the text. The most frequent rhetorical change involves diction. For example, when the novel's hero Monsieur George ponders Dona Rita's response to the presence of her mad cousin, the first issue reads: ". . . but my pity went out not to him but to Dona Rita" (p. 305). In the second issue, the initial conjunction is changed to "yet". If there is a semantic distinction separating the two words it is

---

[12] *Last Twelve Years*, p. 72, p. 73.
[13] Jocelyn Baines, *Joseph Conrad: A Critical Biography*, London: Widenfeld and Nicolson, 1959, p. 410; hereafter cited as Baines.

one so subtle as to evade the common reader. The revision merely eliminates an awkward repetition of words. One suspects Conrad of having a similar motive when he removes the first of a pair of "even's" from the sentence "He pointed out that things had been stolen even out of the Louvre, which was . . . he dared say, even better guarded" (p. 83). Here the double emphasis of the original sentence is inherently awkward. Such revisions are consistent with Conrad's usual practices. We see a similar concern with repetitious diction in the revision of *The Nigger of the "Narcissus"* where Conrad used the phrases "I never saw them again" and "I never saw one of them again'" in close proximity.[14] Later, he altered the second sentence to read "I never met one of them again."[15] It is safe to assume that Conrad, whether revising an old text or perfecting a new one, valued varied diction as an effective element in style.

Both early and late in his career, Conrad struggled to achieve correctness in matters of grammar and idiom. One revision reflecting this struggle occurs on page 35 of *The Arrow,* where Conrad eliminates the final three words in the sentence "The play of the white gleams of his smile round the suspicion of grimness of his tone fascinated me like a moral icongruity *would have done*" (my ital.). Elimination of the concluding verb creates the correct grammatical structure demanded by the preposition "like". It is worth noting that Conrad always seems to have been troubled by "like" and "as," words that he used interchangeably. He was chastized for this confusion by W. H. Chesson in 1898 and seems to have been uncertain of the formal distinction between the two words as late as 1916 when he was revising *The Nigger.*[16] Other changes in *The Arrow of Gold* that reflect Conrad's attempt to achieve idiomatic correctness include the change of "these eyes," to "those eyes" on page 81, and the substitution of "from" for "of" in the sentence "He was the only son from a rich farmhouse . . ." (p. 124). Conrad's desire for grammatical accuracy is further revealed in the elimination of an error in subject-verb agreement on page 190.

Other revisions in *The Arrow of Gold* reveal Conrad's ability to heighten the effect of an image, enhance characterization, and strengthen the irony of passages in the novel. Conrad frequently achieved

---

14 Joseph Conrad, *The Nigger of the "Narcissus,"* London: William Heinemann, 1897, p. 119 and p. 120.
15 Joseph Conrad, *The Nigger of the "Narcissus"*, Garden City, N.Y.: Doubleday, Page and Co., 1925, p. 173.
16 For Chesson's letter and Conrad's response, see *A Conrad Memorial Library,* pp. 34-35; for a detailed discussion of the problem of *like* and *as* in *The Nigger,* see Kenneth W. Davis, David Leon Higdon and Donald W. Rude, "On Editing Conrad," forthcoming in an anthology of essays presented at the International Conrad Conference, University of Kent, Canterbury, England.

more vivid effects by changing a word, cancelling a phrase, or even by simply altering the punctuation. Consider for instance, the difference in tonality that Conrad achieves when he alters the punctuation in a section of Captain Blunt's narration. In the first issue, we find the following long utterance:

"I understand it didn't last very long," he addressed us politely again, "and no wonder, the sort of talk she would have heard during that first springtime in Paris would have put an impress on a much less receptive personality; . . . (p. 47)

In his memo to Doubleday's proofreaders, the author asked that the passage be changed, breaking one, long sentence into three distinct ones:

"I understand it didn't last very long," he addressed us politely again. "And no wonder! The sort of talk she would have heard during that first spiring-time in Paris would have put an impress on a much less receptive per-sonality; . . ."

The alterations enhance the reader's comprehension of Blunt's reaction to the situation he has been describing, suggesting greater dismay at the ill-effect of scandal on the young woman who, he has just told his audience, "must have been adorable." The short exclamation "And no wonder!" breaks the rhythm of the sentence, and when read aloud, I think, forces a falling intonation in the next passage, an intonation suggestive of Blunt's cynical awareness of the true nature of the *demi-monde*, and its effect on Rita.

Like Captain Blunt, Conrad was fascinated with Dona Rita. Inasmuch as Conrad regarded the book as the story of Rita de Lastaola and the initiation of Monsieur George into "the life of passion", it is particularly interesting to note the many revisions which Conrad made in Chapters IV and V of Part Four of *The Arrow of Gold*, the sections of the book in which Monsieur George confronts Dona Rita with his passion for her. Modern critics have found his treatment of Rita to be "cliché-ridden," and his depiction of George to be highly conventional.[17] His careful revisions of these chapters may indicate that Conrad himself was aware of the inadequacy of his portrayals and tried with some success to improve his text.

In these chapters Conrad frequently tried to achieve greater precision in description and characterization. He frequently accomplishes this through small changes in diction which add clarifying detail to his work. Note, for instance, the substitution of "enviously" for "curiously" to describe the tone of Rita's exclamation "What freedom!" on page

---

[17] Baines, p. 410.

246. The more precise descriptive term heightens the irony of the fact that Rita, who is apparently liberated, is in fact a prisoner of the freedom she seems to possess. Similarly, Conrad changed the verb "say" to "shout" in Rita's question ". . . why don't you shout *Vive le Roi,* too?" (p. 218), better expressing" the enthusiasm which Rita feels for the pretender and which she demands of her young admirer. When Conrad emends Rita's statement "I have known domination, . . ." changing the verb to "suffered," he better describes the quality of Rita's experience. A similar change of Rita's rather vague declaration "I don't know anything about myself" to "I don't know the truth about myself . . ." (p. 228) hints at Dona Rita's almost naive denial of her need for true, human love.

On occasion, Conrad clarified the emotions of his characters simply by refining the accidentals of his text. Consider the long speech on page 230 wherein Dona Rita condemns Blunt's hypocrisy:

> . . . but I have my own basque peasant soul and don't want to think that every time he goes away from my feet — yes, *mon cher,* on this carpet. Look for the marks of scorching — that he goes away feeling tempted to brush the dust of his moral sleeve. That never.

In the first issue, the punctuation is clumsy. In its revised state, wherein the two parenthetical elements are joined as part of a single outburst, " — yes, *mon cher,* on this carpet, look for the marks of scorching —", the emotional effect of the interruption is more keenly felt. Indeed, the altered punctuation suggests that Rita's anger has become so intense that she cannot, for the moment, continue the logical sequence of her speech.

Throughout the novel, Conrad attempted to make Dona Rita an enigmatic figure. Although she has been a courtesan, she is naively generous; although she has known passion, she fears true love. Frequently, Conrad's revisions heighten our awareness of Rita's paradoxical nature. For instance, when Conrad writes of Monsieur George's having kissed Rita passionately upon the throat, he describes her response as a sort of "stupefaction" suggesting that "she had never been kissed before". He altered the second issue to read "as though she had never even heard of such a thing as a kiss in her life." The revision seems designed to heighten our awareness of the irony Monsieur George finds in her response.

These then are a few of the typical changes Conrad made in the text of *The Arrow of Gold* as he read corrected page proofs for the first American edition of the novel. All were adopted in later printings. They suggest, I hope, something of the care Conrad took with his texts. One would like to think that the story of the novel's revision ended here. But later in 1919, Conrad wrote to Sidney Colvin, expressing his worry over corrections in the British first edition, the proofs of which he had read "innumerable times." "Why, oh! why," he laments, "didn't I send you the revise?"[18] Thus, it is likely that the process of revision continued, as Conrad struggled to make perfect his tale of those 42-year-old episodes from his youth which still produced "a slight tightness of the chest — *un petit serrement du coeur*."[19]

TABLE A

Variants in the first and second issues of the first American Edition of
The Arrow of Gold

1st Issue	2nd Issue
What Mills had learned represented him as a young gentleman who had arrived furnished with proper credentials and apparently was doing his best to waste his life in an eccentric fashion, with a bohemian set (one poet, at least, emerged out of it later) on one side, and on the other making friends with the people of the Old Town, pilots, coasters, sailors, workers of all sorts. (P. 5)	What Mills had learned represented him as a young gentleman who had arrived furnished with proper credentials and who apparently was doing his best to waste his life in an eccentric fashion, with a bohemian set (one poet, at least, emerged out of it later) on one side, and on the other making friends with the people of the Old Town, pilots, coasters, sailors, workers of all sorts.
We three, however (almost absolute strangers to each other), had assumed attitudes of serious amiability round our table. (P. 16)	We three, however (almost complete strangers to each other), had assumed attitudes of serious amiability round our table.
"Yes." he said. *"American, catholique et gentilhomme,"* . . . (P.21)	"Yes," he said. *"Je suis Americain, catholique et gentilhome,"* . . .
There were also a few bottles of some white wine quite possibly, which we could drink out of Venetian cut-glass goblets. (P.22)	There were also a few bottles of some white wine, quite possible, which we could drink out of Venetian cut-glass goblets.
The play of the white gleams of his smile round the suspicion of grimness of his tone fascinated me like a moral incongruity would have done. (P. 35)	The play of the white gleams of his smile round the suspicion of grimness of his tone fascinated me like a moral incongruity.
. . . he went on: "I suppose you know how he got hold of her?"	. . . he went on: "I suppose you know how he got hold of her?"

---

[18] *Life and Letters*, II, 229.
[19] *Ibid.*

in a tone of ease which was astonishingly ill-assumed by such a worldly, self-controlled, drawing room person. (P. 37)

"Does anybody know beside the two parties concerned?" . . . (P. 37)

She lets them, you know, at ex tortinate prices, that is, if people will give them, for she is easily intimidated. (P. 44)

1st Issue

"I understand it didn't last very long," he addressed us politely again, "and no wonder, the sort of talk she would have heard . . ." (P. 47)

With the merest casual 'Bonjour, Allègre' he ranges close to her on the other side and addresses her, hat in hand, in that enormous voice of his like a deferential roar of the sea heard far away. (P. 47)

"Yes, that old sculptor was the first who joined them in the sight of all Paris. (P. 50)

Of course the rooms in the hotel Tolosa were retained for her by an order from royal headquarters. (P. 55)

Some personage from the Foreign department and the Headquarters was closeted for about a couple of hours. (P. 55)

"While the woman herself is, so to speak,priceless." (P. 64)

"Here I come, expecting to find a good sensible girl who had seen at last the vanity of all those things; half-light in the rooms; surrounded by her favourite poets . . ." (P. 81)

---

in a tone of ease which was ill-assumed for such a wordly, self-controlled, drawing room person.

"Does anybody know besides the two parties concerned?"

She lets them, you know, at ex-tortionate prices, that is, if people will pay them, for she is easily intimidated.

2nd Issue

"I understand it didn't last very long," he addressed us politely again,* "And no wonder! The sort of talk she would have heard. . ."

With the merest casual 'Bonjour, Allègre' he ranges close to her on the other side and addresses her, hat in hand, in that booming voice of his like a deferential roar of the sea heard far away.

Yes, that old sculptor was the first who joined them in the sight of all Paris.

Of course the rooms in the hotel Tolosa were retained for her by an order from Royal headquarters.

Some personage from the Foreign department at Headquarters was closeted for about a couple of hours.

"Where the woman herself is, so to speak, priceless."

"Here I come, expecting to find a good sensible girl who had seen at least the vanity of all those things; half-light in the rooms; surrounded by the works of her favourite poets . . ."

It was as though he had borrowed these eyes from some idiot for the purpose of that visit. (P. 81)

He pointed out that things had been stolen even out of the Louvre, which was, he dared say, even better watched. (P. 83)

It was as though he had borrowed those eyes from some idiot for the purpose of that visit.

He pointed out that things had been stolen out of the Louvre, which was, he dared say, even better watched.

*This comma was changed to the full stop Conrad desired in first British edition and the Sun-Dial Edition of the novel.

1st Issue

We couldn't hear what she said but the movement of her lips and the play of her features was full of charm, full of interest expressing both audacity and gentleness. (P. 86)

I gazed frankly at Dona Rita's profile, irregular, animated, and fascinating . . . (P. 86)

I saw a short, frail little man with a long, yellow face and sunken fanatical eyes, an Inquisitor, an unfrocked monk. (P. 91)

"He was the only son of a rich farmhouse two miles down the slope. . . ." (P. 124)

When we got on to the level that man whose even breath no exertion, no danger, no fear or even anger could disturb, remarked as we strode side by side: . . . (P. 142)

. . . the very shape, feel, and warmth of her high-heeled slipper that would sometimes in the heat of the discussion drop on the floor with a crash, and which I would throw back on the couch without ceasing to argue. (P. 181)

Mrs. Blunt's reception of me, glance, tones, even to the attitude

2nd Issue

We couldn't hear what she said but the movements of her lips and the play of her features was full of charm, full of interest, expressing both audacity and gentleness.

I gazed frankly at Dona Rita's profile, irregular, animated and fascinating . . .

I saw a frail little man with a long, yellow face and sunken fanatical eyes, an Inquisitor, an unfrocked monk.

"He was the only son from a rich farmhouse two miles down the slope. . . ."

When we got on to the level that man whose even breathing no ex ertion, no danger, no fear or anger could disturb, remarked as we strode side by side: . . .

. . . the very shape, feel, and warmth of her high-heeled slipper that would sometimes in the heat of the discussion drop on the floor with a crash, and which I would toss back on the couch without ceasing to argue.

Mrs. Blunt's reception of me, glance, tones, even to the attitude of the admirably corseted figure, were most friendly, . . .   (P. 190)

"But you are too young perhaps as yet . . . But as to my John," . . .
    (P. 197)

The few remarkable personalities that count in society and who were admitted into Henry Allègre's Pavilion treated her with most punctilious reserve.   (P. 206)

1st Issue

It lay there prostrate, handless, feetless, without its head, pathetic, like the mangled victim of a crime.
    (P. 209)

My view now was that he was aware beforehand of the subject of the conversation and if so I did not wish to appear as if I had slunk away from him after the interview.   (P. 213)

"An empty coupé came to the door . . . and its still waiting," she added . . .

     . . .

"Oh! There's that coupé going away."   (P. 215)

"*Amigo* George," she said, "I take the trouble to send for you but here I am before you, talking to you and you say nothing." (P. 217)

". . . You might, for instance, say that you were sorry for my tears."
    (P. 217)

". . . Come, why don't you say *Vive le Roi,* too?"   (P. 218)

". . .For after all, in that Allègre Pavilion, my dear Rita, you were but a crowd of glorified bourgeoisie."   (P. 220)

of the admirably corseted figure, was most friendly, . . .

"You are too young perhaps as yet . . . But as to my John," . . .

The few remarkable personalities that count in society and who were admitted into Henry Allègre's Pavilion treated her with punctilious reserve.

2nd Issue

It lay there prostrate, handless, without its dead, pathetic, like the mangled victim of a crime.

My view now was that he was aware beforehand of the subject of the conversation, and if so I did not wish to appear as if I had slunk away from him after the interview.

"An empty *coupé* came to the door . . . and its still waiting," she added . . .

     . . .

"Oh! There's that *coupé* going away."

"*Amigo* George," she said, "I take the trouble to send for you and here I am before you, talking to you and you say nothing."

". . . You might, for instance, tell me that you were sorry for my tears."

". . . Come, why don't you shout *Vive le Roi,* too?"

". . . For after all, in that Allègre Pavilion, my dear Rita, you were but a crowd of glorified *bourgeois.*"

And I thought suddenly of Azzolati being ordered to take himself off from the presence for ever, in that voice the very voice of anger which seemed to twine itself gently round one's heart. (P.223)

If your heart is full of things like that, then, my dear friend, you had better take it out and give it to the crows. (P. 225)

1st Issue

"Listen, *amigo*," she said, "I have known domination, and it didn't crush me because I have been great enough to live with it; . . ." (P. 227)

". . . All lawful conventions are coming to me, all the glamours of respectibility. . . . "

"I don't know anything about myself because I never had an opportunity to compare myself to anything in the world . . ." (P. 228)

". . . I said to him: The trouble is, Don Juan, that it isn't love but mistrust that keeps you here. A parrot would have added here that I had given him no right to be jealous ..." (P. 230)

". . . but I have my own Basque peasant soul and don't want to think that every time he goes away from my feet — yes, *mon cher,* on this carpet. Look for the marks of scorching — that he goes away feeling tempted to brush the dust off his moral sleeve. That never!" (P. 230)

". . . to know her such as life had made her and at the same time to despise her secretly for every

---

And I thought suddenly of Azzolati being ordered to take himself off from her presence for ever, in that voice the very voice of anger which seemed to twine itself gently round one's heart.

If your heart is full of things like that, then my dear friend, you had better take it out and give it to the crows.

2nd Issue

"Listen, *amigo,*" she said, "I have suffered domination, and it didn't crush me because I have been strong enough to live with it; . . ."

". . . All the lawful conventions are coming to me, all the glamours of respectability. . . ."

'I don't know the truth about myself because I never had an opportunity to compare myself to anything in the world. . . ."

". . . I said to him: The trouble is, Don Juan, that it isn"t love but mistrust that keeps you in torment. A parrot would have added that I had given him no right to be jealous. . . ."

". . . but I have my own Basque peasant soul and don't want to think that every time he goes away from my feet — yes, *mon cher,* on this carpet, look for the marks of scorching . — that he goes away feeling tempted to brush the dust off his moral sleeve. That never!"

". . . to know her such as life had made her and at the same time to despise her secretly for every touch

touch with which her life had fashioned her—that was neither generous nor high minded! It was positively frantic. . . ." (P. 232)

"I always thought that love for you could work great wonders. And now I know." (P. 232)

". . . I am no more fair than other people. I would have been harsh perhaps. My very admiration was making me more angry. It's ridiculous to say of a man got up in correct tailor clothes, but there was a funeral grace in his attitude . . . " (P. 233)

1st Issue

Except for the glazed rotunda part its long walls, divided into narrow panels separated by an order of flat pilasters, presented, depicted on a block background in vivid colours, slender, elongated women with butterfly wings and strange, lean youths with narrow birds' wings. (P. 236)

Quickly, with the least possible action, Dona Rita moved it to the other side of her motionless person. (P. 240)

. . . since the evening of our return I had not been near him or the ship, which was completely unusual, unheard of, . . . (P. 243)

"What freedom!" she murmured curiously. (P. 246)

And yet I left her looking at nothing else but me, with a sort of stupefaction on her features — in her whole attitude — as though she had never been kissed before. (P. 248)

---

with which her life had fashioned her—that was neither generous nor high minded: it was positively frantic. . . ."

"I always thought that love for you could work great wonders. And now I am certain."

" . . . I am no more fair than other people. I would have been harsh. My very admiration was making me more angry. It seems ridiculous to say of a man got up in correct tailor clothes, but there was a funeral grace in his attitude . . ."

2nd Issue

Except for the glazed rotunda part its long walls, divided into narrow panels separated by an order of flat pilasters, presented, depicted on a black background in vivid colours, slender women with butterfly wings and lean youths with narrow birds' wings.

Quietly, with the least possible action, Dona Rita moved it to the other side of her motionless person.

. . . since the evening of our return I had not been near him or the ship, which was something completely unusual, unheard of, . . .

"What freedom!" she murmured enviously.

And yet I left her looking fixedly at me, with a sort of stupefaction on her features — in her whole attitude — as though she had never even heard of such a thing as a kiss in her life.

. . . the tobacconist lady at the fashionable Debit de Tabac, . . . (P. 248)

. . . the tobacconist lady at the fashionable *Debit de Tabac*, . . .

My unhappiness became dulled ,as the grief of those who mourn for the dead gets dulled in the over whelming sensation that everything is over, that a part of themselves is lost beyond recall taking with it all the savour of life. (P. 260)

My unhappiness became dulled, as the grief of those who mourn for the dead gets dulled in the overwhelming sensation that everything is over, that a part of themselves is lost beyond recall, taking with it all the savour of life.

One evening I asked the old man to come in . . . (P. 266)

One evening I asked that old man to come in . . .

And for that matter what had she, the woman of all time, to do with the villainous and splendid disguises human dust takes upon itself? (P. 271)

And for that matter what had she, the woman of all time, to do with the villainous or splendid disguises human dust takes upon itself?

1st Issue

2nd Issue

"I am a very good gun-runner, your Excellency," I answered. He bowed his head gravely. (P. 279)

"I am a very good gun-runner, your Excellency," I answered quietly. He bowed his head ,very gravely.

He tried to force a cigar on me. (P. 279)

He absolutely forced a cigar on me.

. . . it would bring about infinite complications beginning with a visit to the Commisaire de Police on night-duty, . . . (P. 299)

. . . it would bring about infinite complications beginning with a visit to the *Commisaire de Police* on night-duty, . . .

. . . and I heard once a high, clear woman's voice stigmatizing us for a "species of swelled heads" *(espèce d'enflés).* (P. 301)

. . . and I heard once a high-pitched, clear woman's voice stigmatizing us for a "species of swelled heads" *(espèce d'enflés).*

She penetrated me, too, my head was full of her . . . (P. 303)

She penetrated me, my head was full of her . . .

. . . but my pity went out not to him but to Dona Rita. (P. 305)

. . . yet my pity went out not to him but to Dona Rita.

And moreover what would a warning be worth in this particular case, supposing it would reach her, . . . (P. 314)

And moreover what would a warning be worth in this particular case, supposing that it would reach her, . . .

. . . her face a little pale now, with a pink lobe of her ear under the tawny mist of her loose hair, . . .
(P. 326)

. . . her face a little pale now, with a crimson lobe of her ear under the tawny mist of her loose hair, . . .

"Don George," she said with lovely animation, "I insist on knowing who there is in my house."
(P. 333)

"Don George," she said with lovely animation, "I insist on knowing who is in my house.

I had an extreme distaste for that sight.
(P. 355)

I felt extreme distaste for that sight.

I had actually to put her arms into the sleeves, myself, one after another.
(P. 361)

I had to put her arms into the sleeves, myself, one after another.

1st Issue

2nd Issue

Then as if I had in sober truth rescued her from an Alpine height or an Arctic floe, I busied myself with nothing but lighting the gas and starting the fire.   (P. 363)

Then as if I had in sober truth rescued her from an Alpine height or an Arctic floe, I busied myself exclusively with lighting the gas and starting the fire.

She stepped forward on her bare feet as firm on that floor which seemed to heave up and down before my eyes as she had ever been—goatherd child leaping on the rocks of her native hills.
(P. 367)

She stepped forward on her bare feet as firm on that floor which seemed to heave up and down before my eyes as she had ever been, a goatherd child leaping on the rocks of her native hills.

— all but the actual facts which round up the previous events and satisfy such curiosity as might have been aroused by the foregoing narrative.   (P. 370)

— all but the actual facts which round up the previous events and satisfy such curiosity as might have been aroused by the narrative.

But if in this she was a comedienne then it was but a great achievement of her ineradicable honesty.
(P. 371)

But if in this she was a *comedienne* then it was but a great achievement of her ineradicable honesty.

The message sounds rather mysterious.   (P. 384)

The message sounds rather cryptic.

TODD K. BENDER

COMPUTER ANALYSIS OF CONRAD

The complete works of Conrad are in the process of preparation for computer analysis in a project involving a number of 19th century authors at the University of Wisconsin-Madison. Scholars interested in Conrad will know our work through the pilot publication *Concordance to Heart of Darkness* (Carbondale: Southern Illinois University Press, 1973) and the description in our article, "Computer Assisted Editorial Work on Conrad," *Conradiana* (Fall: 1973, 37-45). As our work progresses, we hope to make available at interim stages material which promises to be of general use to scholars such as concordances, verbal indexes, tables of word frequencies, and historical collations of texts for all of Conrad's novels. We undertake this work for two reasons: (1) We believe that most problems in the study of literature demand solutions which are publicly verifiable and require the same order of evidential proof as we normally expect in experimental science. (2) We foresee the day, not many years in the future, when the main vehicle for preserving information will no longer be a page of printed paper, but some sort of electronic storage. We are trying to see what the study of literature, especially textual criticism, will be like in the library of the future which will probably be based on electronic data storage and retrieval systems rather than printed paper as the main provide, are well known.

There is a certain ingrained suspicion among literary scholars that computational techniques are somehow frightening, dehumanizing, mechanical, or destructive of sensitive responses to works of art. It is hard to see how the preservation of a literary text by electronic means is more "mechanical" than the printing of that text by a printing machine. Both are means to an end. The end is to understand as fully as possible all features of the work of art and to make that understanding accessible to others. Like any instrument, the computer can be used clumsily and prove inept in accomplishing its end, or it may be used with great delicacy and sophistication so as to reveal aspects of the literary art otherwise unsuspected, nuances and complications of the author's mind incapable of definition without the assistance of the

123

new technology. The main application of the computer lies in the comparison and indexing of features of a text so as to produce tables of information such as concordances or collations of versions of the work. The kinds of critical applications modern indexes and concordances provide are well known.

A simple index of an author's vocabulary is essential to find patterns of imagery, recurring words which tend to define his style, and to provide information for the lexicographer about the development of the language in his work. But such simple indexes can be broken down into more complex units for comparison and become more informative still. We can index the vocabulary of an early novel and compare it to a late work so as to see what words and images drop from the author's mind as he grows older, what new vocabulary enters. We can index one fictional time level of a novel and compare it to another so that as we see in *Heart of Darkness* there is a class of words which occur as metaphoric in the fictional present frame on the *Nellie,* but recur concretely in the Congo tale. For example, Marlow speaks in the fictional present about stepping into the *shoes* of his predecessor Fresleven metaphorically, but concretely he tears off his blood stained *shoes* in the fictional past of the Congo. Such study shows how vocabulary resonates between present frame and past tale and creates an impression in the reader unobtrusively which can only be revealed through analytic indexes like those generated by modern technology. Or, we might index the speeches of one character to compare against another's so as to determine the characteristic vocabulary of Marlow as separate from that of the first narrator in *Heart of Darkness.* Or, instead of treating single words, we could study collocations of words much as psychologists practice word association tests so as to isolate sets of words which occur in close proximity in habitual patterns. Such study gives us access to the subconscious as well as the conscious level of the writer's mind. Or, we might want to study the text so as to find orthographic differences between the author's English spelling and his American spelling of words, or the punctuation practices of a work set up by a printing house as opposed to the author's manuscript version of it. All these critical or analytical operations are commonplace applications of computer technology. While such applications are extremely interesting to the critic, we must limit our discussion here to textual criticism. How does computer technology influence our conception of the very nature of the text of a novel?

We agree with the opinion of Fredson Bowers as expressed in *Textual and Literary Criticism* that literary criticism is directly dependent on expert textual criticism. We cannot describe the style or meaning of a work until we know what the work says. To visualize this situation, we might imagine a Greek play as a work which existed in the fifth century BC in the author's mind complete and perfect in his final intent. The first imperfect physical representation of that work exists in papyri about 400 AD and a series of more and more corrupt versions follow in MS until the first printed version of about 1600 AD appears. We might visualize the situation graphically as follows:

Stable Transmission of a Text

Imperfect Representations
of the *work* in various *texts*

MS 1

The Work as Conceived or
finally intended by author

MS 2   Critical statement
about the *Work*

MS 3

MS 4

The critic confronted with these varying physical representations of the text, wants to make a descriptive or critical statement about the work, yet the imperfections of the transmission of MS versions screan him off from the real work as intended by the author. Bowers would say that prior to making his critical generalization he must compare all the imperfect physical representations of the work so as to arrive as nearly as possible at the author's final intention. This is why expert textual criticism must logically precede literary criticism. But the problem as conceived by Bowers holds true only for what is sometimes called a *stable* transmission of the text as illustrated above. In a *stable* transmission of the text, although the various physical representations of the work are imperfect; nevertheless, we assume that they all refer to a single, clearcut ideal work which once existed in the final intention of the author. The duty of the textual editor is clear: by a careful examination of all the existing versions of the text, to discover as nearly as possible the author's intent and to create in a scholarly edition a representation of that intent, which will be the only sound basis for subsequent descriptive statements about the work. The textual critic operating under Bowers' principles believes that the *representation* of the work in a single printed verision in his final edition can be made essentially the same as the *work* itself.

Electronic technology when applied to the problem of the textual critic, however, suggests that no printed version no matter how careful and painstaking can be an adequate representation of the *work* and that much of the careful collation of MSS and editing procedures recommended by Bowers are in fact distortions of the *work* which make the final printed critical edition inherently misleading as to the nature of the author's intention.

Note that in the stable transmission, the author has died before the earliest MS or printed representations of his work are made. The transmission of the work therefore can only be a degenerative process, each version deviating more and more from the true work until a modern textual critic steps in to examine and reverse this process. Moreover the assumption must be that the *work* is in its essential naure very similar to a printed text. For example, even though we may know that a Greek playwright was conscious of the music or the dance movements in his chorus, we assume that such features of the *work* are safely omitted from any literary representation, that the *work* is very like a printed text and that whatever cannot be noted in a printed text is peripheral to his intent.

But the transmission of Conrad's texts, or of any modern author's work, is quite different. More often than not the transmission of a printed text in the 19th century is an unstable transmission, which might be visualized as follows:

Unstable Transmission

Author's Expression of Intention for the *work* vs.	Physical Representation of the *work*
Jan. 1900 author dictates	Pencil draft
Feb. author corrects draft	Typescript I
March author revises typescript	Proof sheets for serial
April author approves proof sheets	Serial publication
Jan. 1901 on advice of his agent author goes back to typescript I and rewrites considerable portions of the work for book publication	Typescript II
Feb. author corrects typescript II	Proof sheets converting all spelling and punctuation to American usage
March author approves proof sheets	First American edition
Jan. 1902 working from proof sheets of American edition author cuts down the length of the work at British publisher's suggestion	Proofs for shorter text set from American plates but inserting British spelling and punctuation
Feb. author approves proof sheets	First British edition

This unstable transmission differs remarkably from the stable transmission because the author is living and participating in the production of the physical MS, typescript, proof sheets, etc., so that the process of transmission and the author's creative act become inextricably interwoven. Thus the changes in the physical representations of the text between one state and another are not merely degenerative (mistakes) but can be creative (improvements intended by the author) in the light of his more mature judgment. Advice about spelling, punctuation, or even tempo and length of the story or vocabulary may be the result of intervention of the copy editor or typist, but when accepted by the author they may become truly part of his intent as legitimately as his first thoughts. In this way the *work* is not a single clearcut entity, but a shifting or unstable set of intentions which differs from time to time as his intention develops or as his audience shifts. The editor of a modern novel does not have a stable entity to recapture through analysis of degenerate representations, but a constantly shifting, growing, unstable work, which is nowhere represented adequately in a physical text, even though the author may give his approval to one version, or favor one version at one particular time. The introduction of simply the typewriter into the chain of textual transmission complicates the problem of authorial intent in a way peculiar to modern bibliography and demonstrates how new technology in handling information always both opens opportunities and poses problems for the scholar.

How can a critic proceed most efficiently when he is faced with the problem of describing or indexing the vocabulary of a text such as *Heart of Darkness* which exists in an unstable transmission? In our pilot study *Concordance to Heart of Darkness,* we devised a new format for a literary index in which we tried to preserve and develop advantages unique to electronic procedures. We began by building a data base composed of the 1921 Heinemann text of *Heart of Darkness* encoded in electronic storage. We might conceive a page of this text as a checkerboard in which each square is occupied by a letter, a space, or a mark of punctuation, making a two-dimensional array of information. If we indexed this single text, we would misrepresent Conrad's authorial intent insofar as we omitted variations from the 1921 Heinemann text which appear only in other versions of the work. We therefore superimposed on our initial checkerboard, or two dimensional array, of the Heinemann text a second checkerboard representing the 1924 Kent Edition of *Heart of Darkness.* By stacking one checkerboard on the other, we are able to compare or collate the two versions. Economy dictated for the pilot study that we collate by superimposition only these two versions. We chose the 1921 because it is generally thought to be the nearest to Conrad's mature intention; the 1924 is the last possible version to register changes authorized by Conrad's hand. We might, however, have continued stacking up two-dimensional representations of the text until all significant versions stood stacked up like so many checkerboards in a three dimensional array. In our pilot publication for *Heart of Darkness,* the index of vocabulary refers not to a single printed version (for that would be only a partial representation of Conrad's intention) but to our constructed field of reference which is composed of two versions superimposed so that all variations between those two versions are marked as variants and indexed. For a complete and definitive model of the complex variability of the textual transmission we should build a checkerboard for each version of the text and superimpose them all before making an analytic statement. And, indeed, such work is going forward at the moment in our program.

Our pilot *Concordance to Heart of Darkness* falls into three parts: (1) The field of reference composed of different versions of the work stacked up and compared so as to identify and locate all variations in spelling, vocabulary, and punctuation among them. (2) The index which lists all vocabulary alphabetically with identifying information so that the context of each word can be located within the field of reference. (3) Tables of information such as word frequency, sentence length, tables of punctuation marks, *etc.* If an editor wants to determine the single, authorial intent of Conrad in his work, the format we have devised will be of great assistance to him. It will show the editor where versions differ and so require his editorial decision. And in many cases the index of vocabulary will aid in determining what the habitual, more common, or usual practice of the author may have been in a doubtful situation. The index is thus cut free from dependence on previous editorial decisions. It becomes a tool for determining the final intent of the author if the editor aims to produce a printed critical edition.

But let us imagine a library in the future in which the basic storage vehicle is electronic, like our data base, not printed paper. Such a library could be very small in size but immense in the amount of data contained in electronic memory cones recording information in the format which we have visualized as the field of reference for our index. Telephone circuits might connect this single data bank all over the world to optical screens like television screens, or to printing devices like Xerox machines. The scholar could call in from his home and get a paper copy of the pages he wants to read, or he could ask for specific information such as the number of times and contexts in which Conrad uses the word *Heart* and the number of times he uses *Kernel* and whether the Polish words for these two concepts were ever used in his work—all useful and pregnant questions, we know, for in the Polish translation of *Heart of Darkness* authorized by Conrad the meaning of *Heart* and *Kernel* become intermingled. In such a library, what will be the conception of the *work* of Conrad? What will be the role of the textual critic then?

Today the textual critic approaches the three-dimensional array of author's first draft, a copy text, a first printed edition, a second revised edition, as so many checkerboards stacked one on top of the other. He collates or compares the first letter in all versions, then the second letter, and so on. When all four texts agree, he accepts that letter as a true expression of the author's intent and inscribes it in his definitive text. But when his collation shows a difference between, say, the copy-text and the second edition, he has to decide as nearly as possible what the author's final intent was and that letter goes in the final text while the other versions are considered inferior, perhaps corrupt, variants to be preserved in an inferior status in the apparatus or deleted altogether without trace. What the editor is doing when he makes his editorial decisions is reducing a three-dimensional array of information to a two-dimensional array represented in his final text. He is making the information contained in a stack of checkerboards fit into the single checkerboard of his final critical edition.

The literary editor may not recognize his procedures as involving the reduction of a three-dimensional array into two dimensions, but if he asks a computer programmer about different ways to frame his collation problem, he will soon learn that he does so whenever he tries to determine as nearly as possible the author's single, final intent and to print only that as the definitive text. But what should be done with the cases where the author's intent is legitimately equivocal? Does the editor mean to choose the *artistically final* or the *chronologically final intent.* What if the artist, for example Wordsworth in *The Prelude,* writes one line when he is thirty and blots it when he is fifty? Does not the activity of the editor in such a case appear to be a falsification, a reduction of the complexity of the work and the author's mind exactly to the degree that the editor chooses one reading over another where the author hmself was in doubt? The process of collation as practiced by the best modern editors is appropriate only insofar as the transmission of the text is stable. The author's intent where equivocal or wavering is best represented as a three dimensional array. But the literary editor at the present time is committed to producing a single printed text as his definitive edition and this edited text is itself limited to two dimensions. To some degree at least, what we think of as a definitive edited text may be a simplification of the author's much more interesting wavering, hesitating, shifting intent which the editor is forced to reduce to the limitations of his own published medium. Modern textual scholarship as defined by Fredson Bowers in the "preface" to the *Works of Stephen Crane,* for example, attempts to accomplish two essentially contradictory aims. It tries to establish a reading text in which all decisions have been made as to authorial intent and hesitation, so that the reader can rely on the "authority" of the words before him as if they were coming directly from the author's mind. At the same time, the modern editor is trying to build a structural model of the complex variables in the acts of creation and of transmission of the text. The reading text printed on paper must be a two-dimensional representation. In extremely awkward apparatus and notes the editor tries to mount onto that text other dimensions of variability in textual creation or transmission, indicating shifts and development of authorial intent. Because of the limitations of the printed medium, the model of complex variables cannot be represented completely and so some, perhaps most, variables are judged to be insignificant and dropped completely from record while others are preserved as significant variants in printed notes. It is possible that what is currently thought an "exhaustive" edition is to some degree a simplification of a set of data much more accurately represented as a multi-dimensional array. Such an array can be constructed by superimposing as computer input all significant versions of a text. Any single printed version of the text will be a partial and less accurate representation of the author's complex intent. In this way, a computer concordance based on prior editorial decisions may be farther from the true authorial intent than one which is generated from the input of all significant versions superimposed. In theory, might not a concordance and a "definitive" text be visualized as two different expressions of the same set of data, rather than the concordance standing in a dependent relationship to a previously printed text. Or might we go a step further and say that any edition is a simplified expression of a matrix of complex variables. At some date in the future might the role of the textual editor be the construction of the model of variables, which is inherently more suited to electronic storage than to paper. The reader will come to the electronic data and ask for a provisional expression shaped to his needs—the first printed edition, or the last revised edition, or the two superimposed, or perhaps those parts of the text which are entirely the work of the copy editor. A printed text is not the *same* as a poem or a novel, it *represents* the author's verbal structure in the shifting process of artistic creation and the counter movement of disintegration in transmission. The model and the medium which represents that structure best may well prove finally to be electronic.

The question raised here about the principles of textual criticism in the theories of Fredson Bowers is, finally, a question about the role of ambiguity in art. A few years ago, critics would come to a poem like Keats's "Ode on a Grecian Urn" and see there opposed two contradictory sets of attitudes. On the one hand, the poem celebrates the virtues of permanence in an unchanging world of art depicted on the side of the urn which is very like the world of Platonic essences. On the other hand, there is the sensual world of life and death, change and decay, in which the speaker of the poem lives. Everyone agrees that the poem is structured so as to oppose the phenomenal world of the senses to the permanent unchanging world of Platonic essences, the world of *becoming* and the world of *being*. But for years fruitless controversy argued whether Keats endorses the values of the sensory world or those of the ideal world. In short, a tremendous amount of effort has gone into arguing that the poem must "mean" one thing or the other, that Keats argues that value resides in the life of the senses or it resides in the world of Platonic essences. Most critics now feel, however, that this sort of argument is an attempt to answer a pseudo-question generated by the critics' naive understanding of language. Keats's poem need not endorse either the world of the senses or the world of permanent form. It can be a model for a mental state which holds in a balanced tension attitudes which would be in everyday life mutually exclusive, but which it is the function of art to hold in a delicately balanced ambiguity. Most modern critics following the work of I. A. Richards and William Empson now recognize that the translation of an ambiguous statement in poetry or fiction into an unambiguous paraphrase is not an adequate treatment of artistic language. Rather than resolving ambiguity in literature, a powerful and coherent movement in modern literary criticism demands that we recognize ambiguity as essential to art, providing a model for attitudes in which conflicting impulses stand revealed in a tension which in our day-to-day life would have to be suppressed. Such critics will not try to make Keats's poem say either A or B, but describe how Keats's work says both A and B at once.

The modern textual editor is now at the stage of intellectual sophistication of the literary critic before Empson's ideas became widely known. When the textual critic finds that the author intended to say A in his first edition, but said B in his final revision, the editor resolves the ambiguity by suppressing one or the other possibility. But a far more interesting intellectual problem develops if the editor recognizes that the transmission of the work says both A and B, and tries to see why this should be the case. When Marlow lies to Kurtz's Intended at the end of *Heart of Darkness* and tells her incorrectly that Kurtz's last words were of her, a modern critic does not expect to find a single unequivocal motive explaining once and for all why Marlow lies. There are a range of sometimes contradictory possibilities implied in the work. We expect the critic to lay out the range of possibilities for us, but not to dictate one as the correct answer and exclude all others in order to make the work tidy for us. But the textual critic will come to line 22 of our collation of the 1921 Heinemann and the 1924 Kent edition of *Heart of Darkness* and find his first variant, *realise* spelled with an S in one text but with a Z in the other. The textual editor will decide for the reader whether Conrad intended British or American spelling usage. Is it not the case that Conrad *intended* both at once? Is it not the case that such a contradictory intent cannot be represented on a single printed page, but can be visualized mentally and constructed easily in an electronic model?

In the library of the future the work of Conrad will be conceived in a way radically different from the conception of his work edited in printed editions according to current practices. The process of creation; the variations of spelling, punctuation, and style to suit shifting audiences; the development of his thought and attidudes in sequences of revisions will not be simplified and reduced to an editor's single choice. Ambiguities of the textual transmission will be preserved and investigated as a source of interest and not resolved or hidden in editorial selection. This more sophisticated view of the work is possible only when the work is conceived free from the limitations of printed paper as the vehicle for its representation. We hope that our work with Conrad's texts will not only assist the critic and editor of today, but explore how best to preserve Conrad's work for future generations. We have selected Conrad as one of the subjects of our study because we feel that the complexity of form and ideas in his work and the relevance of his thought to enduring human problems will make him one of the first figures from our age to demand study by scholars of the future.

BRUCE E. TEETS

REALISM AND ROMANCE IN CONRAD CRITICISM

One of the major aspects of Joseph Conrad's art noted by critics during the period of almost eighty years from 1895, the date of publication of Conrad's first novel, to 1974, is the persistent question of Conrad's realism and his romanticism. A substantial study of more than 3000 items published since 1895[1] reveals two extremes, which can be illustrated by brief quotations. The first, from an early review of *Almayer's Folly* in 1895, emphasizes the realism in Conrad's first book: *"Almayer's Folly* breaks new ground in presenting unfamiliar pictures evidently drawn from life; Conrad's overloaded but powerful description of the Bornean forest shows the influence of Zola" (No. 1); the second, from a book, *Conrad's Romanticism,* published by David Thorburn in 1974, indicates some of the importance of Conrad's romanticism:

Repeatedly in *The Mirror of the Sea* Conrad deepens . . . the theme of personal nostalgia by insisting on the larger, communal implications of his connection with the seafaring life. And it is this recurring assertion of his typicality, of the extent to which his experiences and responses at sea have been shared by many other human beings, which most significantly links the autobiographical volume with Conrad's best fiction, and which, together with its statement in the fiction, defines one of Conrad's enduring qualities. As Ian Watt has shown, "In the centrality of his ultimate purpose Conrad is akin to Wordsworth."[2]

Between these two statements come both much agreement and much disagreement with each attitude and, no doubt even more importantly, further new concepts evolving from these two opposing views.

The early reviewers of Conrad's works seemed to note especially his realism, which they frequently called impressionism without making any particular distinction between the two terms; but they also wrote

---

[1] These items are found in Bruce E. Teets and Helmut E. Gerber, eds., *Joseph Conrad: An Annotated Bibliography of Writings About Him* (DeKalb, Ill.: Northern Illinois University Press, 1971), and in more than 1000 additional items annotated by Bruce E. Teets for a forthcoming supplementary volume to this work. References to this book are indicated by entry numbers in the text.

[2] David Thorburn, *Conrad's Romanticism* (New Haven and London: Yale University Press, 1974), pp. 90-1.

about the romance of the Far East and compared Conrad's tales with Loti's exotic romances. A writer of 1899 declared that "Heart of Darkness" is not fiction because it is literally true in every detail (No. 31); Conrad's realism included the vivid portrayal, in *The Nigger of the "Narcissus"* of life on board a sailing vessel (No. 8); and Edward Garnett attributed to Conrad in 1898 a quality of poetic realism like that of the great Russian novels (No. 15). In 1903, one reviewer noted Conrad's exceptional power to portray extraordinary scenery and to impress a character upon the credulity of his readers (No. 62). But with the appearance of *Nostromo* in 1904, critics began to observe more distinctly the glamor and romance of the characters (No. 68) and the romanticism, in this instance, of this tale of South American politics (No. 74). In *The Mirror of the Sea,* the author's language is accurate (No. 90), accuracy being an element of realism, but as late as 1908 Conrad is, according to one commentator, not romantic but consistently and effectively realistic (No. 105); and in 1912, another writer thinks his is not an easy realism (No. 134). These confused and conflicting comments indicate that for the first fifteen years or so Conrad produced a kind of work which was so new that it, like all major writing, could not be precisely classified. A helpful concept, however, soon appeared. Although not entirely new, this concept, noted at least as early as 1912, became of increasing importance to critics. Conrad's romance and realism were seen to be related in various ways: for example, in his method of characterization, in his ability to create atmosphere, and in his powers of description. In 1915, Richard Curle found Conrad to be a "romantic psychologist" (No. 205), thereby relating, as many future commentators were to do, either the realism or the romanticism, or both, with still other characteristics. In 1916, Hugh Walpole decided that for Conrad "realism alone was not sufficient; he had a poet's mind, a romantic mind, and he therefore used romance realistically" (No. 244). In 1918, Ernst Bendz found Conrad to be a curious specimen, "a romanticist with the backbone of a realist" (No. 274). At last, the interest in a combination of realism and romanticism was given a strong impetus in 1922 by Ruth M. Stauffer in her book, *Joseph Conrad: His Romantic Realism*. She found in Conrad an "almost equal balance" between the two attitudes and asserted that the "Romantic-Realist" "aims to translate into the medium of fiction life as it actually is." Conrad, therefore, with "the poetic imagination of the Romanticist and the minute observation of the Realist," assembles in his words "an impersonal study of motives, conduct and character" that is at the same time "as restrained and as passionate as life itself." The epitome of his art, according to Stauffer, is "realistic photographic detail side by side with the Romantic interpretation of the meaning of things and the yearning for beauty." His "dominant strain" is "an abiding realization of the mystery that shrouds life" (No. 394). Stauffer's influential book led critics for ten years or more to an investigation of Conrad's basic peculiarities, many arising from his realism and romanticism, which were found, in due time, to be, among others, his tendency to melodrama (No. 475), his own "kinship of soul" with the Polish Romantic movement,[3] his opposition of romanticism and the "control, normality, and unification of experience" of classicism (No. 897); his philosophical idealism (No. 918); his psychology (No. 934); his fatalism (No. 936); his tragedy (No. 1064); and his irony (No. 1065). In his book, *The Polish Heritage of Joseph Conrad* of 1930, Gustav Morf found that Conrad and his father had similar temperaments, including the same romantic realism; and "the conscious Conrad," he said, "was realistic, the unconscious Conrad, ever dissatisfied and unhappy, was incurably romantic" because he could express that which tortured him "only in an irrational, symbolic form." This deep delving into Conrad's personality soon led to further interest in the psychology of the writer as artist (No. 913); to Conrad the realist as a fatalist and his romantic interlinkings of the senses with imagination, together with his conviction of the necessity of human solidarity, which is "almost Wordsworthian" (No. 973), [here Pelham Edgar anticipated a major insight into Conrad's works which David Thorburn was to develop more fully in 1974]; to the opinion that Conrad deflected tragedy from its traditional course by a combination of romanticism and irony (No. 1064); and to William McFee's eccentric thought (in 1938) that Conrad was an entertainer in the most exalted sense, an ironist, neither a romanticist nor a realist, but an impressionist who painted pictures of "something his imagination had conceived" (No. 1065).

From 1939 to 1958, Conrad criticism continued to expand, in volume, in complexity, and in ingenuity; but realism and romanticism securely retained their places. In 1939, David Daiches added an "inner conviction of optimism" to the general concept of Conrad and his writings, relying partly on *Lord Jim* and *Victory* to support his conclusion (No. 1077); in 1942, Gordon Hall Gerould found value in Conrad's work as "romance of adventure" (No. 1114); in 1949, Walter F. Wright held that although Conrad had no one consistent attitude toward life, his points of view could be grouped under two major divisions: romance and psychological tragedy (No. 1210); and in 1954, Lord David Cecil stated that Conrad's view of life was a mixture of "pessimistic skepticism

---

[3] Marie Dąbrowska, "Joseph Conrad and Poland: Lord Jim's Burnt Boats," *New Age*, 3 Mar. 1927, pp. 208-09.

and romantic faith" (No. 1298). In 1958, one critic believed that Conrad participated in romantic, aesthetic, and realist traditions, but yet remained free in originality (No. 1460); in the same year, David Daiches alleged that the "subtler and more profound" Conrad of the middle novels, from *Nostromo* to *Chance,* was "the novelist of moral exploration and discovery presented through particularized detail of character and action" (No. 1463); and Marvin Mudrick, in the same year, considered Conrad's symbolism "as unallegorical as possible" — it is "severely realistic," he insisted, and even in "Heart of Darkness" Conrad's imagination and technique fail because the theme is too great for him; the evil he must project "exceeds his capacity" to imagine it (No. 1496).

So intent had the critics become on producing an original (original usually meaning ingenious) interpretation of Conrad or of his works that one of them, if unable to stem the flood of writing about Conrad, at least delightfully called its attention to his confreres. In 1958, Ian Watt, astute enough to observe the excessive romanicism of many commentators, wrote that the literary critic "typically functions as the romantic seer": that is, each critic tries to demonstrate how "he saw the book first, or at least that his reading of it is the first *real* one"; and the urge to read a literary work in a new manner has led to symbolic interpretations which are incapable of empirical proof or disproof (No. 1517). Regardless of the degree to which Watt was able to influence the production of Conrad criticism, he must have been both pleased and dismayed by what followed in the 1960's. He must have been delighted, for example, with Adam Gillon's perceptions. Gillon noted that critics had failed to "pigeonhole Conrad into a precise literary category" because of his "individualism both as a person and as a novelist." Still considering realism and romanticism, Gillon defined specifically each aspect as it applied to Conrad: Conrad's romanticism, he said, was "not quite English nor wholly Polish. He is a realist, but his realism is different from that of other men of his age. He is an impressionist, yet his impressionism is but one of the many aspects of his art of fiction." Conrad therefore belongs to no specific school (No. 1580). Gillon also associates Conrad's theme of romantic love with the theme of isolation, which, Gillon notes, is of special significance in the twentieth century. Conrad wrote about the world as he saw it and of its few virtues, with the result being a "strange blend of romanticism and realism" with counterparts in the novels of such authors as D. H. Lawrence, Virginia Woolf, and James Joyce (No. 1581). Gillon thus considers mainly Conrad's place in the modern world. Ian Watt may have been distressed, though, when in 1962, Jerry Allen emphasized

Conrad's realism by maintaining that during World War II American troops used his novels as guides (No. 1661), scarcely, this seems, a valid way of determining the quality of realism in literature.

Another example of the critical interest in Conrad's romanticism appeared in 1964: D. A. C. Maclennan found "at the center of things" in Conrad's universe, chance, disorder, relativism, and a "philosophical romanticism" which, he thought, went easily with nihilism (No. 1814); and nihilism was to appear frequently in Conrad criticism in future years. V. S. Pritchett, for example, believed that Conrad suffered from living before his time, being a man in what we may call the post-1940 situation but obliged to conceal the fact under a fog of rhetoric which, a generation or so later, would have been called nihilism.[4] In 1965, J. Hillis Miller also considered nihilism as one of the possible consequences of romanticism, but he averred that Conrad follows this nihilism into its own darkness and "so prepares a way beyond it" (No. 1897). Alan Sandison found, in 1967, that for Conrad the alien natural world was a source of moral danger. Nature was thus a hostile principle, but engagement with it was essential to self-consciousness, as Stein's advice to Jim makes clear. The paradox of an essentially destructive nature offering nevertheless a method of salvation has much in common with an ambivalence recognized among the Romantic poets. The basic character of Conrad's work lies in his great awareness of man's essential estrangement, and the best he offers as a *modus vivendi* is a steady, ever-conscious fidelity to one's own selfhood.[5] And Tony Tanner believed that Conrad eventually came to see life in its ambiguity; his "Polishness," Tanner thought, consisted of tensions between "individual romantic impulse and commitment to group endeavor," between "betrayal and fidelity," and between "idealism and work" (No. 1837).

Within the past ten years, Conrad has been seen as both realistic and romantic, but with some strong emphasis on his leaning toward romanticism. This tendency of critics has been perpetuated by such major commentators as Thomas Moser, Zdzisław Najder, and Julius Kagarlitzkii.

The year 1974 produced a strong emphasis on Conrad's romanticism. Perhaps the view of realism has been previously more fully considered than has that of romanticism, or perhaps our own romantic age (or possibly neo-romantic age), in searching for solutions to its problems, has turned our attention more fully to Conrad's romanticism.

[4] V. S. Pritchett, "A Pole in the Far East," *The Living Novel* (London: Chatto & Windus, 1946), pp. 139-44.
[5] Alan Sandison, "Joseph Conrad: A Window on to Chaos," *The Wheel of Empire* (London: Macmillan; New York: St. Martin's Press, 1967), pp. 120-45.

Ian Watt states recently, unequivocally, for example, that "the basic terms of Conrad's position were set by Romantic tradition." He believes that Wordsworth, Coleridge, and Shelley conceived the challenge which Conrad accepted, the value of constituents of human personality, usually described as "the imagination or the sensibility, which were not available to scientific psychological study, but were nevertheless necessary to explain not only man's aesthetic impulse but the grounds of his religious, moral, and social life."[6]

David Thorburn's recent book, *Conrad's Romanticism*, actually, according to the author, a "revisionist" survey of Conrad's work,[7] contains several kinds of emphasis on his romanticism. Conrad has deep affinities with the *fin de siècle* tradition of the adventure story as found in Robert Louis Stevenson, Anthony Hope, Stanley Weyman, Rudyard Kipling, John Buchan, and Rider Haggard, and ultimately with the Romantic poets, especially with Wordsworth. At his best, Conrad forces the stereotyped figure of the popular adventure story hero to abandon its promise of the genuinely universal and "strike through" the stereotype by recognizing and dramatizing the defining and unique integrity of a critically rendered character or a fully explored situation, like those of *Nostromo* and *Lord Jim* (pp. 53-54). Conrad's characteristic and recurring story is a "romantic bildungsroman." Also, since such able critics as Geoffrey Hartman, Northrop Frye, Robert Langbaum, M. H. Abrams, and Harold Bloom have seen an essential continuity between modernism and the Age of Wordsworth, Conrad's similarities to the Romantic poets emphasize the importance of his romanticism (p. 106). Then, too, Conrad had a fundamentally Romantic view of art: in his work, the typical first-person narrator of the conventional adventure story turns his attention to his own anguish in creating the story he is telling, so that the novel, *Lord Jim,* for example, is a novel about itself (p. 121). Still other elements of romanticism in Conrad are (1) his faith in the power of language to "make sense of the world" and "however imperfectly, to recreate it" (pp. 123-27); (2) the "gesture of community" present in a teller's decision to relate a story (p. 128); and (3) Conrad's definition of the artist in his famous preface to *The Nigger of the "Narcissus,"* which is strikingly similar to parts of Wordsworth's preface (pp. 149-52). Conrad's best work has, then, a double appeal in being modern and romantic simultaneously.

We may ask, at this point, what conclusions may be firmly drawn from the preceding discussion. The most exact reply seems to be,

---

[6] Ian Watt, "Conrad's Preface to *The Nigger of the 'Narcissus,'*" *Novel: A Forum on Fiction*, 7, No. 2 (Winter 1974), pp. 101-15.

[7] Thorburn, p. 30. Further references to Thorburn appear in parentheses in the text.

"None at all." Surely, no human being can read everything that has been published about Joseph Conrad in all languages or even become reasonably familiar with it; and the total of more than 3000 items on which this survey is based, many of which, of course, do not consider Conrad's realism or romanticism, is not fully representative of the entire corpus of published writing on Conrad. But perhaps we may suggest a few conclusions which have at least some validity as well as importance. First, the necessity to see Conrad as both a realist and a romanticist has been generally recognized; second, from 1895 to the present, the problems arising from Conrad's realism and romanticism have revealed new aspects of Conrad's art; third, this consideration in depth of Conrad's art gives new insights into individual works; and, four, from seeing Conrad essentially as a modern writer who is "one of us" and as a Romantic writer firmly steeped in the nineteenth century, he may justifiably be seen as realistic, romantic, and also transitional and ambiguous, in other words, a product representative of his own time and prophetic of—indeed, an initiator of—certain major interests of the modern world, of which he saw only the beginnings.

III Conrad's Art and Life

HARRY T. MOORE

LEITMOTIF SYMBOLISM IN "THE SECRET AGENT"

Commentators have noted various symbols in *The Secret Agent,* among them the circles which Stevie draws in Chapter III. I don't know whether the fullest possibilities of the latter have been followed through in the immense area of Conrad criticism, but perhaps I can add something to the subject. As they occur throughout the novel, developing suggestions and images of rondure, these symbols cross and intertwine with others that flash with fire. As we examine some aspects of this method, we may consider it as a leitmotif symbolism.

In emblematic usage, circle and fire appear together in Stevie's obsession with the former; he draws "circles, circles, circles; innumerable circles, concentric, eccentric; a coruscating whirl of circles that by their tangled multitude of repeated curves, uniformity of form, and confusion of intersecting lines suggested a rendering of cosmic chaos" — and note that Conrad then adds, "the symbolism of a mad art attempting the inconceivable."

The "rendering of cosmic chaos" as well as the "mad art attempting the inconceivable" reflect Conrad's attitude toward the anarchists. In letters of 1906 to his publisher Methuen and to his friend Galsworthy, Conrad spoke rather lightly of his treatment of the anarchists in *The Secret Agent,* which he was then writing, but in the preface to the 1920 edition he wrote of the unsuccessful "attempt to blow up the Greenwich Observatory" as "a blood-stained inanity of so fatuous a kind that it was impossible to fathom its origin by any reasonable or even unreasonable process of thought." He also said, in the same preface, that the story was suggested by "and centered round the absurd cruelty of the Greenwich Park explosion." Note the "cruel absurdity" as well as the circular symbolism of "centered round."

An investigation of the novel itself shows us that circles, sometimes

140

in the form of globes or domes, often accompanied by the coruscation image, manifest themselves throughout the book. Just how much all these are purposeful, and to what degree they are part of the unconscious operating in the process of art, it is of course impossible to determine exactly; but some of them certainly seem deliberate. In their blending of recurrent pictures and themes, they are to literature what the leitmotif is to music and are often so-called in literary criticism.

In the first chapter, for example, a flashback—and it is really that—shows us Stevie at fourteen, despite his feeble-mindedness hired by a businessman friend of his late father, setting off fireworks on the staircase outside the office: "He touched off in quick succession a set of fierce rockets, angry catherine wheels, loudly exploding squibs . . . An awful panic spread through the whole building." Stevie is discharged, and his sister finally draws him into "a misty and confused confession. It seems that two other office-boys in the building had worked upon his feelings by tales of injustice and oppression till they had wrought his compassion to the pitch of that frenzy." His motivation resembles those of the anarchists, and certainly the explosion of the squib, the ferocity of the rockets, and the circularity and coruscation of the catherine wheel not only fit into the leitmotif symbolism of the story, but also prefigure the way in which Stevie is to die.

In Chapter III, when Stevie is drawing those flashing circles in the kitchen, their element of fire is matched by conditions in the nearby parlor, where the anarchists are meeting: it has two burning gas-jets and a "glowing grate" which has made the parlor "frightfully hot." When Verloc opens the door to the kitchen in order to make the room cooler, we see Stevie making his circles. In the parlor, the gouty anarchist Karl Yunt is attacking the theories of Lombroso, wondering whether the then-famous criminologist has heard about "the pretty branding instrument invented by the overfed to protect themselves against the hungry" — the overfed who apply to the hungry "red-hot applications on their vile skins — hey?" Stevie hears this on his way to bed: "The sheet of paper covered with circles dropped out of his fingers, and he remained staring at the old terrorist, as if rooted suddenly to the spot by his morbid horror and dread of physical pain. Stevie knew very well that hot iron applied to one's skin hurt very much." This entire episode is another symbolic preparation of Stevie's death by the red-hot explosion of the bomb. The suggestion is emphasized a few moments later when the coals in the grate settle down with a slight crash.

The fire-and-light images continue. In Chapter IX, a savage irony comes through Winnie Verloc's statement to her husband that Stevie "would go through fire for you." Other instances of the red glow appear in Chapter XII, after Winnie has murdered her husband because it was his fault that Stevie was carrying the bomb when it blew him up with a coruscating circle of explosion. Winnie, who after she has murdered Verloc is ironically called his widow, rushes through the night streets of Soho, sees the curtained window of one of the cafés as making "a soiled blood-red light." This suggests not only the redness at the core of the explosion, but also Verloc's blood which, in dropping to the floor from the dead man's wound, as his body lies on the sofa, has the tick-tock sound of an instrument for measuring time, which also plays an important symbolic role in the story. (At the beginning of Chapter II, Conrad has Verloc leave his house at 10:30 in the morning; and the Greenwich Observatory, which is to be destroyed, is the custodian and determinator of time.) Interestingly, in the third paragraph of the novel, Conrad names only two of the "obscure" newspapers which Verloc sells in his shop: *The Torch* and *The Gong*. Verloc leaves his house under a "bloodshot" sun.

Again, soon after she has killed Verloc, Winnie, as she drags herself along the street, sees once more "the red glow of the eating-house window," still another accentuation of the red which is the dominant color of the story, as the circles and globes insistently give it a series of recurrent shapes that, in a leitmotif way, present another fundamental theme-symbol.

A highly ironic use of this occurs in Chapter IV, in which the explosives expert known as the Professor, the man who devised the bomb that killed Stevie, talks with Comrade Ossipon in a restaurant which has "many globes" depending from its chandeliers. During their dramatic conversation, the Professor tells Ossipon why the police will never arrest him under the suspicion of manufacturing bombs: the Professor has in his pocket an object he always keeps his left hand curled around, a device which, when squeezed, would within twenty seconds blow him to pieces as well as everyone else within sixty yards. The Professor tells Ossipon what this detonator is: an india-rubber ball.

The most emphatic use of the symbol of rondure, however, may be found in an aspect of the buildings which Verloc is to blow up, thus casting discredit on the anarchists against whom Verloc is working as a secret (today we would say double) agent. Mr. Vladimir, the First Secretary of the Embassy (undefined, but obviously Russian), tells Verloc that "he couldn't deceive an idiot, a particular irony because Verloc does indeed deceive an idiot when Stevie trustfully takes from him the tin varnish can containing the bomb which explodes when he stumbles in Greenwich Park before he arrives at the Observatory, the target designated by Mr. Vladimir.

The Observatory itself, with its various big and little domes, concentrates the recurring symbols of roundness. Conrad doesn't deal to any extent with the essential function of the Observatory (whose other services have since his time been moved away because of factory-smoke pollution), to determine the Greenwich Mean Time. It may be no more than an ironic coincidence that the object which exactly sets the time each day, and is dropped from one of the towers, is a colored ball.

Possibly (and this may be shown in the forthcoming volumes of his letters) Conrad visited the Greenwich Observatory while working on *The Secret Agent,* if he had not done so earlier, as a nautical man with a natural interest in the stars.

Indeed, he may have seen the Observatory domes from the Thamesside wharves when ships he had sailed in docked in that area. Even from the river the Observatory is visible, on its high hill; an engraving of 1840 shows that the domed towers could be seen from the wharfs of the Isle of Dogs. (They are glimpsed beyond and above some other domed turrets, those of the river-edge buildings of the Greenwich Hospital.)

As Stevie walked across Greenwich Park, his last sight on earth was probably those Observatory domes. This brings us back to the circles, the coruscating circles he drew while the anarchists in the next room talked of destruction by fire.

Conrad in most of his imaginative (and even in some of his autobiographical) work makes use of various kinds of symbols. In "Heart of Darkness," for example, the title of the story is repeated in the narrative; and the ivory of the Congo is another principal symbol, and certainly Kurtz's evil rituals and his deathbed cry, "The horror! The horror!" suggest, along with other clues in the story, cannibalism. (And the idea of cannibalism is used in several other instances by Conrad, even to a limited extent in *The Secret Agent.*) Elsewhere we have other symbols: the silver of the Sam Tomé mine and the shadow-line vision of the young captain seeing his ship as a floating grave. Examples abound. But Conrad nowhere else uses recuring theme-symbols so consistently as in *The Secret Agent* (there are others in that book which I have not mentioned), and in the manner of leitmotif: the anarchist circles become the circles of Hell.

LEON GUILHAMET

CONRAD'S "THE SECRET AGENT" AS THE IMITATION OF AN ACTION

When Mr. Vladimir calls Mr. Verloc to the Embassy, thereby setting in motion the incredible chain of events that compose the novel *The Secret Agent,* the First Secretary of the Embassy presents what he calls his "philosophy of bomb throwing." This includes, in Vladimir's words, "that appallingly absurd notion" that "you anarchists . . . are perfectly determined to make a clean sweep of the whole social creation" (p. 32).[1] Before specifying the Greenwich Observatory as the target, that Verloc is to have "a go at astronomy" (p. 34), Vladimir indicates that they are taking aim at something inconceivable:

> what is one to say to an act of destructive ferocity so absurd as to be incomprehensible, inexplicable, almost unthinkable; in fact, mad? Madness alone is truly terrifying, inasmuch as you cannot placate it either by threats, persuasion, or bribes. (p. 33)

It should be noted that by choosing Verloc as his instrument, Vladimir attempts to preserve himself from direct participation in the proposed "outrage." But his absurdly bad choice leads to his destruction, especially since Verloc, in attempting to spare himself the danger, makes an even worse choice, Stevie.

Curiously enough, however, Stevie, Verloc's peculiar brother-in-law, shares a strange and mysterious inclination with Vladimir. It is Stevie's wont, while the anarchist meetings are in progress, to sit in the kitchen drawing circles:

> . . . Stevie, seated very good and quiet at a deal table, drawing circles, circles, circles; innumerable circles, concentric, eccentric; a coruscating whirl of circles that by their tangled multitude of repeated curves, uniformity of form, and confusion of intersecting lines suggested a rendering of cosmic chaos, the symbolism of a mad art attempting the inconceivable. (p. 45)

Stevie's circles, rather too-obvious symbols of perfection, lead us to

---

[1] All citations to The Secret Agent are to the *Collected Works of Joseph Conrad* (Garden City, N.Y.: Doubleday, 1925), IX. Page references are included in my text.

another significant motif implicit in the mad designs which abound in this book. Perfection of one sort or another, it should be noted, is the intellectual object of every character important to the central action. The fact that actual perfection is "inconceivable" indicates the irony with which Conrad treats this motif.

The Professor is a case in point. His life is dedicated to the creation of an instrument of destruction, the perfect detonator. "I am trying," he tells Ossipon, "to invent a detonator that would adjust itself to all conditions of action, and even to unexpected changes of conditions. A variable and yet perfectly precise mechanism. A really intelligent detonator" (p. 67).

The word "perfect" has an ironic resonance throughout the book, since nothing, not even a detonator, can be perfect, as the Professor unwittingly admits when he describes the accident at the observatory: "there are more kinds of fools than one can guard against. You can't expect a detonator to be absolutely fool-proof" (p. 76). The Professor characteristically looks about himself with "perfect indifference" (p. 77), and is later described by the narrator as the "perfect anarchist" (p. 95).

It is the quest for perfection which unites those characters in the book who contemplate violence and those who are devoted to the ideal of personal ease or inaction. The narrator tells us that Verloc "was too lazy even for a mere demagogue, for a workman orator, for a leader of labor. It was too much trouble. He required a more perfect form of ease . . ." (p. 12). Behind Verloc's choice of profession as secret agent is his desire for uninterrupted indolence, for the comforts of domestic bliss. The profession, as he conceives it, is one of observation, not of action. When Vladimir decides that the duties of a secret agent must include action, Verloc is rendered unfit for his profession. It is inconceivable that a man of such disposition should succeed in an act of violence, but in a desperate attempt to preserve what he has, he succumbs to Vladimir's threats.

The grounds of Verloc's domestic bliss bear some looking into as well. It is an unorthodox family that Verloc has acquired. Not only does he inherit a mother-in-law, when he marries Winnie, but a peculiar brother-in-law, the "half-idiot" Stevie, who, the women imagine, will be like a son to him. Though Verloc is loved for what he can provide for Stevie, and only that, he is ultimately victimized by his idealistic belief that he is loved for himself alone (p. 288). Since the motives of Winnie in marrying Verloc will crystallize later into a design for destruction more explosive than any material the Professor can provide, it may be useful to consider them here.

"Devoted Winnie Verloc," David Cecil calls her,[2] and she is surely that. But we should not, in recognizing her heroic qualities, miss the serious defects in Winnie. Her devotion to Stevie, whom she regards as her own child, causes her to miscalculate badly in marrying Verloc. Her decision to marry was not a clear-eyed, rational decision of self-sacrifice. A woman of sexual passion, as her attachment to Ossipon shows, Winnie's initial inclination was toward a youth of her own age, the butcher's son. But the father of the young butcher could not accept her deep and abiding belief that Stevie is her own and that life must center about his welfare. Thus Verloc, who seems indolently willing to accept the myth, becomes Winnie's choice.

Beyond this Winnie and her mother harbor the fantastic belief that Stevie's condition is improving: "Winnie maintained that he was much less 'absent-minded' now. They agreed as to that. It could not be denied. Much less—hardly at all" (p. 164). Additionally Winnie believes another absurdity, that Verloc actually expresses paternal love for Stevie:

"Might be father and son," she said to herself. She thought also that Mr. Verloc was as much of a father as poor Stevie ever had in his life. She was aware also that it was her work. (p. 187)

Later she observes to her husband, not realizing that Stevie is already dead, "You . . . seem to have grown quite fond of him of late" (p. 189).

These fantasies show just how far from reality Winnie has always strayed. Though she preens herself on being a martyr to the realities of the socio-economic world, she preserves a kind of innocence by never looking deeply into things. It is this incapacity that will lead to her destruction. Surely Winnie's characteristic weakness, the substitution of an absurd fantasy for reality, is not unlike the failings of the other characters in the book.

The psychic movement of all the characters described thus far is based on the assumption that the Aristotelian conception of *praxis* is really a movement of minds (*moto spirital,* Dante calls it), toward something that is regarded as good.[3] The point to understand is that the major characters share in a unified movement of mind. Although their goals may seem to be different, they are actually similar when understood by means of a relevant generalization. Characters within

---

[2] *The Fine Art of Reading and Other Literary Studies* (London: Constable, 1957), p. 144.

[3] For this sense of the term *praxis* see S. H. Butcher, *Aristotle's Theory of Poetry and Fine Art* (New York: Dover, 1951), p. 337, and Francis Fergusson, *Aristotle's Poetics* (New York: Hill and Wang, 1961), pp. 8-13.

a unified work do not have different actions but participate in a single, complete action.

Conrad's classical education and his reading in French literature and Shakespeare make it probable that he inherited an Aristotelian teleological sense; but whether the reader is willing to grant this or not, *The Secret Agent* is of interest when read from this perspective. Not only do the major characters participate in a unified action, which we may state tentatively as "to grasp the inconceivable," but the minor characters seem almost perfectly to imitate the action too.[4]

Both the terrorist, Karl Yundt, and Michaelis, the ticket-of-leave apostle, two members of Verloc's coterie, share the vain attempt to grasp the inconceivable. Yundt dreams of men who would accept the name "destroyers" and show "No pity for anything on earth, including themselves, and death enlisted for good and all in the service of humanity—that's what I would have liked to see" (p. 42). Michaelis, on the other hand, a gentle proponent of ease, holds that the essence of anarchy exists in the passive expectation of capitalism's dissolution. Like Stevie, for whom he has affection, Michaelis passes his time constructing a chaotic memoir, and characteristically is blissfully unaware of Stevie's attempt at terrorism.

Divergent as the views of Yundt and Michaelis might be, they are essentially alike. Yundt is a terrorist in name only. He "had never in his life raised personally as much as his little finger against the social edifice. He was no man of action . . ." (p. 48). Michaelis, who, ironically, had once participated in an act of terrorism, is now, by his bulk and indolence, relegated to a world of impotent vision: "Round like a distended balloon, he opened his short, thick arms, as if in a pathetically hopeless attempt to embrace and hug to his breast a self-regenerated universe" (p. 50). More ingratiating than Yundt because of the tenderness of his sentiments, Michaelis shares with the terrorist an inconceivable, indeed mad, dream, not unlike Stevie's program of

4 Eloise Knapp Hay has made brief use of Aristotle's *Politics* in her study of Conrad's novels, *The Political Novels of Joseph Conrad: A Critical Study* (Chicago: University of Chicago Press, 1963), p. 13. She has not, however, argued for the direct influence of Aristotle on Conrad. But Adam Gillon's convincing studies of Conrad's indebtedness to Shakespeare ("Joseph Conrad and Shakespeare" in three parts, *Conradiana*, 1, No. 1 (1968), 19-25, 1, No. 2, 15-22, and 1, No. 3, 41-50) tempt me to believe that Conrad developed an approach to art similar to Shakespeare's use of "analogical action." This use of action by Shakespeare has been demonstrated brilliantly by Francis Fergusson in "*Macbeth* as the Imitation of an Action" in *The Human Image in Dramatic Literature* (Garden City, N.Y.: Doubleday Anchor, 1957), *The Idea of a Theater* (Princeton: Princeton University Press, 1949), especially chapter 4, and *Shakespeare: The Pattern in His Carpet* (New York: Delacorte Press, 1970). See also my forthcoming article "*A Midsummer-Night's Dream* as the Imitation of an Action," *Studies in English Literature, 1500-1900*, (1975).

taking the suffering horse and cabman to bed with him (p. 167). The difference, of course, is that Michaelis and the other anarchists are mad (p. 110), and Stevie is not (p. 167).

Finally, a clear similarity exists between the anarchists on the one hand and Verloc and Vladimir on the other. None seems willing to involve himself actively for the causes to which he is ostensibly committed. The irony with which Conrad treats this inaction would seem to contradict Joseph I. Fradin's contention that "All programs of action are morally, humanly dangerous: *that* is the "political" message of *The Secret Agent*."[5] Though action may be dangerous and destructive, the "perfect ease" sought by Verloc, and everyone else in the novel to some degree, is equally dehumanizing. The comforts of the pub, sought by the cabman and Mrs. Neale, as a relief from the sufferings that man is heir to, turn men and women into Verloc's "Hyperborean swine" (p. 212).[6]

This same action is imitated in several lesser keys by the Assistant Commissioner, the Great Lady, and Sir Ethelred. For the Assistant Commissioner everything is subservient to his own domestic bliss, which would be ill-served by implicating Michaelis in the bombing. The Great Lady's sympathetic acceptance of Michaelis's belief that the economy of the West will fail, has as its corollary that her own superior social position is unshakable (p. 111). This, of course, is nonsense, and her faith in such an absurdity is as fatuous as Winnie's faith that other persons, especially Verloc and Ossipon, have a sincere regard for Stevie. Sir Ethelred, "vast in bulk and stature" and deeply entrenched in the government to which anarchists pose a threat, is the architect of the revolutionary "Bill for the Nationalization of Fisheries" (p. 145). His "private secretary (unpaid)" is a perfect reflection of the attitudes of the Great Personage: "Toodles was revolutionary only in politics; his social beliefs and personal feelings he wished to preserve unchanged through all the years allotted to him on this earth which, upon the whole, he believed to be a nice place to live on" (p. 217). Generally, then, all of these characters dabble in revolutionary schemes without ever risking the loss of their present social comforts.

Though Chief Inspector Heat may seem to be an exception to the rule, he does share some of the weaknesses of the other characters. Most important he harbors the delusion that the police have the

---

[5] "Anarchist, Detective, and Saint: The Possibilities of Action in *The Secret Agent*," *PMLA*, 83 (1968), 1416.

[6] In conjunction with the many allusions to the *Odyssey* in chapter IX, the swine image might suggest a Circean motif. But the Hyperboreans were a legendary race whose name the Greeks took to mean "beyond the North Wind," locating them somewhere in Northern Europe. Since Vladimir is evidently Russian, Verloc characterizes him accurately as "Hyperborean."

anarchists under adequate surveillance: "There isn't one of them, sir," he tells a high official, "that we couldn't lay our hands on at any time of night and day. We know what each of them is doing hour by hour" (p. 84). But this is theory, not experience, and Heat is forced to recognize that "A given anarchist may be watched inch by inch and minute by minute, but a moment always comes when somehow all sight and touch of him are lost for a few hours, during which something (generally an explosion) more or less deplorable does happen" (p. 85). Heat, in seeming to recognize this yearns for a predictable, conformist opponent: "Thieving was not a sheer absurdity" (p. 91). But anarchism is, and in order to comprehend it, Heat moves out toward the limits of the inconceivable, as when he contemplates that "heap of nameless fragments" which was Stevie:

> The man, whoever he was, had died instantaneously; and yet it seemed impossible to believe that a human body could have reached that state of disintegration without passing through the pangs of inconceivable agony. No physiologist, and still less of a metaphysician, Chief Inspector Heat rose by the force of sympathy, which is a form of fear, above the vulgar conception of time. Instantaneous! He remembered all he had ever read in popular publications of long and terrifying dreams dreamed in the instant of waking; of the whole past life lived with frightful intensity by a drowning man as his doomed head bobs up, streaming, for the last time. The inexplicable mysteries of conscious existence beset Chief Inspector Heat till he evolved a horrible notion that ages of atrocious pain and mental torture could be contained between two successive winks of an eye. (pp. 87-8)

This perception, which comes early in the tale, is similar to the tragic insight of Winnie later on. Thus Heat, like Winnie, is satisfied with the limits enforced upon him by his calling. He fears to look deeply into things, but the requirements of his profession press him to exceed his personal limitations. This awareness of restrictions is articulated by the Assistant Commissioner as he admires his own inconceivable achievement:

> "Look at this outrage; a case specially difficult to trace inasmuch as it was a sham. In less than twelve hours we have established the identity of a man literally blown to shreds, have found the organizer of the attempt, and have had a glimpse of the inciter behind him. And we could have gone further; only we stopped at the limits of our territory." (p. 227)

This sense of limitation, the capacity to grasp the inconceivable in order to control it, but never to be consumed by it, is the genius possessed by the police officials in *The Secret Agent*. But if they are models of sanity (to set aside their little mad ventures), they do not attain real wisdom: "Chief Inspector Heat was not very wise—at least not truly so. True wisdom, which is not certain of anything in this world of contradictions, would have prevented him from attaining his present position" (p. 84).

Thus all the characters seem to share a delusive sense of well-being. Each places his faith in an uncertainty, whether in one's marital or social position or profession, or, like the Professor, in his detonator. That delusion, whether Heat's belief that he can really arrest the Professor when he wants to, or Winnie's that Verloc and Stevie are coming closer together, leads either to potential or actual destruction once madness incites action. The Professor consciously and ingeniously designs his own destruction, but so, Conrad shows us, does everyone else, each in his own way.

To see just how Conrad draws together the strands of a unified action and moves it beyond delusion and madness, it will prove helpful to look closely at Winnie in her emergence as the book's heroine.

When Winnie murders Verloc, she is at first treated with the irony appropriate to her situation: "She had become a free woman with a perfection of freedom which left her nothing to desire and absolutely nothing to do . . ." (p. 263). Such perfection is indeed a form of death, reminiscent of the Professor's commitment to the idea of a perfect detonator; and if the book ended here, it would be possible to believe, as a recent critic puts it, that "Conrad stops at a sardonic pessimism in *The Secret Agent*."[7] But Winnie and her effect on Ossipon continue for many more pages, and Conrad discovers there a truth which adds a significant dimension to the book.

In Winnie Verloc a kind of tragic rhythm, abortive in everyone else, but completed in herself, may be discovered. We have already noted that delusion is common to everyone in the novel, but the impetus to rare activity is a wholly different matter. In the half-idiot Stevie a strong capacity for sympathy causes him to turn vicious (p. 169). Vladimir's plan is probably the result of political pressures, since the bomb outrage is to be a reaction to the Conference in Milan. But whatever the emotional source, whether love, sympathy, or the fear of losing one's position, a palpable form of madness is the result, and action follows from that. Thus we can outline a pattern of behavior which holds good for most of the characters.

First there is an anger at injustice, anger fostered by a commitment to an absurd ideal of perfection. This burst of emotion leads to and

---

[7] Joseph I. Fradin, "The Possibilities of Action in *The Secret Agent*," p. 1422.

is a form of madness. The next step is the act of violence, and, if it is successful, it causes death. The next possible step is the contemplation of death, not as something theoretical but as a reality, and then follows the fear which is necessary to the final insight: that life is what matters. Only Winnie emerges as heroic enough to carry through a program of action and thus realize on what false assumptions her action was based. This process produces in her an incredibly intense love of life at the very instant when death has won the victory.

After murdering her husband, Winnie appears to Ossipon as "death itself—the companion of life" (p. 291). But if it is the vision of Winnie as death which terrifies Ossipon to the verge of profound understanding, in the key phrase, "the companion of life," he seems to recognize the essential truth toward which Winnie has preceded him. In coming face to face with death as a concrete reality, Ossipon recognizes that Michaelis's hospital-like utopia and the Professor's dystopian "world like shambles" (p. 303) are beside the point. Ossipon understands that the Professor does not grasp death as it really is: "Wait till you are lying flat on your back at the end of your time," he tells him, "Your scurvy, shabby, mangy little bit of time . . ." (p. 306). Ossipon sees that the Professor's knowledge of death exists on a theoretical plane only. He has not feared its concrete reality as Winnie, and even he, Ossipon, had done. And it is this fear that humanizes even the hopelessly inhuman, and had begun to humanize Winnie: "Comrade Ossipon knew that behind that white mask [of Winnie's face] there was struggling against terror and despair a vigour of vitality, a love of life that could resist the furious anguish which drives to murder and the fear, the blind, mad fear of the gallows. He knew" (p. 308).

Ossipon's insight is that the anarchist assumptions that "the middle classes are stupid" (p. 29) "Everybody is mediocre" (p. 309) are simply wrong. Ossipon sees through the "impenetrable mystery . . . This act of madness or despair" by which the newspaper characterizes Winnie's suicide. He alone heard her as "She lamented aloud her love of life, that life without grace or charm, and almost without decency, but of an exalted faithfulness of purpose, even unto murder. And, as often happens in the lament of poor humanity rich in suffering but indigent in words, the truth—the very cry of truth—was found in a worn and artificial shape picked up somewhere among the phrases of sham sentiment" (p. 298). Ossipon flees from Winnie who is death, but in viewing death closely, he begins a process of understanding that will paralyze his former motives and precipitate his fall into the gutter (p. 311).

In her concluding insights Winnie becomes a candidate for tragic stature. She imitates the action of the novel by grasping at the impenetrable mystery, the love of life which the inevitability of death makes incumbent upon man. Winnie's achievement in the death of Stevie and the killing of Verloc is not merely murder rising out of anguish but liberation from the oppressive fantasy of her marriage and devotion to her brother. In her pathetic attempt to turn herself over to Ossipon, "The memory of the early romance with the young butcher survived, tenacious, like the image of a glimpsed ideal in that heart quailing before the fear of the gallows and full of revolt against death" (p. 275).

Of all the characters in *The Secret Agent,* Winnie alone attains the freedom to act, to see death as it is, and thus set an appropriate valuation on life. Her tragedy is that such energy, having its source in delusion similar to the child-like sympathy of Stevie, must have as its result violence and death. The concomitant realization of the importance of life is compensation enough, perhaps, but it comes only at the price of tremendous suffering.

Thus in violence and death, madness and despair, the truth of life emerges tarnished but hopeful. It is the human spirit, reaching out beyond the limits of the inconceivable to confront death and opt for life, which provides the object and justification of art, even in this, Conrad's darkest of novels.

PETER SLOAT HOFF

"THE SECRET AGENT":
A TYPICAL CONRAD NOVEL?

Conrad scholars have for decades stressed analysis rather than syn-thesis. They have mainly attempted to show how Conrad's novels differ from each other, categorizing and distinguishing them to help account for readers' tastes and preferences. This analytic tendency has especially affected our view of *The Secret Agent,* a novel which appears, especially on first reading, to be among the most anomalous of Conrad's works. In this Conrad obviously departed from the surface textures he had been used to working with. Instead of remote jungle or seascape, England's most exotic major novelist chose to place his story in the heart of London. The surface of the plot is also unusual for Conrad, for it has all the makings of a spy thriller or detective story. Further-more, considering the thoroughly ironic mode of narration and a pecul-iarly Dickensian rhetoric,[1] it is easy to succumb to the urge to read *The Secret Agent* as a profound departure from the pattern set by "Heart of Darkness," *Lord Jim,* and *Nostromo.* Considering the esthetic success of those earlier masterpieces, this "departure" might also appear to be ill-advised. However viewed, *The Secret Agent* has been consistently seized upon by critics as a sign of a major turning point in Conrad's career: a sign that he was tired and ill and that his novelistic powers were flagging,[2] or a sign that he now wanted to forsake art for "popularity,"[3] or a sign that he had turned away from the impressionistic method that had served him so well;[4] in any case a sign that Conrad had turned to something different. I submit that we have tended to overstate the degree of difference in *The Secret Agent.* This novel in

---

[1] The irony is universally acknowledged. J. Hillis Miller comments on the Dicken-sian rhetoric in *Poets of Reality* (Cambridge: Harvard U.P., 1966), p. 22.

[2] Gérard Jean-Aubry, *The Sea Dreamer* (New York: Doubleday, 1957; rpt. Archon, 1967), p. 245.

[3] *Ibid.,* p. 252.

[4] Albert Guerard considers all three of these theses, partially accepting and par-tially rejecting them, in *Conrad the Novelist* (Cambridge: Harvard U.P., 1958; rpt. Atheneum, 1967), p. 218. Or we may choose to accept Bernard C. Meyer's psycho-analytic thesis that *The Secret Agent* "may be considered a literary accompaniment to [Jessie Conrad's] pregnancy and to the immediate postpartum period." *Joseph Conrad: A Psychoanalytic Biography* (Princeton: Princeton U.P., 1967), p. 188.

fact incorporates many of the themes we have come to identify as distinctly Conradian, themes which define the essential nature of his other masterpieces. In terms of theme, *The Secret Agent* paradoxically seems different because it is in such an intense way the *quintessential* Conrad novel.

At least four crucial themes comprise the fabric of *The Secret Agent*. First, the "ideal conception of the self," and whether a man can be true to it, which is so concisely exposed in "The Secret Sharer," and which proves vital to *Lord Jim* and *Nostromo*, forms a thematic *raison d'être* for every character in *The Secret Agent*. Second, the theme of betrayal, which defines *Lord Jim* and *Under Western Eyes*, and figures so prominently in *Nostromo*, binds together a diverse set of characters in *The Secret Agent*. Third, the doubling of characters, which is not only a technique but a central theme in "The Secret Sharer," *Lord Jim*, and *Nostromo*, develops in kaleidoscopic fashion in *The Secret Agent*. Fourth, as we would expect from any typical Conrad novel, *The Secret Agent* forces its readers and its central characters to look directly at the Horror at the *Heart of Darkness*. In essence, then, the surface trappings of setting and plot constitute the main differences between *The Secret Agent* and other great Conrad novels. The thematic core remains essentially the same; and the more heavily ironic treatment of *The Secret Agent's* materials guarantees, more than anything else, an intensity of theme and tone.

"I wondered," says the Captain in "The Secret Sharer," "how far I should turn out faithful to that ideal conception of one's own personality every man sets up for himself secretly." Conscious or not, this question is crucial to the personalities of so many Conrad characters. The gap between the ideal conception and the reality is essentially what defines Lord Jim's personality. Nostromo is a man obsessed by the outward manifestations of this ideal. He desperately wishes that those who know him will recognize his faithfulness to an ideal self. Kurtz's ideal conception of himself becomes perverted and inverted by his encounter with the Horror. On a thoroughly ironic plane, the ideal conception of the self defines the characters and the moral world of *The Secret Agent*. The epithets which accompany the characters, repeated in almost Homeric fashion, identify them not in terms of their actual nature, but in terms of their ideal conceptions: Yundt, the "terrorist," has never lifted a finger to generate any terror; the "robust" Comrade Ossipon, "nicknamed the doctor," is a pseudo-scientific washout whose robustness exists mainly in his false mask of machismo; the "apostle" Michaelis has lost the power of consecutive thought necessary to spread his apostolic creed, or even to formulate it beyond his vision of the world as one vast hospital; and of course Verloc, the secret agent himself, constantly appears clad not only in his overcoat but in the rhetoric of his ideal conception of himself: "the tried revolutionist —'one of the old lot'—the humble guardian of society; the invaluable Secret Agent of Baron Stott-Wartenheim's despatches; a servant of law and order, faithful, trusted, accurate, admirable, with perhaps one single amiable weakness: the idealistic belief in being loved for himself" (p. 235).[5] These characters' self-images are absurd, which may indicate that *The Secret Agent* differs from other Conrad novels mainly in its degree of irony. The characters here exist entirely in what Northrop Frye labels the "ironic mode:" they are "inferior in power and intelligence to ourselves, so that we have the sense of looking down on a scene of bondage, frustration, or absurdity."[6] Whereas in other Conrad novels at least the *possibility* of being true to an ideal conception of oneself exists, the characters in *The Secret Agent* are denied even that possibility. This gap between conception and execution also marks characters other than the impotent anarchists. Chief Inspector Heat displays "the pride of a trusted servant" and is certain that a "valuable chief inspector" is worth far more than his bureaucratic higher-ups. Even the quixotic Assistant Commissioner, with whom the reader is inclined to sympathize, takes excessive pride in his ideal conception of his quixotism, and relishes his "evil freedom" perhaps too much when he escapes from his desk and the snake-like speaking tubes.

The only characters who—in any sense—prove true to ideal self-conceptions demonstrate by their very proof the untenability of the ideal. Stevie, insofar as he is capable of forming an ideal conception, lives up to it. And he is blasted to fragments for his trouble. And the Professor, who acts out his conception of a "moral agent" dedicated to "the destruction of what is," forces us to realize that if this nihilism is the only ideal conception which can be actualized, it virtually negates the concept of actualizing an ideal.

The standoff which results when Heat and the Professor confront each other represents the most society can hope for when pitting the social ideal—i.e., "the game"—against the nihilistic ideal of the "perfect anarchist." "I'll have you yet," asserts Heat, with the "austere quietness" of a man who has mastered the game. The Professor, who also knows the moves, counters with an appeal to the Chief Inspector's ideal conception of himself: "Doubtless . . . but there's no time like the present, believe me. For a man of real convictions this is a fine opportunity

[5] References to *The Secret Agent* are drawn from the Anchor Books edition (Garden City, N.Y.: Doubleday, 1953). Hereafter they are cited by page number only.
[6] *Anatomy of Criticism* (Princeton: Princeton U.P., 1957; rpt. Atheneum, 1968), p. 34.

of self-sacrifice. You may not find another so favourable, so humane. There isn't even a cat near us, and these condemned houses would make a good heap of bricks where you stand. You'll never get me at so little cost to life and property, which you are paid to protect."

"You don't know who you're speaking to, said Chief inspector Heat, firmly. If I were to lay my hands on you now I would be no better than yourself."

"Ah! The game!" (p. 87).

In fact it remains questionable how much better than the Professor Heat really is. For not even he, with his developed sense of the game— an ideal conception of society—can live by its rules. A close correlative to the theme of the ideal conception is the theme of betrayal. The failure to be true to an ideal takes the tangible form of betrayals—be-trayals of fellow men as well as betrayals of the rules of the game. The clearest example of such betrayal in the novels of Conrad is Jim's leap from the *Patna*, his betrayal of the ship of pilgrims. Nostromo, beginning with his night in the dark gulf, betrays not only his ideal self, but by degrees his entire society. *The Secret Agent* is laced with a series of betrayals which not only objectify the theme but—interest-ingly enough—function to tie together many of the various characters.

Verloc's behavior again strikes the keynote. He betrays in all direc-tions, dealing with anarchists, foreign diplomats, police, whoever can offer him money or security in exchange for his information.[7] To Verloc's moral insensibilities, his career as betrayer actually harmonizes with his ideal conception of himself. " 'There isn't a murdering plot for the last eleven years,' " he tells Winnie, " 'that I hadn't a finger in at the risk of my life. There's scores of these revolutionists I've sent off, with their bombs in their blamed pockets, to get themselves caught on the frontier. The old Baron knew what I was worth to his country' " (p. 197). Verloc is himself no stranger to being betrayed, ever since a "fatal infatuation for an unworthy" woman caused him "five years' " rigorous confinement in a fortress" (p. 30). When, ironically, his bomb plot is betrayed by Winnie's foresight—sewing Stevie's name in the coat—Verloc is ready to betray everyone involved. In a vengeful mood he swears to "teach them yet what it means to throw out a man like me to rot in the streets." This prompts a narrative comment: "It was a very appropriate revenge. It was in harmony with the promptings of Mr. Verloc's genius. It also had the advantage of being within the range of his powers and of adjusting itself easily to the practice of

---

7 John A. Palmer characterizes Verloc as a "betrayer of betrayers," and points out his relationship to figures like Jim and Razumov, in *Joseph Conrad's Fiction* (Ithaca: Cornell U.P., 1968), p. 105.

his life, which had consisted precisely in betraying the secret and unlawful proceedings of his fellow men. Anarchists and diplomats were all one to him" (p. 202).

Verloc is by no means the only betrayer. Betrayal is a practice which spreads through all levels of characters, until anarchists and diplomats become all one to the reader. The police, in particular, work at odds to each other. Chief Inspector Heat has for years used Verloc as a private source of information, without letting the rest of the force know. When the vital shred of evidence—Stevie's address—appears, Heat snatches it and plans on keeping it to himself. Ironically, the confrontation between Heat and his superior, the Assistant Commissioner, reveals that both men are protecting anarchists—Heat protecting his source Verloc and the Assistant Commissioner protecting his wife's friend's friend, Michaelis. Not surprisingly the Chief Inspector gets the distinct impression that he is being betrayed. "He felt at the moment like a tightrope artist might feel if suddenly, in the middle of the performance, the manager of the Music-Hall were to rush out of the proper managerial seclusion and begin to shake the rope" (p. 104). The Assistant Commissioner likewise feels that old department hands like Heat are in the habit of betraying him, prompting his remark, " 'Your idea of secrecy seems to consist in keeping the chief of your department in the dark' " (p. 116). And when the betrayed Assistant Commissioner quixotically decides to take up the investigation himself, the Great Personage Sir Ethelred admonishes him, " 'Your idea of assurances over there . . . seems to consist mainly in making the Secretary of State look like a fool' " (p. 119).

The chain of betrayals thus links many characters. Verloc, in order to keep his job at the embassy as a betrayer, betrays Stevie, and by extension Winnie, who quite understandably betrays Verloc in return with a carving knife. Winnie is ultimately betrayed by Comrade Ossipon, whose leap from the train is not altogether unlike Jim's leap from the *Patna.* Winnie ends her own life by leaping from the Cross-Channel Boat.

All in all, the betrayal patterns reinforce other major themes. They are prime agents in undercutting the ideal conception of self held by each character. They reveal the more immediate and universal motivations which win out over ideal conceptions. Or, as Conrad's narrator remarks, "the way of even the most justifiable revolutions is prepared by personal impulses disguised into creeds" (p. 77). And this process of disguising vanity, selfishness, and greed in terms of ideology is not limited to the revolutionaries. It marks all characters and creates a complicated network of unlikely relationships. These relationships finally grow into a third major theme, the doubling and redoubling of characters which denies any person, class, or group a claim to the novel's moral ethos.

Various characters assert in various ways the sameness of all groups. "Anarchists or diplomats were all one" to Verloc. Chief Inspector Heat recognizes that the mind and the instincts of a burglar are the same as the mind and the instincts of a police officer" (p. 85). And the Professor insists that "the terrorist and the policeman both come from the same basket" (p. 68).

While Conrad thus allows his characters repeatedly to assert this theme, he carries it out with an intricate development of plot and imagery. While the impressionistic time scheme of the novel employs frequent time shifts, flashbacks, and background fillers, time present continues to move directly forward as a series of confrontations involving two characters apiece: Verloc and Vladimir, Verloc and Winnie, Ossipon and the Professor, the Professor and Heat, Heat and the Assistant Commissioner, and so on. Twenty years ago John Hagen, Jr. recognized the structural importance of these confrontaions (it may be significant that his generation called them "interviews").[8] Hagen discusses the ways in which the interviews are paired, repeating important material, emphasizing crucial themes, and generally forming the spine of *The Secret Agent*'s structure. What Hagen does not mention is the relationship of the confrontations to the time structure of the piece, and the degree to which the pairings emphasize character doubling. In a sense, the confrontations which shape *The Secret Agent* amount to a kaleidoscopic multiplication of the doppelganger motif which Conrad so artfully isolates in "The Secret Sharer," and which is never far from the thematic core of his major fiction. Here, in *The Secret Agent,* we have a dynamic and shifting set of relationships which show at once the bonds of humanity and inhumanity linking anarchists and public servants, plus—ironically—the ultimate inability of even the most intimately linked characters to communicate.

The lack of communication in *The Secret Agent* has frequently been touched upon by scholars and critics, and here we need only remark that the work's conversations are models of what Ford Madox Ford had in mind when he discussed the impressionistic use of dialogue:

> One unalterable rule that we had for the rendering of converstations . . . was that no speech of one character should ever answer the speech that goes before it. This is almost invariably the case in real life where few people listen, because they are always preparing their own next speeches . . .

---

[8] "The Design of Conrad's *The Secret Agent*," *ELH*, XXII (1955), 148-164. See also *Poets of Reality*, p. 62.

He says: 'Right down extraordinary that petunia was—'
You say 'What would you think now of my . . .'
He says: 'Diamond stripes it had, blue-black and salmon. . .'
You say: 'I've always had a bit of a gift . . .'
Your daughter Millicent interrupts: 'Julia Gower has got a pair of snake-skin shoes. She bought them at Wiston and Willocks's.'[9]

Conrad uses this technique to perfection in *The Secret Agent*. Each of its confrontations presents characters who fail to share the same assumptions or the same factual information, yet who talk to each other as if they did. The culminating, and most ironic, scene of this kind occurs when the distraught Winnie stumbles into the arms of Ossipon. Ossipon believes Verloc blown up in the Greenwich explosion; Winnie is of course all too aware of his actual fate. Since conversation between Winnie and Ossipon goes on here for pages, without either character becoming aware of the other's actual perceptions, tremendous ironic tension builds up. Such is the level of tension that it explodes with the force of the Greenwich bomb when Ossipon, casually entering a room to put out a light, discovers the body of Mr. Verloc, "reposing quietly on the sofa."

A yell coming from the innermost depths of his chest died out unheard and transformed into a sort of greasy, sickly taste on his lips. At the same time the mental personality of Comrade Ossipon executed a frantic leap backwards. But his body, left thus without intellectual guidance, held on to the door handle with the unthinking force of an instinct. The robust anarchist did not even totter. And he stared, his face close to the glass, his eyes protruding out of his head. He would have given anything to get away, but his returning reason informed him that it would not do to let go the door handle. What was it—madness, a nightmare, or a trap into which he had been decoyed with fiendish artfulness? (pp. 232-233)

Ossipon's shock of recognition brings us to the fourth major theme to be considered. As J. Hillis Miller has demonstrated so convincingly, no self-respecting Conrad novel would be complete without rendering a vision of the Horror at the Heart of Darkness. And since Miller has done justice to *The Secret Agent* as Conrad's most intense exploration of this theme, we need not detain ourselves by retracing his steps.[10] In fact Miller is one of the few scholars to recognize not only the greatness of *The Secret Agent* (most scholars have come round to granting that), but also its centrality in the corpus of Conrad novels. What

---

[9] Frank MacShane, ed., *Critical Writings of Ford Madox Ford* (Lincoln: U. of Nebraska Press, 1964), p. 77.
[10] "In *The Secret Agent* Conrad's voice and the voice of the darkness most nearly become one. To explore the meaning of this novel will be to approach as close as possible to the dark heart of Conrad's universe." *Poets of Reality*, p. 39.

we should bring into focus at this point is the relationship of the other major themes to the transcendent vision of the Horror. Various characters are allowed a vision of that Horror. Their individual responses are determined much by their ideal conceptions of themselves, the degree to which they have betrayed those ideals, and the network of doubling relationships which links all of Conrad's humanity in a chaotic universe.

As Miller observes, "In novel after novel Conrad presents characters driven to passivity or death by a confrontation with the darkness: Marlow, with his Buddha's pose, Winnie Verloc, driven to suicide by 'madness and despair,' Lingard, Razumov, Kurtz, and many others."[11] It is appropriate that Miller should single out Winnie; for her experience with the horror is central, though it is shared by others. Circumstances force Winnie, who "felt profoundly that things do not stand much looking into," to look quite profoundly into the nature of things. The source of Winnie's horror is not just the demolition of her brother— though that would have been quite enough. It is that, along with Stevie, Winnie's entire perception of reality explodes. Verloc, to whom Winnie had attached herself and Stevie for the sake of security and stability, proves to be an agent of total instability. When the bomb goes off, everything Winnie could count on as true disappears, and she must face the darkness of a chaotic universe.

The Horror recognized by Comrade Ossipon is similar. It is not just the sight of a dead body that shocks him; again it is the demolition of his conception of order and reality—the vision of a man he believed blown to smithereens instead "reposing in the fulness of his domestic ease on a sofa." Ossipon's response is the one repeated by various characters in the novel: "he turned away from the glazed door, and retched violently." Ossipon, the believer in science, has had his idea of orderly relationships in the material world shaken almost beyond repair. The bomb, ironically, has had its intended effect—for those who glimpse a vision of the Horror, it is as if the First Meridian *has* been destroyed. Time and space no longer assume the relationships counted on.

Verloc too faces the Horror. But in his corpulent insensibility, it makes little impact on him. The great ironic tension of the murder scene depends on Winnie's recognition of the darkness and the new but negative "freedom" it affords her, stretched against Verloc's failure to recognize how utterly his own universe is shaken. Through Chapter XI, Verloc continues to exist as he had, finding fault in others—in-

11 *Ibid.*, p. 34.

cluding Winnie—for what has happened, and blandly making plans for a continued life of slothful ease. Verloc's inability to see the Horror is itself a motivating force driving Winnie to her nihilistic vision and her fatal deed.

Stevie has been the Teiresias of The Heart of Darkness all along. The outward blindness of his simple mind has been a means of his seeing and expressing depths unacknowledged by Winnie. Of all the characters, only Stevie can state succinctly the nature of the social universe: "Bad world for poor people;" and "Shame!" Only Stevie finds a means of expressing the actual chaos lying beneath the surface of things where other characters refuse to look. This much almost all readers have recognized in the obvious symbolism of Stevie's circles: "innumerable circles, concentric, eccentric; a coruscating whirl of circles that by their tangled multitude of repeated curves, uniformity of form, and confusion of intersecting lines suggested a rendering of cosmic chaos, the symbolism of a mad art attempting the inconceivable" (p. 49). The fragments into which Stevie is blown reinforce the image of cosmic chaos. Verloc is allowed to look at the Horror, but he never really gets beneath the surface of things. Winnie does, and is driven first to murder, then to suicide. Ossipon, like Marlow, assumes the Buddha's pose: "he sat up suddenly, drawing up his knees and clasping his legs. The first dawn found him open-eyed in that same posture" (p. 245). He remains shaken by his confrontation with the darkness.

As Hillis Miller concludes, "people in Conrad's world are in an intolerable situation. The Apollonian realm of reason and intention is a lie. The heart of darkness is the truth, but it is a truth which makes ordinary human life impossible."[12] Perhaps that is why the only personally viable position left at the end of *The Secret Agent* is the socially inviable one. The only ideal conception of the self which seems attainable is the search for the perfect detonator, the dedication to the destruction of what is.

This essay has concerned itself with the *thematic* relationship between *The Secret Agent* and other Conrad masterpieces. What remains to be explored is the relationship of method—the ways in which Conrad continued in this novel to develop his impressionistic technique. Some aspects of this technique I have unavoidably touched upon in my discussion of theme. Conrad's impressionistic time structure, we have seen, reinforces the patterns of character doubling and draws the reader into the tale as a participating character. We have also looked briefly at the impressionistic rendering of dialogue, and the use of such dialogue—ironically—to show the noncommunication of intimately

---

[12] *Ibid.*, p. 32.

linked characters. These and other matters of structure and style generate in *The Secret Agent* an intense *progression d'effet* seldom matched by Conrad himself or by other impressionist writers who strove for this goal. A careful study of the technique of *The Secret Agent* would, I am convinced, strongly confirm what I have attempted to show in terms of theme: that in spite of surface differences, the essential substance of *The Secret Agent* is very much like the substance of Conrad's other great works. Like the author's favorite symbol and metaphor—the sea—his novels exist most meaningfully beneath the surface ripples of time, place, and circumstance.

"TO MAKE YOU HEAR . . .": SOME ASPECTS OF CONRAD'S DIALOGUE

" 'And what is the use of a book,' Alice thought, 'without pictures or conversations?' "[1] Most readers of Conrad, I suspect, find the first of Alice's requirements to be satisfied much more abundantly than the second. To a degree such an impression reflects fairly accurately the priorities in Conradian fiction. In many of his stories the play of rapid and varied dialogue is secondary to the compulsively linear flow of monologue. Elsewhere the very conception of a character hardly allows for many developed verbal exchanges: some of Conrad's major characters are habitually withdrawn or stubbornly taciturn, others are inarticulate solitaries, and many more are valued for voiceless strengths which speak far louder than words. Indeed in general it may be thought something of a questionable service to draw attention to a good deal of Conrad's dialogue. At its poorest, it is very poor indeed—in the early Malayan novels tending to be stiffly operatic or full of factitious pauses and agitated silences, and in his very late books markedly limp. In addition even Conrad's more major works can be disconcertingly uneven by virtue of the fluctuating quality of their dialogue. *Victory* comes dangerously close to comic pantomime in the words given to Jones and Ricardo; in *Nostromo* Monygham at one point accuses Nostromo of speaking "drivel,"[2] a habit becoming unfortunately widespread among the Italian population at the end of the novel. Whether from tiredness, or a faltering grasp on colloquial English, or over-ambitiousness, Conrad's hold upon dialogue is subject to severe temporary strains and lapses.

Undistinguished ordinariness in some areas, however, has to be weighed against very substantial achievement in others. Much of Conrad's dialogue is, I think, worthy of Ford's comment that his

---

[1] Quoted by Norman Page, in *Speech in the English Novel* (London, 1973), p. 1.
[2] *Nostromo*, p. 462. All page references to Conrad's works are to the Collected Edition, 21 vols., published by J. M. Dent (London, 1946-1954), and will normally appear in parentheses after quotation. Spaced dots indicate my ellipses in the quoted material, unspaced dots represent Conrad's own use of the punctuation.

"marvellous gift of language was, in the end, dramatic,"[3] though one may have to look in somewhat unusual areas to see why this is so. It is fair to say that generally Conrad has only average success with the kinds of finely shaded and continuous dialogue which many traditional novelists handle so well; he tends to be even less successful, as many critics have noted, with the intricate spoken record of high passion between men and women. Like Henry James, Conrad flirted with the theatre but came to doubt whether his language could ever meet the requirements of the stage; he even felt the dialogue in his novels to be "never very literary."[4] This is a revealing and challenging disclaimer, though what it implies about Conrad's strengths, weaknesses and idiosyncrasies as a dialogist has never been made clear. How, and in what ways, does he most characteristically make us "hear" the spoken word?

Conrad's dialogue in general has two main characteristics, the first and most important being that it is invariably subject to the selective and ordering devices of his impressionism. What he sometimes offers is not a conversation at all but the swift and dramatic impact of things heard upon a detached listener. To a degree unusual in more traditional novels, he draws his material from typical and luminous fragments of speech, fragments heard with an illusion of spontaneity, carefully edited and then recombined in a concentrated speech-burst. Hence specific conversations are often much less important than the piecing together of illuminating moments which capture people in the act of revealing expression; and, given the need to unify these moments, Conrad relies very heavily upon the implied centrality of a sensitive listener who, at his most characteristic, tends to fugitively *over*hear spoken words which are then impressionistically telegrammed to the reader. At one extreme such dialogue leads to some highly colored minor characters who come to us, as in the best tradition of caricature, via oddities speaking very directly of habitual tics and traits. Their speech, invariably rendered as a thumb-nail sketch, usually has a spontaneous surface appeal, even a visual dimension in that it implies gestures, grimaces and nervous twitches. At another extreme the sharply rendered fragment often combines with other methods to give clearer definition to major figures: the latter are not merely the sum of their verbal mannerism, but those mannerisms at least provide one way of access to them. In so far as such dialogue always posits a responsive listener who hears sensitively and indirectly, it is obviously not easily adaptable for the stage; its end may be dramatic, but its means belong to the

---

[3] Ford Madox Ford, *Joseph Conrad: A Personal Remembrance* (London, 1924), p. 202.
[4] *Joseph Conrad: Life and Letters,* ed. G. Jean-Aubry (London, 1927), Vol. II, 269.

printed page. Equally the technique of "rendering" speech may be unfamiliar and not very "literary" to many English readers—though not to those acquainted with the works of Flaubert and Maupassant where it figures extensively.

A second main feature of Conrad's dialogue is the extent to which it exploits broken and interrupted speech, short bursts of conversation and indeterminate pauses which, in form as well as function, seem much nearer to latter-day Pinterese than Edwardian stage-language. The general intention behind interrupted and discontinuous speech is, according to Ford, to capture "the sort of indefiniteness that is characteristic of all human conversations."[5] More impressively, Conrad always has an ear trained to detect the dramatic and psychological resonance inherent in agitated pause and silence. Here again what he offers his reader is, properly speaking, not conversation but the momentous self-colloquy which centres upon the silence of unspoken or unspeakable inner tension. Both the form and content of Conrad's fragmentary dialogue reflect his skeptical attitude to language as a means of communicating with the self and others. Spoken words may sometimes be luminous and revealing. But at best they offer only a partial index of a man's true feelings and, as the narrator of *Under Western Eyes* says, may ultimately be "the great foes of reality" (p. 3). Words, like appearances, are destined to have their opaque surfaces and—even more mysteriously—an impenetrable emotional logic behind them. What is said often proves much less important than what is left unsaid or the way in which something is said. Silences too are revealing, a truth usually implied in the fragmented from and content of Conrad's dialogue. Some of his major figures stumble clumsily with language, their agitated outbursts made up of pauses, repetitions and broken fragments which, disappearing into highly charged silence, seem to offer the reader little solid information; all of these signs in combination may hint at a reality lurking beneath spoken words, but we may have to strain after it for ourselves, sometimes with and sometimes without the author's help. In pursuing the emotional sub-text beneath language, Conrad probably had good reason to feel himself hopelessly at odds with the highly articulate Shavian theatre of his own day. In dramatic terms he is much nearer to the contemporary playwright who exploits the interaction or contradiction between speech and silence to compress a wealth of dramatic hints about submerged motives. Caught in the act of struggling for language, figures like Jim and Razumov are as interesting when they are lost for words as when they find them: they may never be very articulate about themselves but their words—

---

5 Ford, p. 135.

and silences—always prove to be intensely expressive. In the remainder of this paper I want to extend these general observations into three areas where Conrad's ability to make us "hear" seems to me most striking: the materials and methods of character individualization; the dramatization of more subtle motives, inner tensions and tangled communications; and the role of the extended conversation-piece in relation to its total dramatic context.

I

In the presentation of dialogue most authors face the task of recapturing the authenticity and spontaneity of commonplace conversation without, at the same time, being limited to its pace and trivial repetitiveness. The problem is particularly acute for Conrad who often works within the narrow confines of the *nouvelle* and many of whose simpler characters are barely articulate. His main solution is to use a range of devices which "render" speech—that is, which conflate picturesque fragments to convey the flavour of conversation without giving all of its substance. The process is most evident in the case of minor characters, who are not simply a convenient starting-point for discussion but an illustration of how his dialogue works at some of its strongest moments. Each one tends to be a very distinct "voice," a Micawberish compendium of all the more obvious oddities of speech—muddled syntax, extravagant intonation, repetition, exotic pidgin-English and mispronunciation; very often the spoken word alone performs the task of animation, its colorful bric-à-brac concentrated into a speech-burst which is suggestively poised between monologue and conversation, report and mimicry:

"There's some sort of white vagabond had got in there, I hear . . . Eh? What you say? Friends of yours? So! . . . Then it was true there was one of these *vordamte*—What was he up to? Found his way in, the rascal, Eh?" . . . "Look here," says he, mysteriously, "if—do you understand?—if he has really got hold of something fairly good—none of your bits of green glass —understand?—I am a government official—you tell the rascal . . . Eh? What? Friend of yours?" . . . (*Lord Jim,* p. 279)
His flowing English seemed to be derived from a dictionary compiled by a lunatic. Had Mr. Stein desired him to "ascend," he would have "reverentially"—(I think he wanted to say respectfully—but devil only knows)— "reverentially made objects for the safety of properties." If disregarded, he would have presented "resignation to quit." Twelve months ago he had made his last voyage there, and though Mr. Cornelius "propitiated many offertories" . . . on conditions which made the trade "a snare and ashes in the mouth," yet his ship had been fired upon . . . (*Lord Jim,* pp. 238-9)

An almost Dickensian relish for "lunatic" oddity combines with the miniaturist's love of *le mot juste* to give these speeches an engaging zaniness. They are not a complete record of what takes place, but abbreviated reports in which Marlow's replies are often implied but totally omitted. Lovingly chosen fragments form the main substance, but fragments stripped of irrelevancy and then rendered in racy, continuous speech-bursts. The narrator plays the careful editor, selectively combining direct and indirect speech in order to focus attention upon one speaker and so exaggerate the impact his words make. The effect of a long conversation can be given but with no loss of onward momentum; what finally emerges is the animated skeleton of a conversation without its total body.

Distilled fragments of speech invariably appear at the fringes of most of Conrad's stories: they convey MacWhirr's commands during the typhoon, animate the crew of the *Narcissus,* depict the snatches of conversation overheard by Marlow in *Heart of Darkness* and in these cases generally reflect Conrad's endeavour to bring both color and swift pace to commonplace speech. To this end he has the habit of drawing freely upon the more exotic sides of spoken language. I doubt if any other author has so fruitfully exploited the possibilities of broken— and pidgin-English—its opacity and color as well as the strange surprises it can hold. The foreign speakers in his fiction—including Stein, the French lieutenant, Madame de S—, Hermann, Siegers and Schomberg—testify to an astonishingly alert ear for the idiosyncrasies in various racial types. With the more important of such speakers, like Stein and the French lieutenant in *Lord Jim,* oddities are not exploited simply for their surface colour: they have a careful thematic and dramatic value. Both men have the status of spokesmen, taking on an air of authority and mystery by their foreign language; but equally they are quite different in the words they command to grapple with the problem of "How to be." They scholarly Stein with his "voluminous and grave" voice (p. 213) uses elusive fragments, his elliptical sentences punctured by studied pauses, exclamations and foreign words; his sensitivity to the claims of both imaginative and practical life emerges uniquely in the combination of "impalpable poesy" (p. 215) and the powerfully literal superimposition of German syntax upon English. Also his contorted language, if sometimes irritatingly obscure, reflects an intellectual agitation totally absent from the Frenchman's more conventional response. The latter initially attracts Marlow by his slang, nautical terms and bluntness; his language even adds a touch or drollness to the proceedings. But our final impression is of the contrast between the Frenchman's placidity when he offers his philosophy and the spluttered "empty sounds" of his exit-speech: "The honour . . . that is real—that is! And what life may be worth . . . when the honour is gone— *ah ça par exemple* — I can offer no opinion" (p. 148).

Many of Conrad's strengths with dialogue—colour, thumb-nail economy, concentrated vigor—announce themselves flamboyantly in the impressionistic speaking-picture. If sometimes uncertain with the cadences of conversational English, he seems entirely assured in distilling its more unusual or colorful extremes—the fatuous political jargon of Peter Ivanovitch, the grimly rational tones of the Professor, or the youthful naiveties of Scarfe and the Russian harlequin. "The rhetorical will pass when it comes in a human voice."[6]—Conrad's skill lies in reconciling his natural inclination for the picturesque and exotic in speech with the recognizably human note. More than this, his methods of indirect rendering allow him to exploit the flow of colorful monologue while, at the same time, submitting it to the normalizing response of a listener; he ensures that the impact of things heard strikes the reader's ear with measured discipline and a hint of the prosaic.

The concentrated burst of typical speech-fragments is not incompatible with subtle characterization, though Conrad tends to use it sparingly with main figures. It appears in "Heart of Darkness" to give a symbolic force to the "voice" by which Kurtz is chiefly remembered; in *Lord Jim,* especially to convey the habitual quality of Jim's "elated rattle" (p. 234); and widely in *The Secret Agent* and *Nostromo,* two novels where even major figures have to be drawn very quickly.[7] But if in general concentrated and flamboyant impressionism is used sparingly with major figures, the detached and impressionable listener hardly ever disappears. In constructing particular exchanges, Conrad always seems to seek the mobility of stance allowing him to "hear" very variously, to move freely from direct to indirect speech as well as to exploit a variable mixture of the two. Even in dialogue appearing to have the powerful impact of direct speech there are invariably vestiges of indirect report to suggest the silent and bemused listener:

> He [Michaelis] a pessimist! Preposterous! He cried out that the charge was outrageous. He was so far from pessimism that he saw already the end of all private property coming along logically . . . Yes. Struggle, warfare, was the condition of private ownership. It was fatal. Ah! he did not depend upon emotional excitement to keep up his belief . . . Not he! (*The Secret Agent*, p. 43)

Mr. Verloc, in a soft and conjugal tone, was now expressing his firm

---

[6] Ford, p. 146.

[7] See, for example, the way in which Conrad introduces Decoud in *Nostromo* (pp. 152-3) by combining an outline of his past life with some of his typical moments of dandyish eloquence.

belief that there were yet a good few years of quiet life before them both. He did not go into the question of means. A quiet life it must be and, as it were, nestling in the shade, concealed among men whose flesh is grass; modest, like the life of violets. The words used by Mr. Verloc were: "Lie low for a bit." And far from England, of course. It was not clear whether Mr. Verloc had in his mind Spain or South America; but at any rate somewhere abroad. (*The Secret Agent*, pp. 250-1)

Both passages have the flexibility which comes from a free mixture of direct and indirectly rendered speech forms—a flexibility allowing the listener's presence to be felt almost as fully as the speaker's. The first extract captures, in vocabulary and syntax, the full exclamatory force of Michaelis's oratory; but the heated oration mingles freely with devices suggesting that author's cooly detached summary—the absence of quotation marks, past tense and third-person pronouns. The second exploits much more markedly the coolness and remoteness to be gained from indirect rendering and mockingly plays with the contrast between authorial eloquence and Verloc's poverty of language. After opening as indirect and largely neutral report, it quickly accommodates the author's more individual tones. This voice develops a mock-pastoral fantasia on Verloc's behalf, but then suddenly spirals down to the bathos of direct speech. The remaining lines might be seen as indirect mimicry of Verloc's afterthought; but some of them (which Mrs. Verloc *hears*) are nearer to informal direct speech without quotation marks and so maintain a flavour of the conversation taking place. Effects like these are not restricted to *The Secret Agent* though they have a special aptness in this ironic novel. Indeed the variety of speech presentation in Conrad's fiction generally has received something less than the justice it deserves. His methods at their most fluid concentrate the effect a speaker makes, place spoken words within a distancing frame and allow the author's own response to be felt as a pervasive undertone.

Increasingly, however, Conrad seems more confident in allowing dialogue to make a direct impact through the give-and-take of conversation when speakers are not always aware of what they say and when contrast heightens their differences. His most successful major characters have a carefully conceived voice with distinctive and recurring nuances: Massy's discreet glibness in "The End of the Tether" for example, Monygham's bad-tempered sourcess, or Decoud's alternations between fine raillery and earnest intimacy, French and English language. Some of these voices are often defined by jarring contrasts—which can at times inhere in the speech of a single person. In *Victory* Heyst's lacerated feelings momentarily surface in his quarrelling tones. He is a man with two voices—on the one hand the urbanity of polite discourse, on the other the self-torturing outbursts of the misanthrope. At recurring points the ironic clash between the two is painfully evident:

> "No!" he cried roughly. "All this is too unreal altogether. It isn't to be borne! I can't protect you! I haven't the power." . . .
>   "I ought to beg your pardon for these antics," he said, adjusting his hat. "A movement of childish petulance! Indeed, I feel very much like a child . . ." (p. 347)

Conrad is increasingly adept at making difficult nuances and tones cohere in an identifiable speaking voice, and he often does so with an unfussy directness which makes one wonder whether Guerard is quite fair when he says that "the skillful, innovating Conrad often showed less than average skill when trying to employ the narrative methods of the standard realistic novel; he became, suddenly, amateur."[8] This view should not be taken as a fixed rule, as it often is. Conrad can and frequently does take up the settled stance of a silent listener *within* a conversation, allowing contrasts to emerge dramatically and using standard speech presentation to capture the tangled knot of feeling among people who are locked together in mutual evasion or animosity:

> "It has always been the same. We are a wonderful people, but it has always been our fate to be"—he [Decoud] did not say "robbed," but added, after a pause—"exploited!"
>   Mrs. Gould said, "Oh, this is unjust!" And Antonia interjected, "Don't answer him, Emilia. He is attacking me."
>   "You surely do not think I was attacking Don Carlos!" Decoud answered. (*Nostromo*, p. 174)

Elizabeth Bowen's view of speech—that it is "what the characters *do to each other*"[9]—seems aptly to fit the motives leading Decoud to use the barbed word "exploited." The direct thrust and parry of dialogue is not unusual in a novel like *Nostromo*, where it succeeds because Conrad takes up the traditional role of a direct "translator of passions into speech,"[10] allowing dialogue to make its own point. Like other novelists before him, he realizes that the translation works most effectively when it discloses, without giving away the speaker's identity; indeed this kind of dialogue only completes its purpose when the reader's interest is secured and he, too, begins to hear sensitively.

II

Much of the resonance of Conrad's best dialogue comes from its power to suggest conflicting feelings hidden beneath the level of full

---

8 Albert J. Guerard, *Conrad the Novelist* (Cambridge, Mass., 1958), p. 209.
9 Elizabeth Bowen, *Collected Impressions* (London, 1950), p. 255.
10 Author's Note, *Within the Tides*, p. ix.

consciousness, inner tensions pressing for expression but only felt obliquely in spoken words. Returning again and again to situations of deception and self-deception, he records the strain placed upon language in the act of making "a raid on the inarticulate / With shabby equipment always deteriorating." T. E. Lawrence once pointed to the fact—for some it appears a paradox—that Conrad, a man in love with the clear outlines of language, is always straining to capture what the human voice cannot speak and the ear hear properly, so that "all his things end in a kind of hunger, a suggestion of something he can't say or do or think."[11] Lawrence's words are even truer of some of Conrad's self-divided characters who stumblingly make "raids" on their elusive motives yet find language to be a strangely unworkable and alien material. Some of them cling to the clear, monosyllabic language of self-assertion in an attempt to frame and hold silences at bay, while others retreat into the dull thunder of words to escape from moments of accusing silence; but invariably silences appear to contaminate spoken words, obliterate their clear shape and demand to be "heard." And one of the distinctive effects of Conrad's dialogue is that of making the reader unusually sensitive to such para-linguistic features as tone, pause, stress and silence—features designed to alert the ear to the form of dialogue and its relationship to hidden motives. We, too, find ourselves listening to silences and straining for the secret code which unlocks their meaning.

Conrad's ear for the fugitive sub-text beneath conventional language is remarkable. Even in an early story like "The Return" he tries ambitiously to dramatize the intricacies of self-deception in a character who, afraid of accusing silences, struggles to disguise his own inadequacy in the fragile language of social decorum: "One doesn't usually talk like this—of course—but in this case you'll admit . . . And consider—the innocent suffer with the guilty. . . I don't want to say any more . . . on—on that point—but, believe me, true unselfishness is to bear one's burdens in—in silence" (*Tales of Unrest*, pp. 164-5). Too many pregnant pauses run the risk of being as tiresome as too much eloquence: there is no wonder that Ford and Conrad were accused by early critics of simply writing around a plethora of dots and dashes. Hervey in "The Return" is one of the first of Conrad's hollow men to use words like a man walking on thin ice. The real conflict lies within *himself* as the struggle for language indicates, though he quickly becomes more and more facile in using words to avoid the unbearably empty "silence." Dialogue of this kind seems to anticipate the much subtler dramatization of mental agility in *Lord Jim*. Jim is another

---

[11] *The Letters of T. E. Lawrence*, ed. David Garnett (London, 1938), p. 302.

man in dispute with himself who, Conrad implies, cannot explain himself either to Marlow or himself:

"I did not want all this talk . . . No . . . Yes . . . I won't lie. . . I wanted it: it is the very thing I wanted—there. Do you think you or anybody could have made me if I . . . I am—I am not afraid to tell . . . I wasn't going to run away. At first—at night, if it hadn't been for these fellows I might have . . ." (p. 132)

These "dubious stammers" (p. 155) indicate a man who, inscrutable to himself and evidently wishing to confess the truth, only partly rationalizes his motives in speech. His pauses and contradictions are hardly a sign of deliberate evasion, and Marlow rightly accepts them with sympathetic understanding: all words, it is implied here, are the "great foes of reality" even for those who earnestly and energetically seek to know themselves.

If the obscure emotional logic underlying speech always demands to be heard in Conrad's fiction, it is rarely elaborated so opaquely and minutely in dialogue as in *Lord Jim*. Economy rules in *Nostromo*, for example, and produces Gould's memorable stammerings to Emilia after his father's death: "I've come to you—I've come straight to you—" (p. 62). Elsewhere Conrad works more explicitly in his exposure of conscious and unconscious subterfuges. He allows us to become privileged listeners with access to the often ironic clash between secret motives and public language. The hero of *Under Western Eyes*, for example, resembles Jim in that his moral confusion finds an apt correlative in his failing control over language. At the beginning of the story Razumov successfully silences the voice of conscience (while betraying Haldin) by embracing the language of official Russian politics; like most Russians, according to Conrad, he finds himself in love with high-sounding words, which in Razumov's case help him to escape accusing moments of silence. Words, it seems, can delude the moral sense, especially in the case of an habitually silent student like Razumov. A further irony is that words later betray Razumov in a different way—by tempting him to reveal his inner confusion in public situations which also have their awkward silences:

With a great flow of words he complained of being totally misunderstood. Even as he talked with a perception of his own audacity he thought that the word "misunderstood" was better than the word "mistrusted," and he repeated it again with insistence... "What am I talking about?" he thought, eyeing him [Mikulin] with a vague gaze. Mistrusted—not misunderstood— was the right symbol of these people. Misunderstood was the other kind of curse. Both had been brought on his head by that fellow Haldin. And his head ached terribly. (p. 87)

In *Lord Jim* Jim's dialogue resembles a frustrating secret code or puzzle and becomes something of a fixed symbol for an inherently unknowable reality. In *Under Western Eyes* Razumov's spoken words are accompanied by a more or less complete sub-text in the form of his agitated consciousness. The resulting ironic tension—between private and public voices, the need to confess and the recoil from it—leads to a much clearer articulation of the movement through and beyond self-deception. Jim is imprisoned within erratic stammerings, a man trying to speak of an inner voice which he hardly understands. Razumov, on the other hand, penetrates beyond spoken words to the heart of silence where he learns to listen to the promptings of conscience; his final deafness is a symbol of both his freedom from the toils of a poisonously corrupted language and his ability to commune with inner silences.

In dramatizing the situations within which deception and misunderstanding arise, Conrad often stresses the complexity of the listener's role. Language proves a slippery medium for listener as well as speaker, especially when he is intent upon hearing what he wants to hear. As Marlow says in *Lord Jim*, "the power of sentences has nothing to do with their sense or the logic of their construction," and he goes on to point out that his own "idiotic mumble" is given an entirely private meaning by Jim (p. 75). Conrad's irony often centres upon the simple truth that dialogues can be perversely two-sided, the speaker's intended meaning frequently at the mercy of his listener's predispositions. Such is the case in *Victory* where Heyst receives and treasures Lena's most trivial words for their "mere vibrating, warm nobility of sound" (p. 75). Tangled communications reach a high point of absurdity in the superbly ironic conclusion to *The Secret Agent*. Ossipon speaks the words of a conventional lover to a woman who, unknown to him, has just murdered her husband and so gives "a special meaning to every sentence spoken by Comrade Ossipon" (p. 282). Spoken accord ironically disguises from him all the horrors of an unspoken nightmare; to his mechanical blandishments Winnie cries out with "a shuddering, repressed violence" (p. 272) and speaks in "a whisper full of scorn and rage" (p. 275). Nowhere else does Conrad dramatize so boldly the incompatible private monologues lurking mysteriously beneath the give-and-take of conversation.

The possibility of rendering such dialogues with an air of disjointed and indeterminate fragmentariness seems also to have been a point of debate between Conrad and Ford. According to the latter, a rule accepted by both was that in heightened dialogue "no speech of one character should ever answer the speech that goes before it."[12] Yet

---

[12] Ford, p. 188.

Conrad, as might be expected, never restricts himself to such a rule; even Ford later testifies to Conrad's expertise in rendering direct exchanges. The truth is that he never uses broken and interrupted conversation indiscriminately: it is reserved for scenes of high tension where the loss of continuity in dialogue signals a breakdown in communication between people who are too afraid or self-engrossed to make contact. One example is the conversation between Marlow and the Intended in "Heart of Darkness," another the dialogue between Razumov and Mikulin in *Under Western Eyes* which culminates in Razumov's meaningless repetition and Mikulin's unanswered question at the end of Part 1. Similarly at the end of *Nostromo* Conrad sensitively captures the frayed edges of feeling in the erratic movement of dialogue:

> "Was it [the silver] lost, though?" the doctor exclaimed. "I've always felt that there was a mystery about our Nostromo ever since. I do believe he wants now, at the point of death—"
> "The point of death," repeated Mrs. Gould.
> "Yes. Yes . . . He wants perhaps to tell you something concerning that silver which—"
> "Oh, no! No!" exclaimed Mrs. Gould, in a low voice. "Isn't it lost and done with? Isn't there enough treasure without it to make everybody in the world miserable?"
> The doctor remained still, in a submissive, disappointed silence. At last he ventured, very low—
> "And there is that Viola girl, Giselle. What are we to do? It looks as though father and sister had—" (p. 557)

Here broken dialogue subtly records the submerged feelings in Mrs. Gould unwittingly released by Monygham; he, at first insensitive to the effect of his words, then tactfully alters the course of the conversation in his final, hesitant sentence. As is often the case, the hidden nerve-ends just below the surface of speech provide Conrad with the substance of his dialogue: what is left unsaid is just as important as what is said. Conrad himself is the most concise commentator on such delicately sinuous dialogue: "Give me the right word and the right accent and I will move the world."[13]

III

Conrad's major stories show his increasing ability in making the extended conversation-piece an integral part of developing action and characterization. It makes its appearance at carefully planned points, is subject to a "dramatic working up"[14] which gives it a gathering in-

---

[13] "A Familiar Preface," *A Personal Record*, p. xii.
[14] Ford, p. 191.

tensity, and invariably casts reflections both backwards and forwards. This last characteristic is important. The conversation-piece plays its part in a whole by engaging us intensively and extensively. While crystallizing local tensions, it also directs our attention to issues in the past and future for which it acts as a concentrated focus. As Heyst comes to realize when he rashly promises to save Lena, the act of speech can be a momentous occasion: it mirrors the developing tensions of the past and irrevocably lays down the course of future action. Some of Conrad's works tend to affirm this truth by being structured around linked conversation-pieces which, it is important to note, are just as essential to narrative and theme as pictorial symbolism. Extended dialogue provides *The Shadow-Line* with its introduction and epilogue, while much of the main body of the tale develops through "short five-minute" confrontations between the Captain, Burns and Ransome (p. 101). Again the narrative involutions in *Lord Jim*, *Nostromo*, *The Secret Agent* and *Victory* co-exist with patterned interviews which, in various ways, give continuity to character presentation and carry a heavy burden of dramatic material.

Conrad's earliest experiments with extended dialogue are, to say the least, inauspicious and erratic. Conversation-pieces in *An Outcast of the Islands* are not wholly typical of his early work, but they are symptomatic of Conrad's uncertainty with the obligatory dramatic scene. Some of its dialogues seem a way of stretching out thin material or of delaying the climax which, when it finally arrives, is weakened by previous intensities. The long fifty-page conversation between Almayer and Lingard in Part 3 is sadly overburdened with exposition which might have been summarized more economically. It does anticipate one aspect of Conrad's later rhetoric by providing a final dramatic surprise to create renewed expectation—in this case, the news that Lingard has brought Mrs. Willems to Sambir; but the dramatic charge is over-delayed and hardly bold enough to jolt us out of prolonged relaxation. The epilogue of the novel tries to relax without dissolving the intensity of crisis by returning to commonplace talk as in *Victory:* but the drunken meandering of the anonymous butterfly-catcher tends to dissipate the total mood, giving the novel something of a limp dying fall.

Conrad's best conversation-pieces have the stamp of individual rhythms which embrace and combine dramatic ups-and-downs: desultory conversation can be punctured by sudden intensities and vice versa, variety of mood created by dialogues-within-dialogues as in *Lord Jim*, or climaxes prepared for by slowly mounting tension. *Nostromo*, *The Shadow-Line*, *Under Western Eyes* and *Victory* in particular have a number of conversational pauses designed mainly to slow down the tempo and provide relief from action. Some of these supply a resting-point after high intensity as well as a detached vantage or a quiet forum where values can be probed. But it is important to note that Conrad increasingly invites our detachment and relaxation only the more forcibly to surprise us into renewed tension; conversational pauses are not simply parallel to the dramatic action but an integral part of it. Unanticipated tension sometimes comes from the immediate background, as when Decoud and Antonia talk intimately in Part 2 of *Nostromo* against a setting of intense political excitement; the contrast between public and private is memorably caught in the very construction of the episode and particularly in Decoud's defiant shout, *"Gran' bestia!"* (p. 191). *The Shadow-Line* begins with a dramatization of what to the young captain appear to be tedious inanities of conversation. In fact they compress a good deal of information about his past, work towards the dramatic surprise of his promotion and—for the reader at least—are not merely a preface to his test but an essential part of the larger ordeal of his growth into adulthood.

It would be impossible, and I hope unnecessary, to analyze in detail the varying rhythms and tones which give some of Conrad's finest dialogue-pieces their overall unity and coherence. His fully achieved successes in dramatic construction would surely include: (i) the conversation between the young captain and Archbold in "The Secret Sharer" (*'Twixt Land and Sea—Tales*, pp. 115-23) in which the captain's uncertain moral balance is reflected in the nervous comedy brought about by his pretence of deafness; (ii) the long dialogue between Razumov and Sonia Antonovna in *Under Western Eyes* (pp. 237-82) where tension gathers as Razumov uses the trivia of conversation to play with his listener, torment himself and covertly "confess" his crime; and (iii) the exchange between Verloc and Vladimir in *The Secret Agent* where a series of comic shocks and surprises culminate in Vladimir's suave exit-speech: "Think over my philosophy Mr.—Mr.— Verloc . . . Go for the first meridian" (p. 37).

Episodes like these succeed not simply by virtue of what they are in themselves but what they do in an entire novel. They mark off a significant psychological phase, foreshorten the presentation of character and memorably concentrate both past and future developments. For example, the figure who disappears for a long period in Conrad's novels always has to be listened to carefully. In Marlow's conversation with Jim in Patusan or the teacher's first meeting with Razumov in *Under Western Eyes* Conrad indirectly reflects a period of time which has not been shown. In both episodes character development is concentrated and summarized in dialogue offering an implied contrast between past and present. Hence Razumov's agitated, yet weary confrontation with the teacher is a revealing miniature of the mental agony he has suffered since meeting Mikulin, his words and manner stamped by an earlier nightmare now leading to crisis-point. Dialogue, in other words, has an important retrospective function which it often fulfils with an element of surprise. Shocks certainly lie in store for the reader of *Victory*. After being introduced to the polite Heyst at the beginning of the novel, we do not see much of him until after his flight with Lena, when Davidson visits Heyst's island. This meeting, conveyed through the astonished Davidson, presents us with the dramatic surprise of a seemingly transformed Heyst:

"I suppose I have done a certain amount of harm, since I allowed myself to be tempted into action. It seemed innocent enough, but all action is bound to be harmful. It is devilish. That is why this world is evil upon the whole. But I have done with it! I shall never lift a little finger again." (p. 54)

Heyst has not "gone mad" as Davidson believes, but he is a victim of events beyond his conscious control. In engaging our interest by way of surprise, Conrad directs attention back to previous circumstances in the light of which such an outburst is credible. Like Hamlet's first soliloquy, Heyst's words suggest a crisis firmly rooted in both the near and distant past.

Elsewhere the extended dialogue is dominantly forward-looking, sometimes a way of tentatively and ironically mapping out an uncertain future. Actions speak louder than words, and for Conrad spoken words invariably imply a future waiting to test the strength of professed intentions and uncertain stammers; loose ends of dialogue, indeterminate hesitations and evasions—these help Conrad to throw our attention forward and give conversations an open-ended flavour. Razumov is asked "Where to?" (*Under Western Eyes*, p. 99), a question ominously hanging over many similar crisis-situations. It is implied in the episode when Heyst makes himself responsible for Lena: "He felt that he had engaged himself by a rash promise to an action big with incalculable consequences" (*Victory*, p. 83): later irony and pathos combine in the fact that Heyst can detachedly speak of a test of character which in practice he will be utterly unable to meet: "I don't know myself what I would do, what countenance I would have before a creature which would strike me as being the evil incarnate" (p. 207). Dialogues like these leave us with a sense of unresolved issues which may later have to be confronted. Such is always the case in the infrequent talks between

Charles and Emilia Gould in *Nostromo*. Because they are so infrequent, their talks have to be made to intensify the sense of a developing estrangement. We usually meet them at crucial points when Mrs. Gould, who is sensitively aware of the need for continuity in life, wants her husband to face the future implications of his actions: "Ah, if one only knew how far you mean to go," she murmurs at one point (p. 208). As in the case of Heyst, one feels that Gould is already being tested by the uncertain future dimly foreseen by his wife. The fact that issues are raised by her but not resolved, and not likely to be resolved, points to their later estrangement which words are powerless to remedy.

Main crises and climaxes in Conrad's fiction always coincide with intensity of unspoken feeling and emotion. Latent or repressed tensions reach a point of unbearable intolerance where they can no longer co-exist; some form of confrontation or confession usually follows, though it often has the air of a nightmare in which words are painfully wrung from a victim. The final testimony of a Conradian character testifies to unspeakable anguish and pain by being a mixture of silence and stammered release. The voice we hear is often that "of an unlucky sleeper, lying passive in the grip of a merciless nightmare" (*Nostromo*, p. 522). Quietly, sympathetically and reticently, Conrad allows inarticulate suffering to speak in its own way and invents no elaborate shorthand for the cry of pain. Much of this is perhaps self-evident. What is often unnoticed is his care in making the form of dialogue at such points an appropriate vehicle for agitated feeling. Each climax makes its own demands. Some exploit virtually unbroken silence as in *Lord Jim* where Jim's response is a characteristic one—he stands "thinking and switching his leg" (p. 387); some are made up of nervous whispers as in "The Secret Sharer" or the lighter-journey in *Nostromo*. In each case the choices seem to be made so that the climax acts as an appropriate coda for the story as a whole. Verloc's confession to Winnie in *The Secret Agent* seems wholly apt in a novel where people habitually talk for their own benefit rather than to others; the dilemma of the isolated man at the mercy of an impersonal world is mirrored in what language has become—"waves of air of the proper length, propagated in accordance with correct mathematical formulas" (p. 260). When confronted by Nathalia Haldin, Razumov finds his words to be obnoxious and poisoned, part of a morally tainted world in which he speaks "with visible repugnance, as if speech were something disgusting or deadly" (*Under Western Eyes*, p. 346). Most moving of all perhaps is the description of Almayer's words when he confronts Nina and Dain: he speaks in a "monotonous whisper like an instrument of which all the strings but one are broken in a last ringing clamour under a heavy blow" (*Almayer's Folly*, p. 193).

The speech of his character presented Conrad with one of the many difficult challenges he habitually liked to succeed in. He admits to a "customary impenitence" as far as his mistakes are concerned, on the grounds that it is better to try and fail than shirk altogether the task of rendering "a crucial point of feelings in terms of human speech."[15] The present paper has emphasized, I hope, that the challenge was taken up repeatedly and with some impressive successes. As Conrad realized, the task of dramatizing speech cannot be shirked if the writer wants to get at the whole truth about people, a truth best served by dialogue which suggestively insinuates, without giving away its meaning. The subtlety of his best dialogue is not one that degenerates into fussiness or needless obscurity. Yet it is capable of capturing psychological niceties and attends sensitively to the pauses, fragments and silences in conversation. His characters are differentiated by their speech but never fully revealed by what they say. Speaking to other people, they are often merely engaged in self-colloquy; or finding relief in words, they are heard by others and become unexpectedly but profoundly engaged in relationships. Like his own Marlow, Conrad strains for clues in spoken language but sometimes with a faltering belief that they can ever be very revealing. When, for example, Marlow asks Jim why he "cleared out" of the *Patna* and Jim replies, "Jumped . . . Jumped—mind!" (*Lord Jim*, p. 131), we become aware of ourselves as rescue-workers in pursuit of the unnameable. Jim's words may throw a sharp light on unknowable feelings, but they can never fully grasp their meaning. Spoken words, Conrad implies, are the novelist's most precious possession; yet in the end they are only small patches of piercing light momentarily rescued from the surrounding darkness.

---

[15] Author's Note, *Within the Tides*, pp. viii, ix.

"ITS PROPER TITLE": SOME OBSERVATIONS ON
"THE NIGGER OF THE 'NARCISSUS' "

In a devastating and hilarious attack upon the "symbolism racket in schools," Vladimir Nabokov tells us, with self-satisfaction, "The notion of symbol itself has always been abhorrent to me, and I never tire of retelling how I once failed a student—the dupe, alas, of an earlier teacher—for writing that Jane Austen describes leaves as 'green' because Fanny is hopeful, and 'green' is the color of hope."[1] Such a preoccupation with the figurative and a twisting of the obvious, against all sense, to fit a preconception of course won't do. But the example *is* extreme. Like Nabokov in his stand against excess, Ian Watt thinks there has been in Conrad studies something too much of delving for and forcing of symbolic significance. Watt has discussed this abuse at length, with reference to *The Nigger of the "Narcissus."*[2] He is quite right but, for all that, a metaphoric dimension of this novel cannot fairly be denied, no matter how much "symbol-juggling" has gone on— as Watt acknowledges.

So much has been said already about the figurative language of *The Nigger of the "Narcissus,"* that, in truth, for me to say anything more on the subject is perhaps superfluous. Nonetheless, I wish to do so, yet only briefly and addressing myself to implications conventional and seemingly obvious—although, so far as I can tell. the implications have been overlooked except for a mere glance or so in passing. In short, I offer a note to the vexed question of metaphor as it applies to more-or-less subtle intimations respecting James Wait and the "Narcissus."

To begin with, the literal narrative of *The Nigger of the "Narcissus"* amounts to less than a compelling story. Such plot-line as it has is commonplace: manned by the familiar miscellaneous crew, the ship voyages from one port to another, experiencing interruptions of routine by reasons of personal idiosyncrasy the standard unexampled storm, the near-foundering of the ship, virtual mutiny, a Coleridgean becalming, and death—all highly usual in sea fiction and become Hollywood stock-in-trade. Conrad recognized the ordinariness of all this and, during composition, defended it to Edward Garnett (29 November 1896), "As

---

[1] "Rowe's Symbols," *New York Review of Books,* 7 October 1971, 8.
[2] "Conrad Criticism and *The Nigger of the 'Narcissus' "* in *Twentieth Century Interpretations of The Nigger of the "Narcissus,"* ed. John A. Palmer (Englewood Cliffs: Prentice-Hall, 1969), 78-99.

to lack of incident well—it's life."[3] Following publication, Conrad asserted to Cunninghame Graham (6 December 1897), "There are twenty years of life, six months of scribbling in that book," but, he conceded, "not a shadow of a story." And he quoted the reviewer for the *Daily Mail,* "The tale is no tale at all."[4]

This "no tale" is of great impact, however, and is the "first masterpiece" of the forty-year-old Conrad. The reason may be sought in features of Conrad's style, which though rhetorical, even ornate, is admirable. Plainly, the realistic depiction of the storm which overturns the "Narcissus" is unexcelled—with the possible exception of that in *Typhoon*—but the figurative aspects of *The Nigger of the "Narcisus"* seem even more important. If Conrad aimed at a faithfully realistic narrative of men aboard a sailing ship, then he faced nearly half-a-year's round of uneventful days, the "lack of incident" which is "life." Naturally, he varies routine with unusual or intensified occurrences: the customary gale off the Cape of Good Hope is so heightened that the heavy weather all but destroys the "Narcissus" and the common disgruntlement and grousing of the seamen is aggravated into the mutinous. An effective way to treat monotony without being monotonous is to undergird the literal narrative with figurative narrative that extends life aboard ship to life universal.

Conrad objected throughout his writing life to being called a writer of sea stories and insisted that he wrote about men, not about seamen. This attitude has a particular force as regards "my Beloved Nigger," for within four months of his death (3 August 1924) Conrad protested to Henry Seidel Canby (7 April 1924): "surely those stories of mine where the sea enters can be looked at from another angle. In the Nigger I give the psychology of a group of men and render certain aspects of nature. But the problem that faces them is not a problem of the sea, it is merely a problem that has arisen on board a ship . . ."[5]

Roughly seventeen years after publication of *The Nigger of the "Narcissus,"* Conrad told his readers in America, "It is the book which . . . as an artist, striving for the utmost sincerity of expression, I am willing to stand or fall."[6] Four years later still, he wrote, "a work of art is very seldom limited to one exclusive meaning and not necessarily

---

[3] *Letters from Joseph Conrad, 1895-1924,* ed. Edward Garnett (Indianapolis: Charter Books, 1962), 79-80.

[4] Quoted by G. Jean-Aubry, *Joseph Conrad: Life and Letters,* 2vols. (Garden City: Doubleday, 1927), I, 212.

[5] Jean-Aubry, II, 342. See also John E. Saveson, "Contemporary Psychology in 'The Nigger of the Narcissus,' " *Studies in Short Fiction,* 7 (Spring 1970), 219-31.

[6] "To My Readers in America" in *The Nigger of the "Narcissus,"* Harper's Modern Classics (New York: Harper, 1951), xxxv.

tending to a definite conclusion. And this for the reason that the nearer it approaches art, the more it acquires a symbolic character."[7]

Nowadays, one observes some predilection for pooh-poohing figurative readings of literary works, and all are chary of the "intentional fallacy." Conrad, however, made quite plain his concern with the metaphoric and we should not ignore it. Certainly, misinterpreation of the metaphoric structures of a highly figurative work is an everpresent danger for the critic. But discussion of conventional metaphors is warranted and useful, even in the face of authorial denial, like that of Ernest Hemingway regarding the conclusion of *The Old Man and the Sea.* He could deny Christian reference as vehemently as he would, but the fact remains that in the Western world cultivated readers understandably will see such references in a novel about defeat in the flesh and victory in the spirit if a fisherman climbing a hill falls under the weight of the mast he carries and has difficulty arising and if he sleeps in an attitude of crucifixion, "with his arms outstretched and the palms of his hands up." Those palms are torn and bloodied by the fishing line—almost as if the nails had been driven through them. Hemingway could say what he pleased, but as an artist, he knew the Western tradition and if he didn't want readers to understand Christian reference, he should not have been so explicit. Nor should Conrad have had the storm wind pin Mr. Creighton's watch to the shrouds "in attitudes of crucifixion" (56), especially aboard a vessel with three masts to recall the three crosses of Golgotha. If Conrad wished to stand or fall "as an artist" by *The Nigger of the "Narcissus"* and if, in his view, for a book to come near art requires that it have "a symbolic character," to argue a figurative significance for this work appears justified.

To reiterate, then, I wish to make a case for given metaphoric implications of the title *The Nigger of the "Narcissus,"* assuming that a title specifies the subject of what follows it. In a work having both literal and figurative narratives, the title may be expected to have both literal and figurative significance—which is the case here. First, the vulgarism "nigger" derives ultimately from the Latin adjective and substantive *niger,* of such meanings as "night," "black," "pertaining to death," "ill-omened," "wicked," "causing blackness," and the like. This "nigger" is set in opposition to "narcissus," a white (or pale yellow) flower, with significations the reverse of those of *niger.* Upon this rests the base for the much-cited antagonisms black/white, land/sea, dark/light, death/life, wicked/virtuous, evil/good, so much a part of Conrad's imagery.

The implications of these antitheses must be extended, because James

---

[7] Letter to Barret H. Clark (4 May 1918) in Jean-Aubry, II, 205.

Wait "belong[s] to the ship"; he is, after all / the Nigger of the "Narcissus." Not only is Wait "black" literally—from his skin color—but also "white" (like the narcissus) figuratively—from his name. Conrad frequently made use of real-life acquaintances as sources for fictional characters; one of two men who were partial models for James Wait was a shipmate of Conrad's on the "Duke of Sutherland" in 1878-79, a Barbados Negro named George White. Richard Curle says that the eighteen seamen of this ship included "a St. Kitts negro called James Wait—a name used just twenty years later for the negro in *The Nigger of the 'Narcissus'*."[8] Curle seems mistaken about the actual name, for Conrad in the "Duke of Sutherland" days knew English primarily by sound and, forty years later, he recalled the name as pronounced.

To a Belgian, Joseph de Smet, Conrad wrote (23 January 1911) of his English speech, "My first English reading was the *Standard* newspaper, and my first acquaintance by the ear with it was in the speech of fishermen, shipwrights and sailors of the East Coast. . . . I've never opened an English grammar in my life. My pronunciation is rather defective to this day. Having unluckily no ear, my accentuation is uncertain. . . . "[9] The maritime individuals from whom Conrad learned oral English were, probably to a man, illiterate speakers of a corrupted tongue marked with cockney dialect and accentuation. The obligatory elementary education for all children required by the Education Act of 1870—however slight its efficacy may have been—was too recent an innovation to have affected seamen, or cabin boys, when in 1878 Conrad began to sail on British coasting schooners and seriously to learn the vocalized language. Of Conrad's defective pronunciation, H. G. Wells recorded, "He spoke English strangely. Not badly altogether . . . but with certain oddities. He had learnt to read English long before he spoke it and he had formed wrong sound impressions of many familiar words. . . . He would say, '*Wat* "wot" for "hwot" shall we do with *thesa* things?' "[10]

The second real-life source for James Wait was another Negro seaman, Joseph Barron, who was aboard the actual "Narcissus" with Conrad in 1884 and died at sea. Apparently, he was born in Charlton County, Georgia, although his place of birth could have been Charleston,

---

[8] *Joseph Conrad: A Study* (New York: Russell & Russell, 1968), 17.
[9] Jean-Aubry, II, 124-25.
[10] *Experiment in Autobiography* (New York: Macmillan, 1934), 525. Wells' statement that Conrad read English "long before he spoke it" appears to be erroneous. Conrad arrived in England at Lowestoft on 18 June 1878 aboard the steamer "Mavis." At that time he had a very limited knowledge of English; he increased it considerably during his subsequent ten weeks of coasting service.
He could barely write English, however. How quickly he advanced in his ability

South Carolina, because the illiterate former slave would have called that city "Charlton". Tidewater speech as spoken in Charleston and as far south as Jacksonville, Florida, having an essential similarity. In any event, Barron probably had a pronunciation in some respects like that of George White, who pronounced his surname "wĭt," not "wāt," as might be supposed from Conrad's orthography.[11] Like Conrad, they both easily could have the phonetic difficulty with "wh" (or "hw") words, in which the loss of the "h" sound produces such pronunciations as "wĕl" for "hwĕl"; "wâr" for "hwâr"; "wīl" for "hwīl"; "wī" for "hwī"; "wŏt" for "hwŏt"; and other such articulations, including "wĭt" for "hwĭt",

This probability increases with the consideration that White was from British Barbados[12] and Barron, whether from Charlton County or Charleston, was from a locality peopled by substantial numbers of Cockneys, a group important in early settlement of Georgia, and the Irish, who have certain linguistic similarities with Cockneys. Another characteristic of Cockney speech is the vowel shift from the "ā" diphthong to the "ī" diphthong, which gives pairs like "păn/pīn", "rālwā trăn/rīlwī trīn", and the famous words of Eliza Doolittle, "The rīn in Spīn stīs mīnly in the plīn", pronunciations which Conrad unquestionably would have been aware of. These speech sounds are regularly heard in Australia ("ŏ strīl'yah) — where Conrad went for the first time as a crewman of the "Duke of Sutherland" — and in Cockney and other British articulations.

Coincidentally or otherwise, Conrad gets double value from his spelling "White" as in the Cockney utterance, "Wait," because for

---

to read and write is difficult to say; of some pertinence may be Conrad's observation about his beginning *Almayer's Folly* in the fall of 1889: "I cannot say what I read on the evening before I began to write myself. I believe it was a novel, and it is quite possible that it was one of Anthony Trollope's novels. It is very likely. My acquaintance with him was then very recent. He is one of the English novelists whose works I read for the first time in English." *A Personal Record*, Kent Ed. (Garden City: Doubleday, 1926), 71.

[11] See Jerry Allen, *The Sea Years of Joseph Conrad* (Garden City: Doubleday, 1965), 101, 165. Conrad had various orthographic problems, particularly with the rendering of Donkin's Cockney speech. Indeed, Donkin's name is Conrad's spelling of a Cockney pronunciation of the actual "Narcissus." Allen, of Duncan, the captain 166.

In Devon, the common surname "White" was spelled "Wayte" and was derived from Old French for "look-out, place to watch from." In the Norman dialect of Old French "Wait(e) was 'watchman.'" See Basil Cottle, *The Penguin Dictionary of Surnames* (Baltimore: Penguin, 1967), 313, 300.

[12] Conrad's making James Wait a native of St. Christopher would not affect his pronunciation, as it was a British possession from 1713. Perhaps the change was to avoid direct identification with George White. Incidentally, St. Christopher is patron saint of travelers and protects against floods.

those readers who take the Nigger's name to be "wāt" a different set of relevant implications arises.[13] This group is accessible also to those who see the phonetic spelling, for "White" and "Wait" are spoken alike, "wīt". Among the applications of "wāt" are:

1. The "Narcissus" waits (delays) for him. His first word is "wīt", but he is giving his name, the last name on the roster, the smudge Mr. Baker can't make out, not asking for delay.

2. As a crewman, he "doesn't pull his own weight" (malingers).

3. Aboard ship, he is a dead weight (a burden). Note that when his body goes over the side, "The ship rolled as if relieved of an unfair burden . . ." (160).

4. The man wait on (serve) him.

5. The men wait for (anticipate) his death.

6. The men wait out (endure) the suspense when his body does not slide off the planks.[14]

To oppose the black "Niger" and the white "Narcissus" in the title is to suggest the customary dichotomy between evil and good and points us toward the widely-recognized Satanic reference of the Miltonically-described James Wait.[15] He is the Black Man, a traditional designation for the Evil One, the chief of devils. Further, the color black symbolizes error, evil, falsehood (the expression "to swear that black is white" alludes to persistence in obvious untruth, as in Wait's craven bluster that he is not grievously ill), and black as a mortuary color represents death. Beyond this, Castor and Pollux were the patron deities of seamen, and the Gemini symbol (of the opposed worlds of positive and negative) is represented by white and black. Black also represents earth, and in *The Nigger of the "Narcissus"* Conrad consistently associates the land with darkness, evil, and death.[16]

Conrad goes further than this simple antithesis of white and black as good and evil; he names the black man "White" and adroitly insinuates the ambiguity of evil and its coexistence with good.[17] The hint of ambiguity is repeated in Wait's evil fellow, Donkin, clad in

[13] Frederick R. Karl, for instance, says, in *A Reader's Guide to Joseph Conrad*, rev. ed. (New York: Farrar, 1969), 113, that Wait's name, "signifying a do-nothing, becomes literally a definition of what he is."

[14] Remembering "tarry thou," I am tempted to suggest an analogy to the Wandering Jew, because Wait has died a spiritual death but waits (lingers) for a physical death.

[15] Interestingly, James means "the supplanter," and Wait, in a sense, attempts to supplant Captain Allistoun, whose name means "temple stone," a rebellious action not unlike the secession of Milton's Satan from God's authority.

[16] In J. E. Cirlot, *A Dictionary of Symbols*, trans. Jack Sage (New York: Philosophical Library, 1962), 54, 51, an apposite coincidence occurs, for Cirlot lists black among "cold, 'retreating' colours, corresponding to processes of dissimilation, passivity and debilitation" (50), and Wait is black, he does create difference between officers

his black coat and described as having white eyelashes (9). Donkin is said also to have a "sallow face" (33), and Wait compares him to "a dirty white cockatoo" (110). The terms "sallow" and "dirty white" may allude to the narcissus flower, which occurs pale yellow as well as white. Conrad takes pains further to have Wait's black body wrapped in a white blanket before it is sewn into canvas for "solemn surrender to the insatiable sea" (157). These examples not only instance the shifting, equivocal quality of evil, but also illustrate Conrad's ability to use the same color symbol in contradictory ways; that is, to imply the mingling of evil and good by reversing the conventional color symbolism, as Melville did in making Moby Dick a white whale.[18] The black/white duality is likewise emphasized in the crew's ambivalent attitude toward Wait, "the object of our exasperated solicitude" (68), whom the men desire to beat "viciously" but handle "tenderly" (73).[19]

Another set of polarities lies between the "Nigger" and the "Narcissus" of the title, the first being the psychological reference to the eponymous narcissism of the beautiful youth of Greek myth who pined away and died for love of his own reflection in a pool of water. Narcissus has become a symbol of the "self-contemplative, introverted, and self-sufficient attitude,"[20] for whom the ship, "alive with the lives of those beings who trod her decks" (29), is most appropriately, because most egocentrically, named. The "Narcissus" functions as a microcosm and, in its imaging capacity, suggests self-love; aptly like the Greek youth and the flower into which he was metamorphosed, the ship is a "reflection" symbol. The crew adores James Wait as Narcissus adored his reflection, and in both cases the object is spurious, not genuine. The ambivalent love/hate attraction to and revulsion from Wait of the crew reflects their own self-contempt and self-admiration: "We were inexpressibly vile and very much pleased with ourselves" (139). They look at the narcissistic Wait and, unavoidably because egotistically, see themselves. "Wait is at once a symbol of the psychological danger inherent in extreme subjectivity and also the realistic object that furthers that subjectivity."[21] They realize that he will die and they are sorry

and men, and he is both passive and debilitated. This of course does not imply such knowledge on Conrad's part, though he doubtless knew about the Gemini.

[17] Compare Thomas Moser's view that "In *The Nigger of the 'Narcissus,'* whiteness has only good connotations...." *Joseph Conrad: Achievement and Decline* (Cambridge, Mass.: Harvard Univ. Press, 1957), 125.

[18] Another comparable paradox is Conrad's use of the name of Captain Duncan, who is a symbol of order, for Donkin, who is a symbol of disorder.

[19] My thanks to Professor Harry T. Moore, of Southern Illinois University, for citing Kipling's analogous reversal in "Gunga Din" (1890):

An' for all 'is dirty 'ide
'E was white, clear white, inside.

[20] Cirlot, 216. See also Donald T. Torchiana, "The Nigger of the Narcissus: Myth, Mirror, and Metropolis," *Wascana Review,* 2:2 (1967), 29-41.

for him, but his unreality (a mirror of their own, which they reject) provokes their resentment: "His obstinate non-recognition of the only certitude whose approach we could watch from day to day was as disquieting as the failure of some law of nature" (138-39). Wait reminds them that they all are human and must die as he must; so, they hate him for forcing them to see that what they dread must and will be. Hence, they symbolically save themselves, if they can save him; at the last, however, they must bury James Wait, as in their turns each of them will be buried.[22]

One additional reason for preferring, as Conrad did, that this book be issued under "its proper title," *The Nigger of the "Narcissus,"*[23] is, as Vernon Young tells us, to take advantage "of the British association of narcissus with death."[24] I hasten to note that both "Narcissus" and "Nigger" are to be associated with death: the narcissus with the fact and the "Nigger" with the fear of that fact. I make the elementary but fundamental points that the flower narcissus relates to death; Singleton says that Wait will die at the first sighting of land; the land sighted is the most westerly island of the Azores chain,[25] Flores (English, flowers); the last earthly sign of Greek Narcissus is the flower named for him; and at the sight of "flowers" Wait dies.

Wait is dead, but the fear of death, which he incarnated, is not dead. At the committing of his body to the deep, "In death and swathed up for all eternity, he yet seemed to cling to the ship with the grip of an undying fear" (159), which is also the individual and collective fear of his shipmates: "A common bond [the refusal to believe that Wait would die] was gone; the strong effective and respectible bond of a sentimental lie" (155). What Wait is each man of the crew is, and egotism causes each man to love him, but as Wait is a *memento mori,* each hates him. Something like this must be the implication of Conrad's calling Wait "the centre of the ship's collective psychology and the pivot of the action" (XXXV). And everything said here may be seen as implications of that superbly metaphoric title *The Nigger of the "Narcissus."*

---

[21] Saveson, 224. Lionel Stevenson in *The English Novel: A Panorama* (Boston: Houghton, 1960), 433, terms *The Nigger of the "Narcissus"* a "sort of allegory of death." A metaphoric work, allegory or not, the novel universalizes; hence, one appropriately may retad Wait ("wit"), as "wight" or "human being."

[22] Donkin, watching Wait die, feels "the anguishing grasp of a great sorrow on his heart at the thought that he himself, some day, would have to go through it all —just like this—perhaps!" (153-54).

[23] The American edition had been issued as *The Children of the Sea.*

[24] "Trial by Water: Joseph Conrad's *The Nigger of the 'Narcissus' "* in Palmer, 28.

[25] Another example of the twice-useful detail, "most westerly" Flores is sound both realistically (for it is situated precisely in the regular trade route for the sailing ships of that day) and figuratively (because of the conventional association of the west with sunset and death).

JULIET MCLAUCHLAN

CONRAD'S "THREE AGES OF MAN":
THE "YOUTH" VOLUME

Most criticism of the *Youth* volume has erred by concentrating too narrowly upon its three stories as quite separate entities. Each can and should be seen as primarily a self-contained artistic unit — in that each would be of great interest and value even if the other two did not exist— but reader and critic can come to appreciate the stories much more fully by looking at each as presenting one of the three ages of man which the volume shows in turn.

The present paper, which will ultimately serve to introduce my book, is intended to indicate more *generally* the major, and recurring concerns of the volume as a whole. Originally, Conrad had firmly intended that *Lord Jim*, then envisaged as simply "a sketch", should stand third in the volume. Indeed "Youth" and "Heart of Darkness" had been written end even "set in book from in anticipation" of the Jim story which would complete the "Three Tales of Land and Sea"[1], when Conrad began to worry about "Jim's length" and wrote to Meldrum: "It would be to my interest to cut it short as possible, but I would just as soon think of cutting off my head".[2] Some seven months later, when *Lord Jim* had grown to novel length, and Blackwood and Sons had written to suggest the advisability of publishing it as a separate volume, Conrad was at first much disturbed by the proposal. *"Jim,"* he wrote to Meldrum,

has not been planned to stand alone. *H of D* was meant in my mind as a foil, and *Youth* was supposed to give the note. All this is foolishness, no doubt. The public does not care — can not possibly care — for foils and notes.[3]

Only a few days later, however, he had accepted the change, and wrote, again to Meldrum:

The book would have been ill-balanced, and I think I've got good matter ("First Command" especially) for the volume of the *Tales*. It will turn out to be a record of personal experience purely. Just as well — maybe![4]

Page references (in parentheses) are to the Dent Collected Edition, London, 1946
[1] Joseph Conrad, letters to William Blackwood and David S. Meldrum, Edited by William Blackburn, Durham, North Carolina, 1958, p. 74 (note).
[2] *Ibid.*, p. 71.
[3] *Ibid.*, p. 94.
[4] *Ibid.*, p. 97.

But it was to turn out otherwise. Some months earlier he had thought of:

two other stories (more in the 'note' of my 'Maga' work) one of them being called *First Command* and the other a sketch entitled *A Seaman*. These are not written. They creep about in my head but [have] got to be caught and tortured into some kind of shape. I think — I think they would turn out good as good as (they say) *Youth* is.[5]

He had also mentioned to Meldrum his idea of giving "Mr. B'wood the sketch of the old Captain Loutit" and another story "after Jim is finished".[6]

It may be inferred that *First Command* was Conrad's original title for what became much later "The Shadow Line", and that Loutit and the "seaman" were the originals behind Captain Whalley. Although we know nothing of the processes of thought and imagination which lay behind Conrad's eventual abandonment of the *First Command* story, we can see that as he wrote the story which was finally to stand third in the *Youth* volume he began to see more clearly what he wanted it to be. He called it:

Characteristic matter suitable for Binding together with what was already written — and essentially auobiographical. That is, more in the note of *Youth* than in that of *H of D*.[7]

If that is not wholly consistent and clear, he becomes much clearer when he explains that "Falk" (which he wrote before finishing the *Youth* volume):

is good . . . In its way it is superior to *Karain*. On the other hand, it is not a thing intimately felt, like Youth or H of D, not to be used in the same volume. I plan another sort of stuff for its completion.[8]

He later assured William Blackwood: "I know exactly what I am doing . . . the writing is as good as I can make it".[9]

Now it is true that Conrad states unequivocally in the Author's Note to the volume (p. v):

The three stories in this volume lay no claim to unity of artistic purpose. The only bond between them is that of the time in which they were written.

But this seems to be an instance of Conrad's frequent unreliability as a commentator upon his own work, and one where he must be called in evidence against himself. The letters to Blackwood and Meldrum, which are contemporary with the actual writing of "The End of the

---

[5] *Ibid.*, p. 54.
[6] *Ibid.*, p. 63.
[7] *Ibid.*, p. 135.
[8] *Ibid.*, p. 140.
[9] *Ibid.*, p. 154.

Tether" carry great weight in themselves (showing, as they do, that a clear artistic purpose developed as Conrad wrote) and they are reinforced by a letter which he wrote to F. N. Doubleday about six months before he died:

> . . . take the volume of *Youth,* which in its component parts presents the three ages of man (for that is what it really is), and I knew very well what I was doing when I wrote "The End of the Tether" to be the last of that trio.[10]

The volume, then is a "trio", and not simply three independent tales.

Obviously, however, it would be a mistake to look at the stories as if actual character or plot were closely linked. Even though "Heart of Darkness" seems to share its narrator with "Youth", it is in no sense a sequel. Indeed the gravest difficulties would arise for any reader or critic who set himself the task of equating the Marlow of "Youth" with the Marlow of "Heart of Darkness". The narrator in "Youth" gives no indication whatever of having experienced anything like the shattering revelations which have come to the narrator of the second story. Even on the purely physical level he can hardly be imagined as resembling the sallow, sunken-eyed, Buddha-figure of "Heart of Darkness". Lack of any consistency between the two narrators is far from being a fault. Within each story, the responses of "Marlow" to the experiences undergone are totally consistent with Conrad's artistic purpose, and this is what matters. He is not the same person in the two stories, and he is not, in any case, meant to be the unifying link, for that link is broken with "The End of the Tether". Such unity as there is is, rather, thematic, and this gives the three stories their great collective distinction. Conceived in terms of the "definite images" with which Conrad reminded Cunninghame Graham that he always began,[11] each shows aspects of Conrad's art at its very highest — so much so that all three, not just "Heart of Darkness", rank among Conrad's most profound and disturbing work.

A key to all that is to be found in the *Youth* volume is contained in Richard Curle's words about the significance of the epigraph:

> Allowing for his devotion to artistic integrity, it was human beings who fascinated him — did he not give as the motto of Youth these words from

---

[10] G. J. Jean-Aubry, *Joseph Conrad, Life and Letters,* London, Heinemann, 1927, p. 338.

[11] The phrase occurs in the first paragraph of a letter dated 8th February 1899, in which Conrad expresses delight that his friend likes what he has so far received (the first part) of "Heart of Darkness": " . . . you must remember that I don't start with an abstract notion. I start with definite images and as their rendering is true some little effect is produced". C. T. Watts, *Joseph Conrad's Letters to Cunninghame Graham,* Cambridge 1969, p. 116.

Grimm's Fairy Tales "But the dwarf answered: 'No, something human is dearer to me than all the wealth of the world' " — and almost every word he wrote about any of his characterers had a bearing upon its interpretation and development.[12]

Curle's extremely perceptive comment can indeed fittingly be applied to most of Conrad's work. Does he not in all his greatest fiction show how much dearer he himself held the "something human" (in astonishing variety) than any sort of material wealth? That magnificent novel, *Nostromo,* adds up to a great oblique statement about true wealth, which is clearly shown to be the twofold treasure of integrity and love, set against the delusive "treasure", not only of the silver but of the variety of corrupting "material interests" by which men are possessed in the novel. In Conrad, material wealth is never of any real importance; problems of fortune are never central. In this volume, Whalley suffers from lack of money, not because he cares for wealth but because without it he cannot provide for his daughter. Even more significantly, any serious concern with material gain is always the target for Conrad's most savage fictional presentation: notably the Company officials and emissaries in "Heart of Darkness", and Massy (the worst of them all) in "The End of the Tether". Considering the three stories, one can discern interesting differences in theme: although they are united in their deep concern with phases of human life, the essential preoccupation of youth, middle age, and old age are clearly differentiated.

Each story involves a voyage, and each voyage provides a fine metaphor for the story's deepest meaning — for the meaning of each is complex and profound. Marlow, in "Youth", makes his first voyage as an officer, and the voyage and story end for him with his successful arrival with his "first command". The bright illusory view of "the East" which he records, embodies the fact that all life seems still before him, beautiful, varied, new. The same voyage, for the old captain and old mate, has been so shattering that in all likelihood it will be their last, or their last in positions of authority. There is, throughout, the poignant juxtaposition of Captain Beard's ill-fated first command with Marlow's unexpected rise to his; from this springs the story's power. In "Heart of Darkness" an older Marlow sets off with curiosity, hope, and some enthusiasm on a quite different sort of voyage which, as a voyage, involves nothing like the physical test of courage and endurance called forth by the "Youth" voyage. But it is long, fraught with tedious navigational problems, and demanding great vigilance, besides some hard jobs of repair and maintenance. Devotion to these demanding tasks in hand provides an important element in Marlow's restraint

---

[12] Richard Curle, *Joseph Conrad and His Characters,* London, 1957, p. 13.

vis à vis any pull he feels from the wilderness. The protracted nature of the voyage is stressed in order to suggest the depths, strangeness, and darkness of the discoveries which must be made in the course of it, and which account for the full significance of voyage and tale. The voyage is necessarily a two-way one. At the end of the up-stream trip, Marlow must invade the wilderness itself and through his close involvement with Kurtz (whose vestigial humanity it is his mission to save), but even more through his final insight into the manager's total lack of humanity, he must look into the lowest depths of the human potential. The return voyage carries him back to "civilization", where he must contemplate the very highest aspirations of humanity through his encounter with the Intended. (Within this avowedly symbolic tale, the full implications of the word "intended", its deliberate ambiguities, must be given full weight). Saving this "soul", he saves what alone may one day save humanity from the otherwise triumphant darkness. In "The End of the Tether", Captain Whalley's voyage is pre-eminently a last voyage: it is totally unlike any of his other voyages, with no proper landfall, no arrival, no return. It is in every sense a voyage into darkness. The old man proceeds to the ultimate darkness of a violent death through ever-darkening stages: worsening physical blindness, a growing conviction of his own corruption, an increasing sense of his abandonment by God, to the final dark insight into unsuspected depths of evil in human nature. Humanity in old age is shown living a sort of prolonged dark night of the soul, with the darkness deepening to the very end of life's pilgrimage.

Each tale involves the presence of darkness, but in each the darkness has a different metaphorical significance. Although "Youth" must be seen very much as a tale of contrasts, of dark and light, and not merely as a bright memory, there is neither the embodied external evil of the manager or (much more aggressively) Massy; there is neither the total degradation of Kurtz nor the partial corruption of Whalley. Instead darkness enters the story as the inescapable darkness of age and death. Towards this dark reality of human existence the voyage carries the old men; indeed they *embody* the inevitable decline and failure of age, and much of the subtlety of the story lies in Marlow's youthful unawareness of this. Marlow sees and recalls details of the voyage vividly in middle life, but does *not* see how true it is that this is one of "those voyages that seem ordered for the illustration of life, that might stand for a symbol of existence" (4) Suggested powerfully, through some of Conrad's finest "definite images", age and failure shadow Marlow's bright voyage. Here, *visualized,* is the ultimate threat (however far in the future it may seem) to every youthful hope, every youthful achievement. The story's darkest irony is that the old men who voyage side by side with Marlow manifest in their courage and determination the spirit of youth, as much as does Marlow himself, but in the natural course of things their powers are failing; because of this they are inevitably "broken" by the ordeal which is the making of Marlow. Even more subtle in this supposedly simple tale is the way the young Marlow's virtual an-awareness of the reality of old age and failure is carried over into the forty-two-year-old Marlow's facile rhetorical comments on the sadness of the passing of time and loss of youth. These do not ring true and are not intended to do so. The different Marlow of "Heart of Darkness" is forced to awareness of darkness, a different darkness which is twofold: the darkness of deep human degradation (Kurtz) and the deeper darkness of inhumanity (epitomized in the manager). Although the manager is to some extent an embodiment of evil as a destructive external force (in so far as his activities of exploitation, and his coldly malevolent nature are destructive of others) the emphasis is on evil which comes from within. The focus here is on humanity in early maturity. Ages are not precisely stated, but like Marlow, Kurtz (whose Intended is no longer a girl) is past his first youth, as are most of the rest of the characters. Much is made of the dark menace of the wilderness, but in fact humanity is not *shown* to be seriously threatened by external forces, except by disease, since where there is sufficient inner human strength (as in Marlow, and to a different and lesser extent in the Harlequin) the wilderness has no power to "invade". When we come to "The End of the Tether" it is evident that the *Youth* volume shows in every sense the beginning, middle, and end of human experience. All the concerns of "Youth" and "Heart of Darkness" come together, though in changed form, in the third story. The shadow of age in "Youth" looks forward to the abysmal darkness of Whalley end in "The End of the Tether," for the threat of age, which for the young Marlow and even for his older self is basically unreal, is the central dark reality, the necessary condition of the tragedy. The relationship between internal and external evil is complex. The threat of inner corruption which is a central con-cern of "Heart of Darkness" is not absent here, but inner corruption is much less extreme and more excusable. Whalley's corruption seems to him a great darkness, but it is not shown to be inevitably self-destruc-tive, as are Kurtz's consuming passions; essential to the tragedy is the dark destructive power of Massy's greed and active malevolence.

The contrast between the "something human" and "wealth" is basic to the volume, despite the fact that in "Youth" wealth in the material sense comes into the story only in relation to Marlow's listeners, as I shall show below. The human values of "Youth" are quite other than money values. The exuberance of youth and the inevitable deterioration of age are two supremely important aspects of human experience; material wealth is simply irrelevant to the sort of juxtaposition which Conrad gives to them in this tale. There is no need to labour the details to show that the wealth of the world enters "Heart of Darkness" throughout. Love of wealth, imbecilic struggles for it, overriding desire for it — these are condemned (not directly but through "definite images") as the most inhuman and darkly evil aspects of human nature. Marlow's "choice of nightmares" is a real one. In "The End of the Tether", wealth, or the lack of it, is important, but not because Whalley loves wealth as such. Obviously during his wife's lifetime he has delighted in having his ship a comfortable and (to him) beautiful home. There has even been the luxury of having a piano on board, but the emphasis is on the pleasure and enjoyment which goes with possessions. It is, first, the love which prompted the gift, and, second, the joy which Mrs. Whalley's playing and singing give which are the values here. Whalley's enjoyment of "things" is always similarly associated with his characteristically zestful pleasure in life, whether it be his *Fair Maid,* with the seaman's independent life which it enables him to lead, or the minor pleasures of good cigars and wine, which paternal devotion causes him to forego most willingly when necessary. Set sharply against Whalley's capacity for enjoying life is Massy's ugly lust for wealth as such, as something which will confer upon him absolute idleness and a contemptuous power over others.

Certainly, the "something human" is the supreme value in all three stories, differing within the different contexts. In "Youth," there is Mrs. Beard's cheerful motherliness and simple devotion to "John", Marlow's boyish deference and attentiveness to the old people, his firm tact in persuading the old skipper finally to leave his ship, the solid good fellowship among the crew and officers, the mate's personal concern for his captain. It is all more implicit than explicit, but it is firmly there. And there are the genuine qualities of the young Marlow as a seaman. Most of all, Marlow, though superficially insensitive, yet does all that can possibly be done to help the old officers, and does it in the best and indeed only way possible. He would achieve less rather than more (and the story would sink into sentimentality) if he rushed about expressing sympathy and offering to do the old chaps' work for them; nothing could be more useful than the young Second Mate's quiet fidelity to duty, his unfailing service during the *Judea's* ordeal. This is a fine and subtle insight, especially since each story in the volume shows the *necessity* for the human to be actively humane, yet at the same time shows that there must always be serious limitations on the extent to which any human being can help another — no matter how great the need on one side, no matter how willing the help on the other.

In "Heart of Darkness" there is "something human" in the innate human dignity ("I wasn't decent") of the Harlequin, in the human restraint of the cannibals, in the boilermaker's sense of decency and sense of humor, in the "good Swede". But the human is primarily and consistently embodied in Marlow himself, in two main ways: in his own fully human responses to the wilderness; in his active humanity. The attraction of the wilderness for him lies simply in its spontaneity and a kind of wild natural beauty. He is most "appalled", even "horror-struck", when he sees its primitive people exploited, degraded, terrorized, suffering — more moved than he is by the horrors of his vision of human debasement in Kurtz. Significantly, Conrad causes him to describe its worst aspects of savagery and superstitious ritual in such a way as to make them seem more ludicrous and pitiful than attractive or horrifying. His manner of reporting the details of the natives' behavior at the departure of Kurtz shows such behavior as observed and recorded by a truly civilized human being. Conrad here is at his most subtle and impressive: the tone of Marlow's account shows how little of real fascination or power the wilderness can possess for a full human being; seen thus it is only a pathetic display of primitive superstition and futile defiance. A full human being has no wish to revert to a past stage in humanity's long development (Marlow never feels more than "remote kinship" with savagery). At Kurtz's departure, the horned figures, the garish painting of the witch-doctors, the pitifully tawdy accoutrements seem in the light of day to be only ridiculous.[18] In this same light of sanity. Kurtz's involvement with these "devils", his crawling back towards their rituals in the darkness (which we have recently watched) also becomes quite ludicrous, almost unimaginable. Two points thus become obvious: Kurtz's participation has been truly aberrational, a literal wandering away from the human; and his worst failure has been to leave these simple people in their benightedness, to encourage them to remain in it, to prevent their progress towards full humanity. What is strange about Kurtz's involvement is that although this sort of ceremonial does not represent the whole of the wilderness, it does seem to be the aspect (closely linked with the sort of godlike power it enables him to exert) which most strongly possesses Kurtz, rather than its more natural and beautiful qualities. It is also the aspect which leads Kurtz

---

[18] To my knowledge only one other critic has seen a similar point here. Przemysław Mroczkowski, *Conradian Commentaries*, Cracow, 1970, p. 41, writes: "With all this, the swaying negroes remain not a little childish and far beyond any full responsibility for their activities or their implications. They call mainly for pity".

so near to being "lost" entirely. Only Marlow's courageous, selfless humanity in invading the wilderness to save what can be saved prevents this. Here, even more than in "Youth", we are made aware of the limited extent to which one human being can help another. Marlow's achievement is not, however, inconsiderable. The humanity which survives in Kurtz is what makes it possible for him at least to look wthin himself and judge. Marlow makes possible Kurtz's "victory", limited as that may be. Marlow's own humanity is triumphant — strong enough to travel to and contemplate the depths of evil in human nature, to choose firmly between nightmares, to return, and finally to come to the contemplation of humanity's most elevated ideas, and to some understanding of the relevance of a "saving illusion" to humanity's future. Although "Heart of Dakness" does not end on an encouraging note, it still seems to show most vividly the necessity for mature humanity to look hard at the realities of human evil, but to recognize finally that to prevent the total riumph of darkness some "saving illusion" must be allowed to survive in the human heart.

In "The End of the Tether," where there is so much of the "something human" is very evident in Van Wyk and Whalley himself. Whalley's careful arrangement of his belongings in his cabin is revealing and touching; it springs nor from undue pride, but from delight in pleasant and homelike surroundings (a direct contrast again with Massy). Endearing, too, and poignant are the remembrance of his wife's part in making the *Condor* a real home, the happy recollections of family life, the remembrance of his little daughter's delight in the sea before her mother's untimely death, the stoical control of deep grief at his bereavement. The selfless, single-hearted devotion of his life to providing for Ivy is almost above the human, embodying something of an "august Benevolence" (in the "Heart of Darkness" phrase), something of the human pushed to the highest degree of self-sacrifice. In his final impossible dilemma, Whalley's "suicide" is a deliberate choice to make the sacrifice of his life for his daughter.

Throughout this story, it is only the warmth and humane treatment of Van Wyk which nourish the otherwise starved affections of Captain Whalley. The sombre tale's happiest moments are those when the reader can delight in seeing Whalley as he ought to be, expansive, at ease, very nearly content. Some of its darkest moments are those when he confides to Van Wyk the horror of his predicament and his sense of his own corruption. It is Van Wyk's "genuine capacity for sympathy" which leads him to an involvement in Whalley's plight, an involvement which is intensely personal, deeply felt. Yet, deeply human as is Van Wyk's response, it is shown to be ineffectual. He has for too long shunned human involvement; he has allowed his "warmth of feeling" to remain "latent" until stirred by Whalley; too late he is jarred into looking with new eyes at his own comfortable solitude. Realizing that "There were many sorts of heartaches and troubles, and there was no place where they could not find a man out . . . he felt ashamed". Now he *means* to "come out into the world" and do whatever is necessary for Whalley. With, again, fine and subtle insight, Conrad suggests the reasons for his failure to help his old friend, and it is within the context of the volume as a whole that the presentation is most striking. In "Youth", the young Marlow does all that can be done in response to human need, simply by his simple *active* devotion to duty. In "Heart of Darkness", Marlow does all that can be done for Kurtz by an *active* rescue operation. In "The End of the Tether", Van Wyk's bungalow may indeed be "a *point* of splendor" (my italics) in the surrounding darkness, but as the related imagery consistently suggests, his humanity does not radiate far enough from this "point". Kindly, affectionate, welcoming, he allows his genuine concern to remain for too long passive. Forced to look into the depths of Whalley's suffering, Van Wyk genuinely comes to see the need for action but, tragically for Whalley, the one action Van Wyk can take (to secure Sterne's silence for the rest of this last crucial voyage) is not enough. In young middle age, human beings often *do* create their own comfortable, civilized shelter from the realities of life; warm in their own humanity, unthreatened themselves by the wilderness, they hope to escape the "heartaches of the world". Especially, they may be blind to the harshness of life for the old in a changing world — a world which makes new and unexpected demands upon fixed skills and deteriorating bodies.

However active Van Wyk might have been upon Whalley's behalf, there is much which he could not have spared him. For Conrad shows, supremely, in Whalley, a man whose whole life has been based upon illusion. "The End of the Tether" shows the progressive shattering of all his illusions, and it is thus closely linked with the two other tales in the volume, for they too are much concerned with illusion, although in different ways. In "Youth" the glamor of youth itself is illusory, and the false glamor is carried right over into middle age. There is no awareness of the fact of age, although juxtaposition of "definite images" brings this awareness to the reader. In "Heart of Darkness" Marlow looks deep into the harshest of realities and, after a period of personal disturbance and disorientation, sees that the "saving illusion" which has "survived" *is* indeed illusory, but that mature humanity cannot allow the illusion to be lost, even though the remote, isolated, tomb-like surroundings of the Intended suggest that there is little hope that illusion can ever become reality. In "The End of the Tether" all the major illusions by which humanity lives are destroyed. As far back as the untimely loss of his wife, Whalley's great good fortune seems to begin to fail him. By that cruel external blow, the warm comfort of his home life is destroyed forever, and with it the happy future near Ivy, which Whalley and his wife imagined "would go on without end". As he grows older, his good luck gradually deserts him altogether: his great professional competence becomes outmoded; he loses his money; his adventurousness and enterprising spirit can find no appropriate outlets; bodily strength remains, but vitiated by one crucial weakness. Even his admirable "simplicity" of heart and "rectitude" turn out to have been based upon illusion, for he has to face the existence of real evil, both internal and external, and to face ultimately an external evil which is actively and totally dectructive. Worst of all, his earnest faith comes to seem illusory, since prayers to God remain unanswered. Conrad's vision of life is here at its darkest.

The ending of each story is wonderfully appropriate. In "Youth" Marlow asks the "man of finance, the man of accounts, the man of law", and the narrator: ". . . wasn't that the best time, that time when we were young at sea *and had nothing . . .* [isn't] that only — what you all regret?" (My italics). And they all:

nodded at him over the polished table that like a still sheet of brown water reflected our faces, lined, wrinkled; our faces marked by toil, by deceptions, by success, by love; our weary eyes looking still, looking always, looking anxiously for something out of life, that while it is expected is already gone — has passed unseen, in a sigh, in a flash — together with the youth, with the strength, with the *romance of illusions.* (My italics) (42)

The first italicized phrase above reveals the relavance to "Youth" of the volume's epigraph. Marlow here specifically challenges his companions, who are clearly wealthy and influential, to weigh the value of their youth against the "success which they have gained. Unhesitatingly, unanimously, they accept Marlow's suggestion that their youth at sea outweighs all else in value. At the end of "Youth" there is nothing but middle-aged regret for the beauty and romance of lost illusions. "Heart of Darkness" ends on a quite different note. Marlow has just remarked that it would have been "too dark — too dark altogether . . ." The "saving illusion" has been saved, but:

The offing was barred by a black bank of clouds, and the tranquil waterway leading to the uttermost ends of the earth flowed sombre under an overcast sky — seemed to lead into the heart of an immense darkness. (162)

Visually, the outlook is made to seem hopeless; it is rather as if the darkness into which Marlow has looked stretches ahead, above, and ("immemse") all-encompassing for these men in middle life. It does serve also to look forward to the "immense darkness" of the third story in the volume. By contrast, "The End of the Tether", although the darkest and most painful of the tales, ends on a note of partial affirmation: "But she had loved him, she felt that she had loved him after all". That, at least, and that only, is no illusion. The daughter whom we have seen once, as a joyous child in her father's arms affirms and repeats in weary middle life the fact of her love. "The End of the Tether" has shown the concrete and dreadful *reality* underlying the middle-aged Marlow's romanticized regret that "youth, strength, genius, thoughts, achievements, simple hearts — all dies". It has shown, that, too, to be the reality which must overtake every youthful conviction such as Marlow's, "that I could last forever, outlast the sea, the earth, and all men . . . that deceitful feeling . . ." . Conrad's artistry is supreme, the link here plain, for Whalley, too, even in old age has felt confidently hopeful of doing this, and has shared that "triumphant conviction of strength" of which Marlow at forty-two has sentimentally regretted the loss. But in this bleak Conradian universe of lost illusions, Whalley's paternal devotion is real. Very shortly before Massy perpetrates his cruel trick:

. . . an immense and fierce impulse, the very passion of paternity, flamed up with all the unquenched vigour of his worthless life in a desire to see her face (320).

This desire in Whalley's heart is answered — too late, but answered. Ivy's realization of her love for him is real, too. At least he has not sacrificed his honor and his life for a total illusion

Central to all the stories in the *Youth* volume is concern with the human heart and with the different flames which may burn within it. Soundness and simplicity of heart characterize young and old in "Youth". Captain Beard's old heart and Marlow's young heart burn with the same ardor. Ardor burns more strongly in Marlow after his long ordeal, but everything suggests that for Captain Beard the flame is all but permanently "quenched" by the same ordeal and, most of all, "by time", and will indeed soon be lost in "impenetrable night".

In "Heart of Darkness" the Harlequin's over-naive heart is aflame with blind devotion to an unworthy object, Kurtz, but through simplicity and selflessness it remains sound and "light". Of Kurtz's once (perhaps) "noble heart", the Intended speaks more truly than she realizes when

she says that "nothing remains". It has been almost wholly emptied of
true human emotions by the consuming egoistic fire of insatiable
desires, its pulse tuned only to the wilderness. The manager's heart
is a darkness, a meanness, its only flame his occasional flashes of anger
and malevolence. On only two occasions does Marlow record awareness
of the state of his own heart: first as he approaches Kurtz in the forest;
second in his meeting with the Intended. On the first occasion Marlow
"confounded the beat of the drum with the beating of my heart, and
was pleased at its calm regularity". That is, again, the response of a full
human being, this time to the beat of the heart of the wilderness, by
which Kurtz's heart has been possessed. Marlow in "Heart of Darkness"
is the human, forced to contemplation of the lowest and highest potential of the human heart. He has never felt more than a faint thrill of
kinship with the primitive; he has felt strong human sympathy with
Kurtz; it is in the scene with the Intended that his heart is most involved.
Marlow experiences *"together"* (my italics) the awareness of the Intended's survival and of Kurtz's "eternal damnation", so much so that
he feels a "sensation of panic in my heart", "as though I had blundered
into a place of cruel and absurd mysteries not fit for a human being
to behold". To "behold" the "mysteries" of these mingled extremes is
more shattering to Marlow's humanity than when he "struggled with
a soul", the "mad" soul of Kurtz. Faced with the Intended's faith in
Kurtz, and with her "You know!", his "Yes, I know" comes "with
something like despair in my heart" — and he bows his head. Her
conviction that Kurtz must have "died as he lived" stirs Marlow to
anger at the inescapable fact of Kurtz's degradation, but this emotion
is quickly replaced by "a feeling of infinite pity" for the human heart's
"unextinguishable light of belief and love". This is what must be saved
(from extinction), but before Marlow actually nerves himself to the
saving lie, he feels something "like a chill grip on [my] chest"; he speaks
"shakily"; stops most uncharacteristically "in fright"; and after the lie,
"[my] heart stood still, stopped dead short . . . by the cry of inconceivable
triumph". The intensity of Marlow's emotional involvement arises from
his *seeing* at one and the same time during this scene the dark "horror"
of a human heart emptied of humanity and possessed by the primitive,
and a human heart aflame with the "unextinguishable light of belief
and love", belief in and love for the highest human values. Marlow
feels his human response in terms of the physical agitation of his heart;
otherwise, throughout "Heart of Darkness" the steady flame of Marlow's
heart is a consistent compassion.

The funeral flames associated with the end of the *Judea* are matched
by no visible flame at the *Sofala's* end. The ship lies "a black mass

upon a black sea", and very soon after the shuddering explosion there is nothing to be seen. Shortly before the end Whalley has felt "in that old heart . . . a horror of death" but this, although *almost* the most powerful human emotion, is replaced by a more powerful one. Personal terror gives way to that final flare-up of his paternal love, and the strength of the enables him to allow his still "unquenched vigor" to be "quenched" in "impenetrable night". The final flame in the *Youth* volume is appropriately invisible, the pure inner flame of a sacrificial love.

PAUL L. GASTON

THE GOSPEL OF WORK ACCORDING TO
JOSEPH CONRAD

Joseph Conrad's "Heart of Darkness", perhaps his richest and most
deeply rewarding work, is, in addition to its other distinctions, the most
thorough and forceful analysis in the nineteenth century of the popular
faith in the value of work.* It is, at least in part, the story of a man who,
believing "devotion to efficiency" the saving grace of European civilization, must survive in a land rife with incompetence and sloth, one
where efficiency itself is corrupt. Yet Marlow, who must withstand
the "flabby, pretending, weak-eyed devil of a rapacious and pitiless folly,"
finds no better weapon than that of his own industry. At first, he
works to sustain the sense of reality he associates with civilization.
Work offers, he says, "the chance to find yourself. Your own reality—
what it really means." Deeper in the heart of darkness, though, as
dark and fearful truths begin to emerge, work offers instead a respite
from too much reality. In the tasks of the moment, Marlow says, "The
inner truth is hidden—luckily, luckily." Finally, when Marlow faces
the critical temptation of "a dance and a howl" on shore, it is not
"fine sentiments" by which he is restrained, but engineering and

* Because the original, much longer version of this paper will appear eventually
as part of a book-length study, that published here is the condensed form prepared
for and delivered at the San Diego conference. Consequently, consideration of the
historical and literary contexts for the work ethic in Conrad and of its presence in
all but the early fiction has been eliminated. Not eliminated, however, is my obliga-
tion, broad if not specific, to the recognized major works on Conrad by Jocelyn
Baines, Adam Gillon, J. D. Gordon, Albert J. Guerard, Bernard C. Meyer, Thomas
Moser, and Paul Wiley, and to those studies which bear even more directly on
examination of the work ethic in Conrad, among which are the following: Donald
R. Benson, "*Heart of Darkness:* The Grounds of Civilization in an Alien Universe,"
Texas Studies in Language and Literature, 7 (Winter, 1966), 339-47; *The Cambridge
History of Poland,* ed. W. F. Reddaway, et al. (Cambridge: Cambridge University Press,
1951); Lawrence Graver, *Conrad's Short Fiction* (Berkeley: University of California
Press, 1969); Leo Gurko, *Joseph Conrad: Giant in Exile* (New York: Macmillan,
1962); Alison L. Hopwood, "Carlyle and Conrad: *Past and Present* and 'Heart of
Darkness,' " *Review of English Studies,* 23 (May, 1972), 162-72; Anthony Low,
"*Heart of Darkness:* The Search for an Occupation," *English Literature in Transition,*
12 (1969), 1-9; Gustav Morf, *The Polish Heritage of Joseph Conrad* (London: S.
Low, Marston & Co., 1930); Zdzisław Najder, *Conrad's Polish Background,* tr.
Halina Carroll (London: Oxford University Press, 1964); William F. Zak, "Conrad,
F. R. Leavis, and Whitehead: *Heart of Darkness* and Organic Holism," *Conradiana,*
4 (1972), 5-24.

navigational problems which require his attention; they are sufficient, Marlow says, "to save a wiser man."

Later works such as *Nostromo, The Secret Agent,* and *Under Western Eyes* also develop the dramatic paradoxes inherent in the Gospel of Work, an idea so simplistic as to be repeatedly susceptible to misapplication, misunderstanding, and deliberate perversion. But it is "Heart of Darkness" which first and most fully reveals the depth of Conrad's concern. It is in "Heart of Darkness" that Conrad most thoroughly exposes the inadequacies of pious exhortations to work, there that he most insistently compels a wider perspective on ethical conventions, there that he most successfully exploits the work ethic in his narrative— as a characterization device, as an ingredient in discredited imperialist orthodoxy, as psychological constant, as moral objective, even as archetypal symbol. In an *ouevre* consistently concerned with the honor of labor, "Heart of Darkness" remains Conrad's ironic, complex, inspired Gospel of Work.

But to students of Conrad's fiction, what is especially interesting about his concern with this ethical principle is the way in which it develops prior to this definitive examination. Attention to the record of Conrad's youth can easily uncover possible sources of his later analytical concern: he grew up in a nation disenchanted with the dangerous idealism of revolution and committed to the principles of organic work, became the ward of an uncle who repeatedly exhorted him to "work and endurance, endurance and work," found confirmation of these ideals in a life at sea, and, on joining British society, discovered that in his adopted, as in his native country, many of the strongest and most influential voices preached the dignity of labor, the Gospel of Work. But attention to Conrad's early fiction is even more illuminating, for it can reveal how carefully and deliberately Conrad refined this most straightforward of Victorian moral assumptions, developing it finally into the complex interest so material to the enigmatic and ambigious moral environment of his mature fiction. In short, to follow the growth of this idea is to glimpse at least one element in the growth of the artist, and to concentrate on this one concern, far from being reductivist, allows an expanded appreciation of the real coherence and integrity of Conrad's ethic.

Almayer's Folly, Conrad's first novel, introduces initial distinctions in his work ethic. While the Gospel of Work according to Carlyle preaches the "perennial nobleness, and even sacredness, in Work," Conrad at once takes up the complex relationship in a man's life between the work he must do and the ends he hopes to achieve by it. Almayer's failure is not the direct result of an unwillingness to work;

he fails because, trapped in a frustrating *cul-de-sac,* he doggedly hangs on to unfeasible plans and unreasonable ambitions. And his attitudes on his work, formed by years of fruitless effort, help to separate him from reality and make him vulnerable to catastrophic disappointment.

As he awaits, in the novel's opening, the momentous return of Dain, Almayer seems idle and feckless, but he has been a worker in his youth, and he seems eager enough to exert himself again if his ambitions can be fulfilled. Indeed, he wants to work, to earn his reward the hard way, to deserve it. He dreams of "gold he meant to secure yet, through his own honest exertions, for himself and Nina" but thinks with contempt of "gold the others had secured—dishonestly, of course." Almayer, willing to assume "the bitterness of toil and strife . . . in the vision of a great and splendid reward," can forget his futile past labors by anticipating his imminent success and avoid "the hated reality of the present by absorbing himself in his work." For Almayer, then, work represents at once an unproductive past effort to be forgotten, a means of distraction from present realities, and the route, in good time, to his future prosperity.

But it is precisely the inconsistencies inherent in these attitudes on work which help to explain Almayer's collapse. His insistence on putting past failures from his mind blinds him to the dubiousness of his treasure hunt in the interior; just such expeditions, once undertaken by Almayer's father-in-law, had so depleted the resources of Almayer's trading station as to destroy his chance for success. And his mindless absorption in present tasks, preparations for the treasure hunt, so blunts his awareness of his surroundings as to preclude his anticipating the thoroughly characteristic treachery of his daughter; he so assiduously avoids the "unpleasant realities of the present hour" that his failure to form the most obvious suspicions is thoroughly credible. But, finally, it is Almayer's view of work as a simple prerequisite to riches, a means to an end, that most directly determines his fate. It was this view which led him as a youth to accept a grotesque arranged marriage and a job managing an unpromising trading station; he trusted that his sacrifice would make him a rich man, a wealthy European. When his despair at his failure is relieved somewhat by the birth of a daughter to whom Almayer can transfer his ambitions, he reveals that he has learned nothing. Almayer sustains himself with a groundless faith in eventual success; when his projections, doubtful in themselves, are forestalled, Almayer has nothing more to live for. He has worked, certainly, but worked singlemindedly in a compulsive quest for extravagant, narrow, and almost certainly inaccessible ends. When his work fails to produce the desired result, Almayer confronts only the vacuum of his unfulfilled greed. Nina, contemplating her love for Dain, understands that "no two human beings understand each other," but Almayer, unable to come to terms either with the work he can do or with the futility of that he wants to do, cannot understand himself. He is the victim of powerful forces, certainly, but his vulnerability to them has at least a partial basis in his selfish and unrealistic views on what he can and must do in the world.

As a man some thirteen years younger, Almayer appears again in Conrad's second novel, *An Outcast of the Islands*. Although he has already lost his simple faith in what good office furniture and neatly-ruled ledgers can accomplish, he can still look forward, at the novel's beginning, to the eventual use of the still considerable capital of his father-in-law, Lingard. Having bartered his life for the promise of wealth, Almayer must endure in *An Outcast of the Islands* the collapse of this promise through the treachery of another of Lingard's protégés. His youthful faith in Lingrad, in the inevitable fruits of earnest enterprise, and in his own capacities, is, after the events which the novel describes, utterly lost. Entirely bereft, he requires another illusion, this one based on Nina, not Lingard, on the hope of instantaneous wealth, not the promise of steady industry. And it is no wonder that these revised ambitions, leading him further and further from the reality in which he lives, will lead him ultimately to the climax of *Almayer's Folly*.

But it is Almayer's "scoundrel," Willems, who is the protagonist of *An Outcast of the Islands,* and it is through the progress of his fortunes that the novel develops a further investigation into the work ethic, through his fall that it qualifies but sustains a fundamental asumption of the Gospel. As the novel opens, Willems seems to know his work and to do it, not out of any regard for the work itself, but because it enables him to continue his enjoyable tyranny over his wife, family, and gaming companions. Having "stepped off the straight and narrow path of his peculiar honesty," he expects the detour to be temporary, but his soft life and moral relativity already lend him the scent of corruption. By comparison, and it is a telling one, there is Tom Lingard, "a master, a lover, a servant of the sea." He knows his work, does it, and likes it "not so much for profit as for the pleasure." By the harsh and uncompromising standards of the sea, standards which are crucial to the later *The Nigger of the "Narcissus,"* Lingard is tested and found worthy. Willems, however, is not. Even as a youth concerned only with getting money, he possessed, Conrad makes it clear, "an instinctive contempt for the honest simplicity of that work which led to nothing he cared for." His instincts, rather, are for the unscrupulous subtlety of that work which leads most expeditiously to money and power. Scruples are, for Willems, the impediments to these self-justifying ends.

It is the delicious irony of Conrad's second novel that Willems loses both money and power by ignoring one scruple too many. Unfit for a life of honor and integrity at sea, he proves himself also unfit for the life of dealing and subterfuge which he has chosen. He has known his work, but not well enough. And he has done it, but not well enough. Viewing his occupation solely in terms of what it can provide, he fails to bring to it the integrity that even a corrupt businesman must employ. And because Willems has sustained himself on the perquisites of his employment alone, dismissal represents the collapse of his existence. Even before boarding Lingard's ship for the second time, he is an exile. "Were he never so benighted, forgetful of his high calling, there is always hope," Carlyle had said, "in a man that actually and earnestly works." But not in Willems. Actual, earnest work has not been enough.

There is a further dimension to Willems's loss that is even more significant. Still smarting under his shame and poverty, Willems discovers that there is nothing for him to do. And just as his career has illustrated a perverse, selfish, but consistent application of the simple premises of the Gospel of Work, so does his dilemma demonstrate those dangers of idleness implicit in the traditional regard for work. In the midst of the fecund, savage-filled jungle, he hears everywhere "the reproach of his idleness" and feels "left outside the scheme of creation in a hopeless immobility." It is to escape this situation that Willems begins the wanderings which lead him ultimately to the native girl, Aissa, and it is this situation which renders him vulnerable to her. Conrad is explicit on the point: "While she was near there was nothing in the whole world—for that idle man—but her look and her smile." At the end, when Willems must face Lingard after betraying him, he complains, "you . . . left me here with nothing to do." *An Outcast of the Islands* is Conrad's first extended study of a problem that will appear frequently in later works, the effects of idleness in men.

But if idleness is immediately suspect in Conrad's developing ethical system, even the most skillful and devoted attention to a life's work need not be unreservedly meritorious. Illicit motives thwart the industry of Almayer and Willems, but the example of Lingard is not nearly so simple. Indeed, his characterization represents yet a further stage in Conrad's progressive refinement of the simple faith in the value of all work. Lingrad is in many ways admirable, but those qualities which make him a successful captain and trader handicap his running people's

lives. The same unreflective decisiveness which enables him to sur-
mount crises at sea makes him vulnerable to an act of treachery he
finds "awful, incomprehensible." Finally forced to concede the perfidy
he has, in a sense, nurtured, he can no longer support any coherent
view of the world; the light dies from his world, the air is already dead.

Almayer, Willems, and Lingard, the principal characters of Conrad's
first two novels, are men destined to understand neither each other
nor themselves. Their respective accomodations with existence reveal
unbridgeable discrepancies suggested in part by the different ways in
which they view their work. Lingard sails complacently in the assurance
of a firm categorical imperative, Almayer rules neat ledgers and thirsts
for European riches, Willems condemns himself to fatal indolence by
sacrificing the egotistical satisfactions of his petty enterprise to insatiable
greed—these are men who, without explicitly violating the traditional
canons of the Gospel of Work, become outcasts of the islands, adrift
far from the convenient standards of civilization's moral concensus,
bound for destruction.

In *The Nigger of the "Narcissus,"* Conrad continues to refine the
ideas on work suggested in the first two novels by further developing
the distinctions they enforce. Yet, Conrad's third novel, his most com-
prehensive early analysis of the work ethic, also represents his strongest
affirmation of it. The microcosm of the ship at sea is the setting for
a struggle which reveals competent work as essential to economic
stability, social order, and survival, as a substantial basis for practical
character judgments, and as a critical requirement for acute psychic
needs.

Singleton's often-praised devotion to the task, crucial to the survival
of his mates and the profitability of the voyage, stands in clear contrast
with the sloth of rebellious Donkin, whose foul-mouthed truculence
exacerbates the tensions rife among the "Narcissus" crew, and with
the apparent malingering of the dying James Wait, who infects his
mates with dissension and brings order itself into question. When the
mutiny fomented by these shirkers has at last been quelled, the captain
concludes, simply, "If you knew your work as well as I know mine,
there would be no trouble." For civilization to exist, men must know
their work and do it—a simple equation, frequently obscured in the
enigmatical world of Almayer and Willems, but sharp and clear, at
least for the moment, on board the "Narcissus."

Conrad's concern for the tangible values of work, so effectively and
comprehensively developed in his first three novels, is however, extended
in *The Nigger of the "Narcissus"* by an obvious interest in more subtle
and profound values, ones implicit in the depiction of the voyage as,

if not archetypal passage, at least communal psychic trial. Prior to the ordeal of the storm and the rescue of Wait which it compels, the crew performs its tasks begrudgingly, sullenly, and, in isolation from one another. But the test of the storm and the rescue provide a restorative confrontation. Even the simple sailors perceive the awesome significance of their efforts: "It had become a personal matter between us and the sea." And, while we may quarrel about the exact nature of the renewal, it is the crew's attitude to its work which confirms that a renewal has taken place: "the wish to do things well was a burning pain."

Three of Conrad's short stories collected in 1898 as *Tales of Unrest* add further dimensions to his developing work ethic, ones which are to be essential to its complex place in "Heart of Darkness" and the later novels. "The Idiots," "An Outpost of Progress," and "The Return," for all their widely disparate subjects and methods, together take up crucial distinctions between private and public morality, distinctions which consistently involve the work ethic. They are all, in effect, stories of relationships which disintegrate when traditional expectations are frustrated, communication is broken, and the ordinary enterprises of life cannot continue.

When Jean-Pierre Bacadou returns to his family's farm after serving in the army, he "remarked with pain that the work of the farm was not satisfactorily done." Driven by his pride in the land, he mends the fences and cares for the cattle. He knows his work and does it. Then, urged by his devotion to the land, he marries to obtain a helpmate and fathers twin sons who soon should be "striding over the land from patch to patch, wringing tribute from the earth beloved and fruitful." The land will always be cared for, will remain always in the family. But they are, it becomes apparent, idiots. And Bacadou's despair, which would be profound enough under ordinary circumstances, is exacerbated by his sense of failure to the land and to the future generations for whom he should preserve it. As one who has measured himself against an uncompromising work ethic, he can evaluate his tragedy only as work somehow badly done. His workman's skill is revealed as inadequate; he is incompetent. Bacadou is not incapable of love, but he places love in the context of a responsibility which must be fulfilled. Thus, when his commitment is brutally blocked by idiot children, or, in his view, by a woman who will not give him the sons he needs, his naive understanding of his tragedy in terms of the work ethic leads to the unbridgeable schism between man and wife that ultimately destroys both.

In "An Outpost of Progress," Kayerts and Carlier, employees of a trading service who have been left to man an isolated jungle station, begin their duty term with shows of assiduousness and gentlemanly competence. So long as they are able to conceive of themselves as partners in a civilized enterprise, they can sustain themselves with the morality of civilization. Knowing their work and doing it, they trust all will turn out well. But two circumstances intervene. First, they are forced to confront in the roving band of slave traders the despicable realities on which their proper enterprise has stood. The obvious rapacity of the undertaking in which they are involved makes a lie of the assumptions of order by which the men have lived. Second, confronted with the hideousness of their circumstances and utterly lacking the opportunity for even the slightest relief from wracking self-scrutiny which might be afforded by some task, they find that their relief does not arrive. They haven't done their job; neither has anyone else. All that remains is character, and unaided character, here weak to begin with, fails miserably.

Finally, in "The Return," Conrad pursues his consideration of the work ethic to what can be seen as its logical conclusion prior to "Heart of Darkness." It is, as nearly everyone agrees, a terrible story, but it does clarify the progression I have been tracing. Having introduced a series of reservations and qualifications to an ethical premise with which he is in fundamental agreement, and having built from these reservations and qualifications the basis of a convincing and eloquent defense, Conrad in "The Return" presses the work ethic to a climactic test by placing it in the mouth of a fatuous fool. "Restraint, duty, fidelity—unswerving fidelity to what is expected of you. This—only this—secures the reward, the peace." What success the story enjoys (and it is not much) has to do with the convincing distinction it makes between the validity of ethics as principles of a life well lived and their perverse and artificial application to the most banal of selfish human desires. It is Alvin who is discredited by the values he mouths, not the other way around. Even in this failed effort, Conrad makes an important additional point: the integrity of ethical values does not depend on the integrity of those who express and apply them. When Conrad describes Marlow's initial fascination with the reputation of Mr. Kurtz, the distinction, inconsequential in this weak story, will be momentous.

GUSTAV MORF

"THE RESCUE" AS AN EXPRESSION OF CONRAD'S DUAL PERSONALITY

The Rescue is one of three novels belonging to what Conrad himself called his "Malayan Phase." *Almayer's Folly, An Outcast of the Islands* and *The Rescue* from what can be called the Lingard trilogy. Contrary to what one would expect, the figure of Lingard is young in the last book and old, powerless and almost forgotten in the first.

The Rescue was begun in 1896, but never grew much beyond its first part. Having written about one fifth of "that accursed thing" (as Conrad told Garnett), he gave it up. Nineteen years later, he returned to the ms. and *The Rescue* was finished in 1919, just at the moment when Poland was reborn as an independent country.

The novel begins with a magnificent prologue — a song of praise for the Malayan freedom fighters and the few Whites who supported them in their valiant struggle for independence, followed by an angry speech against the European powers who divided the Malayan archipelago amongst themselves. On the first page of the novel, Conrad writes: "The vices and the virtues of four nations have been displayed in the conquest of that region that even to this day has not been robbed of all the mystery and romance of its past — and the race of men who have fought against [the European powers] . . . has not been changed by the unavoidable defeat." Of the subdued and "pacified" peoples he says, "They have kept to this day their love of liberty, their fanatical devotion to their chiefs, their blind fidelity in friendship and hate — all their lawful and unlawful instincts. Their country has fallen a prey [to the conquerors] — the reward of superior strength if not of superior virtue." (Conrad of course meant "but not of superior virtue.") There is no hope for the freedom fighters, for, "tomorrow the advancing civilization will obliterate the marks of a long struggle in the accomplishment of its inevitable victory."

Who would not feel in these exalted passages the strong Polish undertones? Who would not be reminded of the letter Conrad wrote in 1885 from Singapore to Joseph Spiridion Kliszczewski and which culminated in this statement, "Whatever may be the changes in the fortunes of living nations, for the dead there is no hope and no salvation. We [Poles] have passed through the gate where *lasciate ogni speranza* is written in letters of blood and fire, and nothing remains for us but the darkness of oblivion."[1] Of the freedom fighters Conrad says in *The Rescue*, "Their lives were thrown away for a cause that had no right to exist in the face of an irresistible and orderly progress . . . but the wasted lives, for the few who know, have tinged with romance the region . . . that lies far East . . ." Had the fate of the Malay peoples and of their native principalities not struck a Polish chord in Conrad, these lines would never have been written.

After the magnificent pathos of the beginning, one would espect action, deeds of heroism. What the reader gets, however, is inaction. The story falls short of its promise. This inability to live up to a grandiose promise of heroic deeds seems to be a very Nałęcz Korzeniowski trait. More: the discrepancy between great words and actual deeds was a trait common to many of the Polish leaders of the time. After the arrival of the yacht *Hermit*, the struggle for independence of a noble people led by a noble prince and princess becomes quite remote. Lingard no longer knows his own mind. He very half-heartedly decides to save the sophisticated English millionnaire at the expense of the native freedom fighters. For two years he had poured his money, time and energy into the great enterprise. Hassim and his people had once saved his life, and according to their code of honor Lingard should stand by them absolutely. Conrad was unable to continue writing shortly after Lingard had reluctantly decided to sacrifice Hassim and Immada and everything they stood for.

This intriguing—and in Conrad's writing career unique — blocking of inspiration can only be explained by an inner conflict within the artist himself. Lingard commits a betrayal. He breaks a word solemnly given. Contrary to Willems or to Lord Jim, he even gets away with it. Was this course too distasteful for Conrad who put such a high value on the concept of honor? I think Conrad became the victim of his own game. As a Pole, he had the highest admiration for the Malay freedom fighters, and the greatest contempt for the imperialistic powers who grabbed the land together with the people. As an English writer, and especially as one who wanted to be successful, he could not possibly let any harm befall the English people who are cruising for their pleasure, and who know so little about the natives, that they call them "Moors." On the other hand, Lingard who identified so readily with the natives, has absolutely nothing in common with the mil-

---

[1] G. Jean-Aubry, *Joseph Conrad: Life and Letters* (2 vols. Garden City: Doubleday, Page & Co., 1927), I, p. 81.

lionnaire Travers and his wife Edith. He has more in common with d'Alcacer who, being a Spanish nobleman (he might just as well be a Polish count), appreciates a point of honor and understands Lingard's situation. (This is probably the reason why d'Alcacer is part of the story at all).

However, the identification with the yacht people is brought about by "love." Here, Conrad tried to kill two birds with one stone. On one hand, he was convinced that in order to sell, *The Rescue* had to be a love story. On the other hand, he could motivate Lingard's betrayal by his infatuation for Mrs. Travers which robs him of all will-power.

The crucial passage, where Lingard motivates his betrayal of the freedom fighters, sounds very contrived. Alluding to her husband's distaste for him, he says to Mrs. Travers:

I suppose I didn't look enough of a gentleman. Yes! Yes! That's it. Yet I know what a gentleman is. I lived with them for years. I chummed with them — yes — on gold fields and in other places where a man has got to show the stuff that's in him. Some of them write from home to me here — such as you see me, because I — never mind! And I know what a gentleman would do. Come! Wouldn't he treat a stranger fairly? Wouldn't he remember that no man is a liar till you prove him so? Wouldn't he keep his word whenever given? Well, I am going to do that. Not a hair of your head shall be touched as long as I live![2]

Psychologically this is one of the most awkward passages in Conrad. At the very moment when Lingard decides to break his solemn word to Hassim and Immada, he speaks of playing the role of a gentleman keeping his word. At the very moment when he is betraying his best friends who once saved his life, he has no better excuses than the conventional English conception of "fairness to strangers." He reminds us of Lord Jim, who (according to Baines) only tried to be "fair" towards gentleman Brown. Unfortunately the principle of fairness, so appropriate to an English cricket field, is incongruously out of place in the setting of *The Rescue,* as it was out of place in Patusan. Of course, Lingard only tries to find a rational reason for what is actually a behavior dictated to him by his infatuation for Edith Travers.

Conrad's conflict connected with *The Rescue* is reflected in his letters, but nowhere does Conrad give the real reason (nor any reason) for the blocking of his inspiration. He began the novel on his honymoon and hoped to write it swiftly. He needed money all the more as he had just lost most of his uncle's inheritance in a speculation. In April 1896,

---

[2] "The Rescue", Complete Works of Joseph Conrad, Garden City, New York, Doubleday, Page & Co., 1924. p. 164.

he told his prospective publisher, "If the virtues of Lingard please most of the critics, they shall have more of them. The theme of it shall be the rescue of a yacht from some Malay vagabonds *(sic.),* and there will be a gentleman and a lady cut according to the regulation pattern."[3] That Conrad was ready to make great concessions to the reading public is indicated in a letter to Garnett, written in March 1896, where he refers to *The Rescue* thus: "It will be on the lines indicated to you. I surrender to the infamous spirit which you have awakened in me and, as I want my abasement to be very complete, I am looking for a sensational title."[4]

Two years later, the abasement had obviously become too much and Conrad felt unable to continue. He had just sold the American serial rights: In March 1898, he told Cunninghame Graham, alluding to his inability to proceed, "Yes, we Poles are poor specimens. The strain of national worry has weakened the moral fibre, — and no wonder when you think of it. It is not my fault; it is a misfortune. Forgive my jeremiads. I do not repine at the nature of my inheritance but now and then it is too heavy not to let out a groan;" At about the same time, he complained to Garnett, "As to the serial it must go anyhow. I would be thankful to be able to write anything, anything, any trash, any rotten thing."[5]

In a letter to Mrs. Bontine, of November 1898, Conrad gave this explanation:

Attempting to tell romantically a love story, in which the word love is not to be pronounced seems to be courting disaster deliberately. Add to this that an inextricable confusion of sensations is of the very essence of the tale, and you may judge how much success, material or otherwise, I may expect. *Le lecteur demande une situation nette et des motifs définis.* He will not find it in *The Rescue.*[6]

In this passage where the word *sensations* obviously stands for *feelings,* Conrad does not really touch the root of the matter, namely the conflict between the Pole Konrad Korzeniowski whose sympathies are all on the side of the freedom fighters, and the English writer who had to satisfy an English public of 1898, which took imperialism and colonialism for granted and for which the rebelling freedom loving natives were just "a bunch of searobbers." One can also get a measure of Conrad's conflict from a letter to H.G. Wells, dated December 1898,

---

[3] Edward Garnett, ed., *Letters from Conrad. 1895 to 1924.* (London: The Nonesuch Press, 192). Pp. 46.
[4] *Ibid.*, pp. 23-24.
[5] Jean-Aubry, *op.cit.,* I, p. 230.
[6] *Ibid.*, p. 255.

"I am eating my heart out over the rottenest book that ever was — or will be."

It was only in 1916 that Conrad took up the novel again, apparently at the suggestion of his wife. England at that time was fighting heroically against Germany, and this in a way justified the rescue of the English yacht. Even so, the novel took three more years to finish. Moreover, Conrad had developed his *persona* of an English writer sufficiently to overcome the conflict which had prevented him from writing the book in the late nineties. Again, he considered *The Rescue* first and foremost as a potential money maker. In a letter to his agent, Pinker, dated January 1919, three months before the completion of the novel, he expresses the hope that it might become "a money hit," more so than the reprinted *Outcast of the Islands*. He based the hope on the fact that *The Rescue* was "picturesque and at the same time more conventional" than the *Outcast*.[7]

One cannot read without astonishment the callous words Conrad wrote in an undated letter to Pinker, at the end of 1918:

You may however assure the representative of the *Cosmopolitan Magazine* that the story will end as romantically as it began, and that no one of particular importance will have to die. Hassim and Immada will be sacrificed, as is any case they were bound to be, but their fate is not the subject of the tale. All those yacht people will go on their way, leaving Lingard alone with the wreck of the greatest adventure of his life.[8]

We have read correctly, "their fate is not the subject of the tale," and, even worse, "no one of particular importance will have to die," considering how much Conrad, and through him Lingard, loved these people at the beginning of the book. Even if one takes these words in a sarcastic sense, it is incredible that a *Nałęcz Korzeniowski* would write this, the descendant of people who had fought for a nation whose fate, indeed, was "of no particular importance" in the eyes of the world. Here Conrad clearly sacrificed his Polish heritage, his loyalty and his innermost convictions to the build-up of the *persona* or image of the successful and talented English writer. Moreover, he did so not when he was poor, but when he was already famous, and at the very moment when the dreams of the Polish freedom fighters finally came true and Poland was resurrected from the dead.

These are hard criticisms, but a close study of *The Rescue* and of the letters pertaining to the novel lead to this unescapable conclusion. The great flaw of the book is that Conrad, who constantly ridicules the

---

[7] *Ibid.*, II, p. 219.
[8] *Ibid.*, II, p. 212.

imperialistic attitude of the English (from Mr. Travers to Carter and down to Lingard's own mate, Shaw) and makes fund of their complete ignorance of the legitimate aspirations and needs of the native peoples, has to protect the lives of the white conquerors throughout at the expense of the noble prince Hassim. About fifty brown men die in the book, against only one white, old Jorgenson — a Dane whose life is expendable. The ammunition ship he blows up is called *Emma.* Since Emmeline (little Emma) was Jessie Conrad's middle name, one may wonder whether the coincidence is not symbolical. One knows how much Conrad was upset at times at his wife's English placidity and blissful ignorance of political problems. At any rate, we know that he "blasted her" many a time.

Speaking of *The Rescue* in a letter to Mrs. Sanderson, in August 1898, Conrad wrote, "The last shred of honor is gone."[9] What did he really mean? On the surface, he was writing about his inability of producing the text according to the agreed time-table, but we may well assume that he meant more than that. Otherwise he would have said "credibility" instead of honor.

Seen as a psychological problem, the writing of *The Rescue,* extraordinarily painful even by Conrad's standards, can be explained by the writer's dual personality. The two parts of his personality had never been so much at odds with each other as when he tried to write *The Rescue.*

To the obvious question, what Conrad should have done with the yacht people, I would not say that they should have perished. Either Conrad should have found a way to avoid the alternative which makes the death of some a condition for the salvation of the others, or he should not have written the book at all. Life often has more resources than Conrad will allow of in his writings.

---

9 *Ibid.,* I, p. 247.

JOHN S. LEWIS

CONRAD IN 1914

The year 1914 cuts a shadow-line across Joseph Conrad's literary career. For nearly two decades he had carved out a secure reputation, but the commercial success that he had deserved, if not sought, had eluded him until the publication of *Chance*. The spring of 1914 saw Conrad working to finish *Victory*. The novel was probably in its last stages when Conrad received a visitor, "a very young and unknown pianist then," at Capel House. Fifty-eight years later, Arthur Rubinstein, the unknown pianist of the 1914 visit, was uncertain of the date of his journey to Kent, but thought "it must have been just before the First World War." Rubinstein's memory, which serves him so well in his profession, had not failed him in this instance either. The external evidence points to the spring of 1914, probably May, as the date of Rubinstein's visit.[1]

When he was asked to recall the visit, December 10, 1972, Rubinstein had just completed writing his autobiography, *My Young Years,* and therefore had the events of the period well in mind. He remembered Conrad as being more correct than cordial. "He seemed stiff and formal," Rubinstein said. "He was trying to adapt to English ways—We had tea." Rubinstein supposed that Conrad's formality came about because the pianist was not well known at the time. More likely, other matters were responsible for Conrad's lack of cordiality. For one thing, Rubinstein had been brought down to Kent by Norman Douglas. Conrad and Douglas had once been friendly, but according to Professor Frederick R. Karl their relationship had begun to deteriorate at this time.[2] Karl

---

[1] Conversation with Arthur Rubinstein. I wish to acknowledge the help of Mr. Rubinstein, his secretary, Mrs. J. N. Clemans, and his traveling representative, Mr. Louis Bender, all of whom were the epitome of courtesy and helpfulness during the preparation of this article. I should also like to acknowledge the friendly suggestions of Edmund A. Bojarski and Adam Gillon, both of whom I am grateful to for saving me from errors of fact and emphasis.

Rubinstein's recent autobiography, *My Young Years* (New York: Alfred A. Knopf, 1973), does not mention the Conrad meeting; however, it carefully indicates the pianist's whereabouts from his own Zakopane holiday in the summer of 1913 to his arrival in England in the early spring of 1914. Consequently, his meeting with Conrad could not possibly have taken place before late in March, 1914.

[2] "Joseph Conrad, Norman Douglas, and the *English Review," Journal of Modern Literature,* 2, 3 (1971-72), 342-56. According to Karl, Douglas' homosexuality had become an open matter by 1915.

attributes the break to Douglas' homosexuality, which Douglas no longer attempted to conceal; however, Professor Karl does not cite Douglas' habitual and indiscriminate swearing, which may very well have annoyed Conrad more than Douglas' homosexuality did.[3]

A second possible reason for Conrad's formality was that he was preparing *Victory,* for publication, an arduous task that finally ended July 18.[4] Richard Curle tells us that "Conrad had a feeling akin to gaiety about *Victory*—that kind of gaiety which comes from accomplishing a work of art in one of those inspired intervals when toil itself is a pleasure."[5] Yet Conrad had spent many months of hard work on that novel and might have been annoyed by what he could have regarded as an interruption. In addition, though he had enjoyed fairly good health during the last months of the previous year, early in 1914 he complained to John Galsworthy, "I have been feeling abominably seedy for the last four months. I've only just got out of bed (gout and a nasty sort of cold) this morning. Everybody tells me I am looking well,—but I know how I feel."[6] The cumulative debility of Conrad's gout may have left him out of sorts.

Lastly, Conrad had ambivalent feelings about his native land and fellow Poles. He had not been in Poland since 1893 and still smarted over Eliza Orzeszkowa's attack on him for deserting Poland.[7] In fact, as Dr. Zdzisław Najder observes, Conrad had mentioned Poland only three times in his published work up till 1914,[8] and sometimes he seemed reticent to Poles. But in May, 1914, Conrad and his family were invited to accompany Józef and Otolia Retinger to Poland to visit Mrs. Retinger's mother's estate east of Kraków. Conrad could take his wife and both his sons, none of whom had yet seen Poland, and he accepted the invitation.[9] The visit to Poland was to mark a decided change in Conrad's attitude toward his native land.

---

[3] See Rubinstein, *My Young Years,* pp. 413, 415.

[4] Exactly when *Victory* was completed is open to some doubt. In the "Note to the First Edition," Conrad declares that "the last word of this novel was written on the 29th of May, 1914" ("Dent's Collected Edition," London: J. M. Dent and Sons Ltd., 1948, p. vii). The final page of the manuscript of *Victory,* now in the care of the Humanities Research Center, The University of Texas at Austin, bears the date of June 27, 1914. I am grateful to the Humanities Research Center for permission to examine the manuscript. In a letter to John Galsworthy, Conrad says that he finished the novel June 28 and adds that he completed revisions on July 18 (G. Jean Aubry, *Joseph Conrad, Life and Letters* [London: William Heinemann, 1927], II, 157).

[5] *The Last Twelve Years of Joseph Conrad* (London: Sampson Low, Marston & Co., 1928), pp. 103-04.

[6] Letter dated March 19, 1914, Aubry, p. 152.

[7] Zdzisław Najder, *Conrad's Polish Background* (London: Oxford University Press, 1964), pp. 22-23.

[8] Najder, p. 26.

[9] In a letter to Galsworthy, July 25, 1914, Conrad remarked that Retinger's invitation "carried such an excitement in the household that, if I had not accepted in-

Earlier, I suggested that Rubinstein's visit to Capel House took place probably in May. My reason for making this assumption was that the Retinger invitation came that month and that Poland was the subject of Conrad and Rubinstein's conversation. After the death of Conrad's uncle, Tadeusz Bobrowski, in 1894, the novelist's principal link with Poland was through his cousin, Karol Zagórski. After Zagórski's death in 1898, he continued to correspond with Aniela Zagórska, Karol's widow, and later with Karol's daughters, Aniela and Karola.[10]

Madame Zagórska had established a *pension* in the Polish resort town of Zakopane where Rubinstein had been a guest for several weeks during the previous summer, 1913. Naturally, Conrad was interested to know about the Zagórski household, and from Rubinstein the writer learned what life in *Pani* Zagórska's villa, "Konstantynówka," was like. It was no ordinary *pension;* during Rubinstain's stay there regular dinner guests included the poet Leopold Staff, the writer Stanisław Witkiewicz, and Józef Piłsudski, the future Marshal of Poland.[11] Most interesting to Conrad, though, was the fact that Stefan Żeromski, at that time Poland's most distinguished man of letters, was a regular paying guest at Madame Zagórska's board. Through Rubinstein, Conrad learned much detail about life at the villa. Later, in Kraków, when word of Austria's general mobilization reached Conrad, after twenty-four hours he and his family fled to Zakopane. In his essay, "Poland Revisited," Conrad implied that the Zakopane trip was a spur-of-the-moment decision to avoid being caught in a war zone. Kraków was only a few miles from the Austrian-Russian border, and no Krakovian could have guessed that the Russian Imperial General Staff, hoping to cripple the German eastern forces, decided to launch their attack into East Prussia. Consequently, the Russian troops on the Austrian frontier withdrew to defensive positions well inside the border. Not privy to Russian and German strategy, Conrad feared an immediate attack, and, according to a letter to John Galsworthy written August 1,[12] he quickly left Kraków for Zakopane.

---

stantly, I would have been torn to pieces by my own wife and children" (Aubry, p. 157). Conrad's indifference, in the Galsworthy letter, to revisiting Poland, whether real or feigned, is one example of his ambivalence toward his native land. Borys Conrad, *My Father: Joseph Conrad* (London: Calder and Boyars, 1970), indicates neither enthusiasm nor indifference toward the trip on Conrad's part.

[10] Najder reprints the text of thirteen letters to Madame Zagórska. These letters were destroyed during the Second World War. Several letters by Conrad to Aniela Zagórska, the daughter, were apparently all wartime casualties. Miss Zagórska, however, made French translations of some of the letters for Aubry's use during the 1920's. The notebook containing these translations, now in the Yale University Library, was used by Dr. Najder for his book.

[11] Rubinstein, *My Young Years*, pp. 416-17.

[12] Joseph Conrad, *Notes on Life and Letters* (London: J. M. Dent and Sons Ltd., 1949), p. 171; Aubry, p. 158.

Zdzisław Najder's shrewd guess that Conrad probably intended to visit Zakopane during the summer anyway[13] is confirmed by Rubinsten's conversation with Conrad and the latter's interest in the Zagórski household. Since he felt close to the Zagórski family, Conrad undoubtedly would have been interested in Rubinstein's details even if he had not been invited to visit Poland with the Retingers. But his interest in details of the house guests and the intellectual atmosphere of Konstantynówka suggests that Conrad had already been invited to join the Retingers.

The Retinger invitation included a stay at Tola Retinger's mother's estate in the Russian zone near Kraków. Doubtless the Conrads planned to stay at the estate a decent interval, but Conrad probably intended to visit Zakopane later.

Events hastened Conrad to Zakopane. In July, Conrad had remarked to Richard Curle that the assassination of Archduke Franz Ferdinand was nothing to worry about[14] and made no alteration of his plan to travel. The Conrad family and the Retingers sailed for Hamburg July 25 and probably arrived in Kraków on July 30.[15] Almost immediately Austria declared mobilization, but Tola Retinger had already left for her mother's estate on the Russian side of the frontier. Conrad's son, Borys, and Józef Retinger spent an anxious night awaiting word from Tola at a guarded checkpoint, but not until Retinger and the Conrads arrived in Zakopane was Tola able to rejoin them. By that time Józef Retinger, determined to get back to England, had already left Zakopane.[16] Thus the Conrads and the Retingers were swept up by the tragic events of the summer of 1914.

Great Britain entered the war when the Germans invaded Belgium; hence, both the Conrads and the Retingers, as British and French subjects, were technically enemy aliens in a potential war zone. Quickly Conrad decided to take one of the last civilian trains out of Kraków and fled to Zakopane where the Conrads and the Retingers parted company. The Conrads were to remain in *Pani* Zagórska's home for more than two months, cut off from sources of money.

The story of Conrad's escape is well known. Through the help of Polish friends and the American ambassador to the Habsburg court,

---

[13] Najder, p. 23.

[14] Curle, p. 171.

[15] Najder, pp. 23-24; Borys Conrad, pp. 85-87. According to Józef Retinger's account, *Conrad and His Contemporaries* (New York: Roy, 1943), pp. 146-62, the party left London July 29 and arrived in Kraków August 1, "the very day that Austria mobilized." Actually, the Conrads and the Retingers sailed for Hamburg July 25, and Austria declared full mobilization on July 31. Retinger's factual inaccuracies have been noted by several scholars. See Jocelyn Baines, *Joseph Conrad: A Critical Biography* (London: Weidenfeld and Nicolson, 1960), p. 401 and n.

[16] Borys Conrad, pp. 87-89; 90.

Conrad and his family eventually escaped to Italy and took ship for England.

Conrad might have chosen to escape with the Retingers if his younger son had not been ill and if his wife had not been partially crippled. He chose, however, to remain in Zakopane; after all, Madame Zagórska was a relative, and her daughter Aniela was the center of the lively intellectual life of the household. After the war, Conrad authorized Aniela Zagórska, the daughter, to translate his works. Had Conrad been forced to sit out the war—a real possibility because the Austrian authorities showed no overt indications of interning the Conrads—where would he have found a more agreeable place than Zakopane?

The importance of Conrad's two-month enforced sojourn in the resort was, as Najder has shown, that Conrad finally became convinced that an autonomous, even an independent Poland was possible.[17] Furthermore, Stefan Żeromski, who had the highest of literary reputations in Poland, welcomed Conrad as a fellow writer and countryman. The Conrad—Żeromski relationship is enigmatic. In a letter to Żeromski, who had written the introduction to Aniela Zagórska's translation of *Almayer's Folly,* Conrad showered the Polish novelist with praise,[18] but in a letter to Edward Garnett, Conrad declared that Żeromski's *History of a Sin* "is disagreeable and often incomprehensible in comment and psychology. Often it is gratuitously ferocious."[19] Scarcely more than two months after the Garnett letter, Conrad was to write Aniela: "Be so kind, my dear, as to remember me to Mr. Żeromski and give him my deeply sincere regards" (Letter of December 14, 1921),[20] and a few months later Conrad was to write of Żeromski in a similar vein to Bruno Winawer.[21] These obvious contradictions, Adam Gillon finds, smack of insincerity, if not sycophancy.[22] Nevertheless, whatever may have been Conrad's opinions of Żeromski's works, he still seemed genuinely pleased that the Polish author greeted him so warmly at Zakopane.

In his 1915 essay, "Poland Revisited," Conrad termed the situation the Poles in Zakopane found themselves in a tragedy. Like Conrad, they too could not return home because some of them lived in potential

---

[17] Najder, p. 27.

[18] Letter 90, March 25, 1923, p. 289.

[19] Edward Garnett, *Letters from Joseph Conrad, 1895-1924* (Indianapolis: The Bobbs-Merrill Company, 1928), p. 280, letter dated September 2, 1921.

[20] Letter 74, Najder, p. 277.

[21] "Faites me amitiés je vous prie à Żeromski pour qui j'ai une vraie affection," Letter 78, Najder, p. 280.

[22] "Joseph Conrad: Polish Cosmopolitan," a paper read at the Joseph Conrad Symposium, Texas Tech University, in January, 1974. Professor Gillon graciously sent me a copy of his paper before its publication in *Symposium Proceedings.*

war zones and transportation was not to be had.[23] They seemed to regard the Great War as a final disaster for themselves and for Poland. Nevertheless, though Conrad's friends, and perhaps even Conrad himself, may have found both Poland and themselves doomed, they had ample time to talk of ideas and events and to discuss what the future held for Poland, if indeed Poland had a future. Perhaps the conversation of Żeromski and the others shone forth with a brilliance born of despair, but a brilliance despite the Miltonic pandemonium that seemed ready to engulf all of Europe.

When the young pianist, Arthur Rubinstein, told Conrad of life at Konstantynówka a few months earlier, neither could have foreseen the way that Conrad and his family were caught up, like characters in a Tolstoy novel, in the swirling winds that were to end *pax* Europa; nor could Conrad have ever dreamed he would spend two anxious months in Madame Zagórska's villa. The enforced sojourn convinced Conrad that Poland could one day be autonomous. Thus a few remarks by a young pianist, who himself was to win great distinction later, to a man thirty years older may have led Conrad across his own shadow-line, an emotional and intellectual return to Poland. Whatever may be the truth, undeniably Conrad had not, from the launching of his literary career to the beginning of the First World War, shown much interest in his native land.

One can only speculate as to how a few chance remarks can lead to an overwhelming alteration of a man's life. Such things happen only in novels, do they not?

---

[23] Conrad, pp. 171-72.

CONTRIBUTORS

ANTONI SŁONIMSKI. Contemporary Polish poet and fighter for democratic freedoms.

SUZANNE HENIG. Professor of English Literature, San Diego State University, Editor of *The Virginia Woolf Quarterly*.

JONAS SALK. Discoverer of the anti-polio vaccine, founding Director and Fellow of The Salk Institute for Biological Studies in California.

ADAM GILLON. Professor of English and Comparative Literature, State University of New York at New Paltz, author of *The Eternal Solitary: A Study of Joseph Conrad*, and other works on Conrad. President, Joseph Conrad Society of America.

RUTH C. BROWN. Associate Professor of English, California State University, San Diego.

FLORENCE TALAMANTES. Associate Professor of Spanish, San Diego State University.

GLENN SANDSTROM. Professor of English and Comparative Literature, San Diego State University.

D. RIDLEY BEETON. Professor and Head of the Department of English, University of South Africa, Pretoria.

PRZEMYSŁAW MROCZKOWSKI. Professor and Chairman of the Department of English, The Jagellonian University, Cracow.

DAVID LEON HIGDON. Associate Professor of English, Texas Tech University, General Editor of *Conradiana*, now preparing a critical edition of *Almayer's Folly*.

DONALD W. RUDE. Associate Professor of English, Texas Tech University. General Editor of *Conradiana*; now preparing a critical edition of *Victory*.

TODD BENDER. Professor of English Literature, The University of Wisconsin-Madison. Director of a Project in Literary Application of Computer Technology which has produced a Concordance to Conrad's *Heart of Darkness*.

BRUCE E. TEETS. Professor of English, Central Washington State College, co-editor of *Joseph Conrad: An Annotated Bibliography of His Writings*.

HARRY T. MOORE. Professor of English, Southern Illinois University, Carbondale, Fellow of the Royal Society of the United Kingdom, author and editor of various books on 20th-century literature, most of them concerned with D. H. Lawrence.

LEON GUILHAMET. Assistant Professor of English, The City College, City University of New York.

PETER SLOAT HOFF. Assistant Professor of English, The University of Wisconsin-Parkside.

OWEN KNOWLES. Professor of English, University of Hull, England.

JACK I. BILES. Professor of English, Assistant Head, Department of English, Georgia State University.

JULIET MCLAUCHLAN. British scholar and writer of American descent; has published works on Conrad, Hardy and Shakespeare; has recently been largely instrumental in forming the Joseph Conrad Society (United Kingdom), and is currently finishing a book, *Mr Conrad's Art;* contributing editor to *Conradiana.*

PAUL I. GASTON. Associate Professor of English, Southern Illinois University at Edwardsville.

GUSTAV MORF. Canadian scholar and practicing psychiatrist. Author of *The Polish Heritage of Joseph Conrad* and of the forthcoming *The Polish Shades and Ghosts of Joseph Conrad.*

JOHN S. LEWIS. Associate Professor of English, The University of Texas at Arlington, Assistant Editor of *Conradiana.*

LUDWIK KRZYŻANOWSKI, Editor-in-Chief, *The Polish Review,* Editor, *Joseph Conrad: Centennial Essays,* co-author (with Adam Gillon) of *Introduction to Modern Polish Literature.*

Other Books of Related Interest

THE WORLD OF DAVID BEATY

The Place of the Images

BY ROBERTA J. FORSBERG

This perceptive study of the English novelist and pilot, who continues the Saint-Exupery tradition, is also a searching examination of the symbolic function of images in literary realism. Dr. Forsberg applies the Dorothy Sayers-Charles Williams critical analysis to the contemporary, realistic novels of David Beaty, a writer concerned with the human being trapped more and more by his own technology.

Beaty explores the moral predicament of the pilot in command, and his dramatic tales, like those of Conrad, present isolated, guilt-ridden men who have broken the code of human solidarity, whose final trial is held in the court of their own conscience. Unlike Saint-Exupery, Beaty shuns emotional terminology. His fiction provides a strange borderland where religion, philosophy, and lyrical imagination meet. His sense of compassion and his indignation at the victimization of man by technology are conveyed by understatement, irony, and symbolic imagery. And though his protagonists know darkness and despair, their tragic fate is an affirmation of man's ideal values. **(224 pages)**

Cloth: $6.95

Library of Congress Catalog Number: 74-151413
ISBN: 0-91 3994-07-3

MALTHUS AND THE CONDUCT OF LIFE

BY SAMUEL M. LEVIN

A stimulating and scholarly discussion of a renowned thinker whose work has acquired a new significance as a result of the population explosion in our time. This study is based on Professor Levin's series of articles on Malthusian thought, published in a number of leading quarterlies and in valumes of the Papers of Michigan Academy of Science, Arts and Letters. He is Emeritus Professor of Economics, Wayne State University.

". . . a serious contribution to the understanding of contemporary population problems . . . suitable for an educated lay audience."
(176 pages)

Harvey M. Choldin, in **The Michigan Academician**

ISBN: 0-913995-11-1   Cloth: $5.95

ASTRA BOOKS, NEW YORK